Immigrant workers in Europe: their legal status

Immigrant workers in Europe: their legal status

A comparative study

Eric-Jean Thomas
Study Director

The Unesco Press

The authors are responsible for the choice and the presentation of the facts contained in this book and for the opinions expressed therein, which are not necessarily those of Unesco and do not commit the Organization.

Published in 1982 by the United Nations
Educational, Scientific and Cultural Organization
7 place de Fontenoy, 75700 Paris
Typeset by Imprimerie des Presses Universitaires de France, Vendôme
Printed by Imprimerie de la Manutention, Mayenne

ISBN 92-3-101867-1
French edition: 92-3-201867-5

Preface

For many years Unesco has been very active in promoting human rights and has striven, in particular, to combat all forms of discrimination in respect of race, sex, language or religion. It was quite natural, therefore, for the Organization to interest itself in the question of immigration inasmuch as that phenomenon has become an increasingly common cause of a cultural clash between individuals, and even societies, belonging to different worlds. This confrontation between cultures and systems stems from the economic disparities existing between the rich countries, which are in need of cheap manpower, and the poor countries, which sell them their labour.

It is clear that the phenomenon of migration is associated with the international division of labour and that it benefits the affluent countries which, in the final analysis, are always in control of migratory flows.

Immigration is in itself a source of discrimination—discrimination between nationals and foreigners, discrimination between the religion of the migrant and that of the host country, discrimination, too, in professional life.

States have a responsibility for determining the status of immigrant workers and their families: just as they regulate the conditions of access to their national territory, so do they lay down rules governing the rights and freedoms accorded to foreigners on their soil. Such regulations can go a long way towards mitigating the effects of discriminatory situations, but they can also aggravate them.

The principal merit of this study is that it shows how the status of immigrant workers is determined with reference to the economic, political and social conditions peculiar to each host country and, above all, how the legal machinery controlling immigration affects the future of migrants.

This publication is a contribution to the implementation of Objective 1.1 (Respect for Human Rights) of Unesco's Medium-Term Plan for 1977–1982. It has been prepared as part of the current effort to arrive at a better understanding of the functioning of the principal types of multi-ethnic societies and the ideological and cultural aspects of ethnic awareness.

We wish to convey our thanks to the contributors; a special acknowledgement is due to Eric-Jean Thomas, Barrister at the Paris Bar, university instructor and former Director of the International Institute of Human Rights, who co-ordinated the preparatory work and also wrote several chapters.

Contents

Note on terminology

Many different terms are used in this work to describe migrants going abroad to sell their labour. Some of these terms convey various shades of meaning, but on the whole they merely reflect a lack of uniformity in the terminology used in the countries studied here.

Thus, in the chapters that follow, the terms 'foreign workers', 'immigrant workers', 'migrant workers' and even Gastarbeiter are synonymous and are to be understood as such. The term 'permanent workers' is used to describe all foreign workers residing on a long-term basis in the host country, as opposed to 'seasonal workers' or 'frontier workers'.

The term 'total foreign population' designates all foreigners living on the territory of the host country. It comprises all active aliens (foreign workers) and non-active aliens (unemployed members of the family of a foreign worker, students, etc.).

The term 'family immigration' covers members of the family of a foreign worker who usually immigrate after the foreign worker has arrived in the host country.

Lastly, 're-migrants' are immigrants (whether active or non-active) who return to their country of origin to re-establish themselves there on a long-term basis, either on their own initiative or within the framework of a host country's policy of aiding immigrants to return home.

Introduction

Eric-Jean Thomas

International migrations of workers are by no means a recent phenomenon. It was already common in the last century for migrants to set out with their families for the New World with nothing else to offer than their labour. However, the migratory flows that characterize the second half of the twentieth century differ from traditional immigration patterns in terms both of space and of time. First of all, in terms of space, because today's migrants are moving towards Europe instead of away from it. Secondly, in terms of time, because they regard their stay abroad as a purely temporary expedient; it is intended to last only as long as is necessary to save up enough money to establish themselves when they return home.

Numerous studies, primarily of an economic and sociological character, have tried to delimit, as narrowly as possible, the problem area of the migratory phenomenon. Yet a perusal of bibliographies dealing with the subject of migrant workers quickly reveals the absence of research work in the legal field. We do not intend here to advance arguments in favour of the autonomy of law as a science, nor to deplore the dearth of studies of a strictly legal nature. The subject that interests us is primarily the concern of the economic and social sciences and no useful purpose would be served by trying to single out the specifically legal elements in order to study them on the pretext that this ground has not been adequately covered. Our intention lies elsewhere. There is no denying the existence of legal data concerning the freedom and rights of immigrant workers, and although they are closely connected with socio-economic factors, they still enjoy some degree of autonomy and are weighty enough to exert, in their turn, an influence on the development of economic and social conditions. What is to be deplored is the fact that these mechanisms have never been the subject of studies that would throw light on the specific role they play in helping to determine the status of immigrant workers.

The legal data with which we are concerned here are woven into the web of laws and regulations which envelops foreigners and restricts their capacity and rights. The decision as to which of these should be singled out *a priori* for consideration is, of course, a difficult and somewhat arbitrary one to take. However, it seemed reasonable to advance the hypothesis that the key elements of immigration policies—that is to say, the mechanisms controlling access to the host country's territory and labour market—play a leading role among the factors determining the freedoms to be enjoyed by migrants. It can be assumed, *a fortiori*, that the social and political rights granted to foreigners by law are equally essential characteristics of the status of immigrant workers and their families.

Moreover, it is not possible to study the status of immigrant workers unless we grasp the position they occupy in the economy of the host country, especially because—if our assumptions are correct—their place in the economy must partly depend on the mechanisms governing the circulation of migratory flows.

It also seemed necessary to extend this inquiry to cover several countries, for a comparative study of the same data relating to various countries is the only sure means of arriving at valid conclusions.

Finally, it did not seem possible to study the status of migrant workers in the host country without trying to discover its effects on their future, that is to say, on the development of what is usually called 'the foreign worker's migratory plan'. In other words, it was necessary to investigate the question of the immigrant's return (or decision not to return) to his country of origin, and also to consider the significance and implications of emigration for that country.

Five country studies have therefore been carried out. The countries were chosen on the basis of various criteria: the size of their population, the nature and origin of their immigration flow and their geographical situation in Europe. While the choice was to some extent an arbitrary one, it was nevertheless dictated by certain logical considerations, for countries having a highly distinctive approach to migratory problems were excluded from the study. For example, the United Kingdom, which has been equipped since 1971 with an extremely elaborate and quite unique set of immigration laws, was omitted in favour of France (likewise a former colonial power, whose resident foreign population is roughly the same size as that of the United Kingdom), for its approach to migratory problems is similar to that of the other countries selected. Moreover, all the countries chosen for this study belong to free movement zones (the EEC, Benelux, the Common Nordic Labour Market), and this fact has some influence on their general immigration strategy.

Each monograph consists of three sections. The first examines immigration policy and the relevant control mechanisms; the second describes the place and role of immigrant workers in the economic structures of the host country; the third section seeks to evaluate the place assigned by the host country to foreign workers, particularly as regards opportunities to participate in social and political activities.

It should be noted that this publication contains only the summaries of the monographs that were submitted to Unesco's Division of Human Rights and Peace. For technical reasons they had to be cut by roughly one-half, with the result that certain passages and certain topics, which were more extensively treated in the original manuscripts may seem to be inadequately developed. We felt, however, that this drawback was of secondary importance by comparison with the advantage to be gained from publishing the condensed versions, especially because the original monographs were taken as the basis for the comparative study that concludes the present work.

Given the magnitude of the task, there could be no question of tackling the whole range of problems raised by the topics selected for study. Two areas of research, in particular, were excluded, one concerning the rules governing the barring and expulsion of foreigners and the other concerning the status of second-generation migrants. Although many references to these matters are to be found in the country studies, it did not seem desirable to treat them as special subjects. Research into the question of the barring and expulsion of foreigners would have involved an analysis of the state's power to direct police action against foreigners, and this goes well beyond the problem area of immigration, even if it is close to it. As regards the question of second-generation migrants, although the problems it raises are directly linked to the status of first-generation migrants, an analysis of those problems also lies beyond the range of the present work.

Lastly, a case-study was carried out in Turkey on the problems raised by the return of migrants to their home country. Since the migrant's return home is considered to be the most desirable conclusion of the migration process, both by the migrant himself, when he sets out, and by a good many host countries, it was important to ascertain the current situation as regards that phenomenon and its real significance. The question of the immigrant's return is linked directly to that of his status, for his situation in the host country necessarily varies according to whether he stays there only temporarily or lives there for many years. Moreover, host countries point to this phenomenon as a reason for the absence of a legal status for immigrant workers on their territories.

The case-study on Turkey, which was largely conducted in the field, has shown to what extent the country of origin has really benefited from the migratory phenomenon, and that is not the least of its merits.

Needless to say, this work, which does not claim to be an exhaustive study, suffers from the shortcomings inherent in any hazardous undertaking. Above all, it seeks to fill a void and provide food for thought.

Some of its conclusions were expected, others are more surprising. It is hoped that they will pave the way for research into certain areas which had been hitherto neglected and that they will alert people to the importance of this problem and make them realize how much remains to be done, even in Europe, to ensure that all men enjoy the same fundamental rights.

The status
of immigrant workers
in Belgium

Herman Debbaut and Johan Declerck

Immigration policy and regulations

Immigration into Belgium from 1945 to the present day

As in most immigration countries, the policy of the Belgian Government concerning *Gastarbeiter* was dictated by the needs of the labour market. During the period between the two world wars (from 1918 to 1940), about 50,000 Poles and over 30,000 Italians settled in Belgium, but it was not until 1944 that an immigration policy was defined.

This is explained by the fact that in 1944 there was a change in the nature of migration. Before the war, immigration was usually a matter of individual movements of persons, but in 1944, the Belgian Government itself took the initiative in encouraging the influx of a large number of people.

In 1946 and 1947, Italians and Poles were recruited in large numbers both in order to compensate for the slow but steady exodus of Belgian workers from the mines and in order to fill the void left by the departure of prisoners of war.[1]

In 1946, Belgian collieries hired 21,329 foreign workers in their countries of origin; in 1947, 40,640 foreigners were induced to migrate to Belgium and in 1948, 40,894 were given jobs.[2] According to the 1947 census, 567,619 persons, i.e. 4.3 per cent of the total population, were foreigners. This represented an increase of 27,820 over the number of foreign residents in 1938. By taking direct action in the matter of the mass recruitment of foreign manpower, the Belgian Government initiated

Herman Debbaut is Chief Adviser, Society for the Regional Development of East Flanders (GOMOV); Johan Declerck is Deputy Adviser, GOMOV.

TABLE 1. The nationalities of foreigners in Belgium: 1920–77 (percentages)

Country of origin	1920	1947	1961	1970	1977
EEC (six countries) of which:	(82.7)	(64.7)	(72.0)	(61.4)	(58.5)
Italy	2.5	22.9	44.1	35.8	33.7
France	45.0	18.1	13.6	12.5	12.6
Netherlands	26.1	17.3	11.1	8.8	8.4
Poland	3.5	15.9	7.0	2.6	1.5
Spain	0.8	0.9	3.5	9.7	7.6
Greece	0.4	0.3	2.2	3.2	2.9
Turkey	0.3	0.1	0.1	2.9	7.0
Morocco	...[1]	...[1]	0.1	5.7	9.5
Others	12.3	18.1	15.1	14.5	13.0
TOTAL PERCENTAGE	100	100	100	100	100
TOTAL NUMBER	149 677	367 619	453 483	696 282	850 917
PERCENTAGE OF TOTAL POPULATION	2.1	4.3	4.9	7.2	8.1

1. Included in 'Others'.
Source: NIS.

a policy for easing the problems of the labour market which was reapplied on an even broader scale in the 1960s.

In 1961, on the eve of a period of unprecedented economic growth, 453,486 foreigners were living in Belgium; they accounted for 4.9 per cent of the total population. In fourteen years, i.e. since 1947, their number had increased by 85,867. At that time, 'foreign workers' or *Gastarbeiter* were identified by the Belgians with miners and, in a few cases, with steelworkers.

By 1961, emigration conventions had been concluded with three countries, namely Italy, Spain and Greece. Between 1961 and 1967, there was a positive migratory balance of 231,623 and during this second migratory period the net annual increase in the number of foreigners ranged from 40,000 to 60,000.

In an effort to remedy the shortage of manpower—especially of unskilled labour—during the boom, the Belgian Government suspended the strict application of immigration regulations. Migrant workers entered Belgium as tourists and had no difficulty in legalizing their situation afterwards. Some foreign workers even carried on a lucrative business of helping their fellow-countrymen to gain a footing in Belgium.

It was then decided to recruit foreign labour in other countries besides the traditional ones (Italy, Spain, Greece) and more emigration conventions were signed, notably with Morocco and Turkey. However, with the growth of unemployment in 1966–67, the government put a stop to the immigration of 'tourists' and a Royal Decree, reaffirming the principles laid down in the Decree of 1936 concerning the regulation of immigration, emphasized in particular that entry into Belgium was conditional upon prior authorization and the possession of a work permit. This was a way of trying to close the frontiers.[3] Since 1967, foreign workers have been recruited mainly on a quota basis. It is note-worthy that there was a net annual increase of 10,000 to 15,000 in the number of foreigners between 1967 and 1970. Since 1970, the annual increase figure has ranged from 20,000 to 30,000. The influx is only partly explained by the recovery of economic activity. There is reason to think that the demand for foreign workers is increasingly due to a shortage of manpower for specific jobs, i.e. those that are regarded as socially unacceptable. As they are at the bottom of the social scale, such jobs are poorly paid and are associated with irregular working hours, shift work or unpleasant working conditions due to extreme tem-peratures, monotony, etc. Socially unacceptable jobs fall into the secondary segment of the labour market.

The principles which originally shaped Belgium's immigration policy may be defined as follows: to offer, within a strictly economic framework (that is to say, with no demographic ends in view and ignoring the process of cultural assimilation), immediate solutions to the problems of Belgian firms. However, neither these principles nor their implications nor, *a fortiori*, possible alternatives were taken into consideration in working out the immediate solutions which were in fact found for the firms' manpower problems.

Access to the labour market

Immigration is regulated mainly by a system controlling entry and residence, on the one hand, and employment, on the other. This has led to the establishment of a system of residence and work cards for migrant workers, and employment permits for employers.

The system does not apply to all migrant workers in the same way. One category enjoys especially favourable treatment: it is the category of migrant workers who are nationals of a member state of the European Economic Community (EEC). Since 1968, these workers have enjoyed the right to freedom of movement throughout EEC territory.

Migrant workers who are nationals of an EEC member state

The freedom of movement of migrant workers who are nationals of an EEC member state and their free access to employment were ensured in three stages, the last of which was reached when the Council of Ministers approved Regulation No. 1612/68, of 15 October 1968, concerning the free movement of workers within the community. This regulation entered into force on 8 November 1968.

Since that date, workers who are nationals of a member state have the right to accept and take up paid employment on the territory of another member state in conformity with the legislative and administrative provisions governing the employment of workers who are nationals of that state.

Any legislative or administrative provisions which are directly or indirectly discriminatory, with the exception of conditions concerning language requirements, are null and void.

Since the right to work is largely determined by individual or collective contracts, it is specified in the relevant provisions that any discrimination based on nationality is likewise prohibited.

Migrant workers who are nationals of non-EEC countries

Immigration to Belgium is restricted. The employment of foreign workers who are not EEC nationals is subject to a system of dual authorization which was introduced by Royal Decree No. 285 of 31 March 1936 and reaffirmed by Royal Decree No. 34 of 20 July 1967.

The purpose of this system is to protect the national labour market by bringing in foreign manpower as and when it is needed by Belgian industry and in particular when the national labour market can no longer satisfy the domestic demand. Immigration countries—particularly those which, like Belgium, resort to immigration in order to make up for the shortage of manpower to perform certain unpleasant tasks—are careful to restrict the entry of migrants to periods when they are needed owing to the state of the national labour market and to channel them into sectors where there is a demand for manpower.

An immigration visa and permission to work in Belgium is granted only to the nationals of countries with which Belgium is bound by international manpower conventions or agreements.

The Minister of Labour and Employment can waive this rule for economic or social reasons.

The employer's employment permit

As a general rule, an employer wishing to hire migrant workers must first obtain authorization to do so; an employment permit is then issued by the services of the Ministry of Labour and Employment. When an employment permit is applied for, the authorities take into account the state of the national labour market (except in certain cases where this rule is waived, for example, in favour of certain members of the family of a migrant worker). Consequently, an employment permit can be issued only when it is impossible to find on the national labour market a Belgian or migrant worker who meets the requirements of the job offered by the employer.

An employer is not required to apply for an employment permit if he intends to hire: (a) a worker who is a national of an EEC member state; (b) a migrant worker who is in possession of any one of the following documents: a work card of unlimited duration (Card A); a work card valid for all employers engaged in the same branch of activity as the prospective employer (Card B); a work card valid for all trades in which the services of a worker are customarily used by several employers (Card C).

It is important to distinguish between two types of employment permits that may be applied for—one concerns the hiring of individuals, the other, the hiring of a group of migrant workers.

An individual application gives the name of the migrant worker to be hired. Several individual applications—as many as fourteen—can be submitted simultaneously, when the workers in question are not available on the national labour market.

When an employer wishes to hire and employ simultaneously fifteen or more migrant workers who are not yet living in Belgium, he applies for a permit to bring in a group of migrant workers.

The migrant worker's work card
As already stated, only those workers who are nationals of a country with which Belgium is bound by a manpower convention or agreement may apply for permission to work in Belgium. Apart from the case of persons who are already legal residents of Belgium, such workers must submit their application to their national emigration services or to the employment office opened by the Belgian Government in their country.

That office centralizes the offers of employment received from Belgium and applications for jobs submitted by local workers willing to emigrate.

Before the would-be migrant worker is granted permission to enter Belgium, he must undergo a general and serological medical examination, as well as an X-ray examination of the lungs, to make sure that he has no contagious or transmissible disease and is not likely to become incapable of work for health reasons in the near future. Other conditions (age, educational level, etc.) are laid down in the bilateral manpower agreements.

The migrant worker signs the work contract in his home country. The Ministry of Labour and Employment then supplies him with a work card. The first work contract, which is based on a model prepared by the ministry, is of limited duration; it is usually valid for twelve months but in some cases for a shorter period.

In the event of the immigrant worker being dismissed through no fault of his own, the employer undertakes to cover his travel expenses.

The different types of work card

As far as the right to work is concerned, migrants are subject to different rules, particularly with respect to their freedom of access to the labour market and the period of validity of their work card.

Workers holding Work Card B. There are two distinct phases: (a) the first year of work in Belgium—when a migrant worker takes up his first job in Belgium, the authorities, or the employer, have supplied him with Work Card B, which is valid for one year and for one employer; (b) the second and subsequent years of work in Belgium—Card B expires at the end of one year (unless this period is extended as provided for in certain special cases). The migrant worker must apply to the Ministry of Labour and Employment to have the card renewed. The ministry takes into account, in particular, the economic situation prevailing in Belgium and the state of the labour market. In the event of a decision being taken in favour of renewal, the migrant worker obtains another Work Card B; this is valid for one year and for a single branch of activity, usually the one in which the migrant has started to work. Every year the migrant worker has to submit a fresh application for the renewal of his Work Card B and a favourable decision depends on the economic situation and the state of the labour market.

Migrant workers holding Work Card C. This card has been introduced to cater for workers whose job demands great mobility for professional purposes; it is applicable to trades and activities in which a worker has to have several employers.

Workers holding Work Card A. Holders of Work Card A enjoy certain advantages: (a) the decision to issue this card does not depend on the state of the labour market ; (b) the card is valid for an indefinite period; (c) the card is valid for all branches of activity and all kinds of paid work. In practice, this card can be applied for only by persons who have lived and worked continuously for quite a long time in Belgium and the decision to grant it depends on their family status and nationality. Currently, Card A can be obtained generally after four, and often after three, years of regular work and continuous residence in Belgium. This period is reduced by one year when the worker's spouse and/or children are living with him in Belgium.

The migrant worker's working conditions and social security coverage

A foreign worker cannot be employed in Belgium unless he enjoys the same working conditions as Belgian workers in similar jobs.

He is accordingly entitled to the same pay and the same working conditions (hours of work, holidays, medical care, etc.) as his Belgian counterpart. The same holds good for working conditions and benefits resulting from collective bargaining.

When the worker has been hired in an irregular way (for example, when no employment permit or work card has been obtained) the work contract is null and void. However, the worker loses none of the rights accruing from the work that has in fact been done. In principle, all workers employed in Belgium are assured of the right to social security.

Accordingly, no distinction is made between Belgian and foreign workers. However, some restrictions exist in the systems governing the payment of unemployment benefits and family allowances. Difficulties arise in respect of eligibility for unemployment benefits; periods of employment abroad and the period of employment spent in Belgium are not totalized unless this is provided for in the social security agreements. As regards the system of family allowances, restrictions exist when the worker's family is living in the country of origin. The social security agreement lacks uniformity on this point.

There are restrictions concerning: (a) the number of children for whom family allowances are paid; (b) the sum paid for each child. These allowances vary according to the branch of activity in which the head of the family is employed. It is the children of Moroccan, Tunisian and Turkish workers who suffer most from the effects of these restrictions.

It should be noted that in accordance with Regulation No. 1408/7, such restrictions are not applicable to EEC nationals.

Residence, establishment and exclusion from Belgian territory

No one has a right to freedom of entry and residence on Belgian territory. Any person wishing to enter Belgium and to spend some time on Belgian territory must first obtain authorization to do so from the Minister of Justice. Therefore, a foreign worker who wishes to emigrate to Belgium and consequently to reside on Belgian territory must comply not only with the regulations governing the employment of migrants, but also with the legislative and administrative provisions concerning the control of movements of aliens.

Foreigners residing in Belgium are still subject to the provisions of an old law, namely the Aliens Control Act of 28 March 1952 (amended several times), and the Royal Decree of 21 December 1965 concerning the application of the Act of 28 March 1952.

As in the case of the employment regulations, a distinction must be made between migrants who are EEC nationals and those who are not.

Migrant workers who are nationals of an EEC member state

Regulation No. 68/1612 concerning the free movement of workers within the community was amplified by Directive No. 68/360 of 15 October 1968, which removed restrictions on the movement and residence within the community of workers of member states and their families.

The Belgian authorities have incorporated the provisions of the Directive into Belgian law.

Migrant workers of the EEC countries therefore enjoy particularly favourable conditions: they can enter Belgian territory to look for work, whereas other migrant workers are, in principle, forbidden to do so.

If they have found work within three months, they are entitled to a residence permit unless a refusal to grant their request is justified for reasons of public order, public health or public safety.

Migrant workers who are nationals of non-EEC states

Residence

Unlike migrant workers of the EEC countries, a national of a state which is not a member of the EEC cannot enter Belgium to look for work. He must be hired by a Belgian employer before he immigrates. Furthermore, before leaving his own country, he must apply for authorization to reside in Belgium on a long-term basis.

Before supplying the migrant worker with a provisional residence permit, the diplomatic or consular services make sure that: (a) his presence in Belgium is not regarded as undesirable; (b) he is not likely to disturb the peace or subvert public order or public safety in Belgium; (c) he has adequate means of subsistence or is capable of earning a regular living.

The first two conditions relate mainly to the personal conduct of individuals. The third condition is a more general one and to meet this requirement the migrant will have to produce his work card. The possession of a work card is therefore a prerequisite for obtaining a provisional residence permit from the Belgian authorities and the migrant worker must have this card before he enters Belgium.

Establishment

The holder of an establishment permit (*permis d'établissement*) enjoys two advantages: more stable conditions of residence in Belgium and special guarantees against the risk of being expelled.

Greater stability is ensured because the establishment permit is valid
   for five years and this simplifies the relevant administrative formalities.

A foreigner who is established in Belgium cannot be expelled from the
   country except for reasons specified in special regulations; the
   decision to expel him is subject to approval by an Advisory Commission for Foreigners and must be taken in the form of a Royal
   Decree (see below).

Only those migrant workers who have been living and working in Belgium in conditions characterized by some degree of stability are likely to

obtain an establishment permit. For example, a successful application for Work Card A may be the first step towards the acquisition of an establishment permit. In order to obtain this permit, a migrant worker must submit a request to that effect, and the decision to grant it is taken independently by the Minister of Justice following an inquiry into the migrant's conduct (verifying, for example, that he has a clean police record) and real interests in Belgium. After obtaining his establishment permit, the migrant receives an identity card and his name is entered on the population rolls.

Exclusion from Belgian territory
In order to obtain entry into Belgium for a stay of no more than three months, all that is necessary, generally speaking, is to hold a valid passport and produce it for inspection at the frontier. Foreigners who enter Belgium in this way and who have not obtained a provisional residence permit must leave the country within three months of their arrival. If they stay longer without authorization, their residence is considered to be illegal.

Illegal residence is often associated with an illegal job, that is to say, a job which has not been authorized by an employment permit obtained by the employer or a work card obtained by the migrant worker.

Apart from punitive sanctions, administrative action may be taken against a migrant who is living illegally in Belgium (except in the event of the situation being regularized). The Minister of Justice or the Director of the Public Safety Department draws up an order to the effect that the foreigner is to be conducted to the frontier, whereupon the police serve him with an order to leave the country.

The order to leave the country is not, as a rule, accompanied by an injunction forbidding re-entry into Belgium: the foreigner may come back to Belgium provided that he follows the prescribed entry procedure.

A migrant worker residing legally in Belgium by virtue of a residence or establishment permit does not, however, have a right to stay in Belgium as long as he likes: he can be sent home (*renvoyé*) or expelled (*expulsé*) from Belgian territory.

Any foreigner residing in Belgium who does not observe the conditions implied by the decision to grant him a residence permit, or whose presence is considered by the Minister of Justice to be dangerous or prejudicial to public order, public safety or the Belgian economy, can be sent home by the Minister of Justice. The decision to send him home is taken in the form of a ministerial decree. Any foreigner who holds an establishment permit and whose presence is deemed dangerous or prejudicial to public order or public safety in Belgium, or who is being prosecuted—even outside Belgium—for extraditable crimes or offences or has been convicted thereof can be expelled from the country. The decision is taken in the form of a Royal Decree counter-signed by the Minister of Justice.

The difference between the 'sending home' (*renvoi*) and the 'expelling' (*expulsion*) of foreigners consists in the fact that the former measure is applied to those who are residing in Belgium and the latter to those who are established there.

Although these two types of exclusion measures have never been applied collectively against a whole group of migrant workers legally established and working in Belgium, the existence of these powers and the danger that they may be used against individuals are particularly detrimental to the legal protection of migrant workers and weigh heavily upon their choice of activities.

Family immigration policy

Reuniting families: conditions and restrictions

When migrant workers are nationals of EEC member states, their spouse and their descendants who are under the age of 21 or are dependent on them for support, and also their forebears including those of their spouse (provided that they are dependent on them for support) have the right to join them and settle with them in Belgium. The members of the family can seek and accept gainful employment. Their nationality is disregarded: for example, a Turkish woman married to an Italian has the same employment and residence rights as her husband. On the other hand, the immigration of the family of a migrant worker from a non-EEC state is subject to strict conditions. They relate, first, to the situation of the migrant worker and, secondly, to the concept of 'family'—as defined by the manpower agreements and Belgian laws and regulations—and the requirements to be met by the members of the family. Before his family is allowed to join him, the migrant worker must have worked legally and factually in Belgium for a minimum of three months.

It is important to note that the migrant worker must immigrate alone. His family may join him three months later provided that he is actually working at that time. If he is unemployed, even after having in fact worked for more than three months, his family may not join him. Furthermore, the migrant must be working in Belgium and not in a neighbouring country. The members of the family authorized to join their relative are specified in restrictive provisions of the regulations. The first to be mentioned is the spouse of a migrant worker who is not divorced or legally separated. It is then stated that the same right is accorded to a migrant's unmarried legitimate, natural or adopted children who are dependent on him for support and are under the age of 21. All these are concurrent conditions.

It is customary administrative practice in Belgium to encourage the immigration of entire families. Accordingly, it is not possible for an immigrant to bring a son or daughter into Belgium (with a view to putting him or her to work).

This practice may, of course, have regrettable consequences. Consider the case of a family which includes a child enrolled in a course of technical or higher education in a college of the family's native country. The family cannot emigrate to Belgium unless the child interrupts his studies, and it will be no easy matter for him to take them up again in Belgium (owing to language difficulties in particular).

The right to work of members of the family

The migrant worker has a Work Card B or C ▮

The members of the family are not automatically entitled to a work card. They do, however, have the right to look for work. If they find an employer, they must, like the employer, comply with the prescribed formalities, that is to say, the employer must apply for an employment permit and the worker must apply for a work card. The application is submitted by the employer to the regional branch of the National Employment Office. The authorities do not take into account the state of the Belgian economy when deciding whether to grant an employment permit and a work card for the spouse of the migrant worker or his unmarried legitimate, natural or adopted children who are living at home and are under 15 years of age or who entered the country before the age of 15 and are taking their first job in Belgium after leaving school. The situation of a child who is over 15 when the family is reunited is much more difficult. In that case, the authorities take into account the economic situation existing at the time when the application for an employment permit and a work card is submitted. The permit and card can be withheld on the grounds of the economic situation. The child will then have to wait until his father has obtained Work Card A (see below).

The work card issued to members of the family who have found a job is a Work Card B (or C). It is therefore valid only for that branch of activity in which the work is performed. It must be renewed every year (and the authorities' decision is taken without reference to the labour market situation).

The migrant worker has a Work Card A

Work Card A is issued to the spouse (not divorced) of a migrant worker who is entitled to Work Card A. It is also issued to his legitimate, natural or adopted children, or to the children of his spouse, provided that they are not married and are members of his household. There is therefore no age limit for the children. The members of the family have a right to this card even if they are not working or have no intention of working.

Work Card A is issued to them on request provided that they prove that their spouse or parent, who is already working in Belgium, is entitled to Work Card A.

Practical results of the legislation

The available statistics do not show how many families of foreigners have been reunited in Belgium. However, there are several signs that point indirectly to the conclusion that a large number of these families have in fact been reunited. For example, we have deduced from the findings of the 1970 census and a sample survey carried out in 1977, that almost as many women as men of foreign nationality are living in Belgium and that the length of their stay is tending to increase.

Moreover, we have been able to establish that in 1974, 89.1 per cent of the total number of foreigners from EEC countries, 93.3 per cent of the Italians and 81.2 per cent of the other foreign workers had their families with them in Belgium.[4]

The place and role of migrants in economic structures

The structures

Foreigners and the economic structures

Following the influx of foreign labour into the Belgian collieries after the Second World War, the 1961 census showed that nearly 25 per cent of the economically productive workers of foreign nationality were still working in the energy sector at that time. Nine years later, that percentage had fallen very significantly: in 1970, 7.3 per cent of the foreign workers were employed in that sector. This trend has continued to the present day. In 1977, foreigners accounted for only 3.7 per cent of all manpower in the energy sector. Nevertheless, half the total number of miners and the majority of miners working underground are of foreign nationality. Table 2 shows the changes that have taken place since 1961 in the distribution of foreigners by sector of the Belgian economy.

As Table 3 shows, the index representing the ratio between the distribution percentage by sector recorded for 1977 and that recorded for 1961 is in excess of 1 per cent for the following branches:[5]

Sector 3: Metal processing industries, precision engineering (1.4).
Sector 5: Building and civil engineering (1.6).
Sector 6: Trade, restaurants, repairs (1.5).

TABLE 2. Distribution of foreigners by economic sector (sample survey, April 1977)

Sector (NACE)	Men %		Women %		Total %	
0	0.8		0.4		0.7	
1	5.1		0.2		3.7	
Of which 11		87.6		25.1		86.6
2	15.1		3.8		12.0	
Of which 22		60.1		19.9		56.6
24		20.1		31.7		21.1
25		14.9		45.6		17.5
3	13.8		6.4		11.8	
Of which 31		34.8		33.4		34.6
32		18.7		13.4		17.9
34		17.6		37.8		20.7
35		21.6		10.2		19.9
4	9.6		13.2		10.6	
Of which 41		25.9		19.3		23.6
42		19.6		18.7		19.3
44		16.3		37.1		17.7
46		7.5		12.2		14.9
5	13.6		0.9		10.1	
6	16.4		24.3		18.4	
Of which 61		29.9		16.0		24.8
64/65		29.9		54.7		38.9
66		21.6		27.0		23.6
67		16.2		1.5		10.9
7	4.5		1.3		3.6	
Of which 72		54.1		15.3		50.1
8	3.1		2.9		3.1	
Of which 83		64.6		53.8		61.8
9	6.3		23.4		11.1	
Unknown	4.2		2.7		3.8	
Unemployed and military	8.5		20.5		11.1	
	100.0		100.0		100.0	
Total number	221 357		85 045		306 402	

Source: NIS (Population Survey, April 1977).

Sector 7: Transport and communication (1.1).

Sector 8: Financing, insurance, business services (1.8).

A comparison of the 1977 percentages with those for 1970 shows that in no industrial sector was the index still in excess of 1 per cent. Since 1961, several trends have emerged:

Foreigners tend to be distributed more evenly among all sectors of the Belgian economy and are no longer primarily employed in the coal fields.

In the first phase, which began during the second half of the 1950s it was the basic heavy industries, in particular, which absorbed a large

TABLE 3. Distribution of the foreign population by economic activity—1961–77

Economic activity	Foreign population			Index		Density index	
	1961 %	1970 %	1977 %	$\frac{\% 1977}{\% 1961}$	$\frac{\% 1977}{\% 1970}$	$\dfrac{\%\ \text{Active foreign population}}{\%\ \text{Total active population}}$	
						1970	1977
0	1.7	0.8	0.7	0.4	0.9	0.2	0.2
1	23.6	7.3	3.7	0.2	0.5	3.2	1.6
2	14.4	14.2	12.0	0.8	0.9	1.9	1.6
3	8.6	13.4	11.8	1.4	0.9	1.4	1.2
4	10.4	13.2	10.6	1.0	0.8	0.9	0.7
5	6.4	9.6	10.1	1.6	1.1	1.2	1.3
6	12.2	14.5	18.4	1.5	1.3	0.9	1.1
7	3.2	3.5	3.6	1.1	1.0	0.6	0.6
8	1.7	2.3	3.1	1.8	1.3	0.5	0.7
9	14.2	12.4	11.1	0.8	0.9	0.6	0.5
00 and unknown	0.4	5.0	3.8	9.8	0.8	2.5	1.9
Unemployed and military	3.2	3.8	11.1	3.5	2.9	1.2	3.6
	100.0	100.0	100.0				

proportion of the migrant work force, and this practice became even more pronounced between 1962 and 1966. At the same time, the building industry also hired a great number of foreign workers: between 1961 and 1967, the number of foreigners employed in Belgium rose by 32 per cent while the number of workers in the building industry grew by 159 per cent. In the tertiary sector, foreigners were employed mainly in the catering and hotel industries and also as personal and domestic servants. Many workers of foreign nationality gained access to the Belgian labour market by finding employment in the collieries. As for the women, a large number entered the labour market by accepting jobs in the personal and domestic services category.

The percentages index in column 6 shows that, in the second phase, it was the tertiary sector that tended to absorb more foreigners as well as more Belgians.

This trend confirms that there is a need for foreign manpower to perform certain tasks which are distributed throughout all branches of the economy. It also reflects the result of the foreign workers' adjustment to the situation prevailing in Belgium. Furthermore, it is important to take into account the fact that some of these foreign workers are second-generation migrants. The socio-occupational characteristics of men and women in this category are not quite the same as those of their parents and now they do not perform the tasks which were assigned to their fathers when they first came to Belgium.

The distribution of foreigners by economic sector must, of course, be compared with that of the total labour force. As Table 3 shows, in 1970 foreigners were overrepresented in the following sectors:

Energy and water: index percentage of foreign population over percentage of total labour force = 3.2.

Mining and processing of non-energy minerals and their by-products, chemical industry: index = 1.9.

Metal-processing industries, precision engineering: index = 1.4.

Building and civil engineering: index = 1.2

At the time of writing this study, figures concerning the distribution of the total labour force by economic activity in the year 1977 had not yet been made available. To calculate the 1977 index, we divided the percentage of foreigners in 1977 by the percentage of the distribution of the total population in 1970. It will be noted that the index obtained is higher than 1 per cent for the same branches as in 1970 as well as for activity 6 (trade, restaurants, hotels, repairs). This index shows that foreigners were more evenly distributed among the various economic sectors, for the difference in relation to 1 per cent is less than it was in 1970.

Table 4 shows the distribution of Greeks, Spaniards, Turks and Moroccans as compared with the total foreign population.

TABLE 4. Distribution of certain nationalities by economic activity (1977)

Economic activity	(1) Greeks, Spaniards, Turks and Moroccans %	(2) Italians %	(3) Foreign population	Index (1)/(3)
0	0.4	0.1	0.7	0.6
1	8.7	3.0	3.7	2.4
2	8.7	18.9	12.0	0.7
3	11.3	14.0	11.8	1.0
4	11.3	9.2	10.6	1.1
5	11.0	11.5	10.1	1.1
6	14.1	15.4	18.4	0.8
7	4.3	1.6	3.6	1.2
8	1.2	1.9	3.1	0.4
9	10.5	6.9	11.1	1.0
00	5.0	3.4	3.8	1.3
Unemployed and military	13.5	14.1	11.1	1.2
	100.0	100.0	100.0	

The *Gastarbeiter* from those four countries are most heavily concentrated in sectors 1, 4, 5 and 7. The greatest difference is found in the energy sector, which employs 8.7 per cent of these foreign workers in Belgium as against an average of 3.7 per cent for the total number of foreign workers. On the other hand, they are greatly underrepresented in sector 8 with an index of only 0.4. This is the sector of financing, insurance and administrative services which employs more white-collar workers than manual workers.

It should further be noted that the distribution of foreigners by economic activity differs also according to the nationality of the *Gastarbeiter*. This is demonstrated by the distribution of Italians. The way in which the employment of foreigners has affected the active population in Belgium likewise calls for comment. In 1977, 36 per cent of the foreign population was working. In 1970, 37.7 per cent of the Belgian population was working as compared with a figure of 36.8 per cent for the foreign population. The drop in the employment rate for foreigners can be ascribed mainly to the following two factors: (a) first, the age structure of the foreign population, which was characterized by a large number of young people who were not yet of working age; (b) secondly, the presence of women who were not accustomed to working in their countries of origin. This was particularly characteristic of nationals of Muslim countries.

The average employment rate for foreign women was 21.3 per cent; the rate for Moroccan women was 8.5 per cent, for Turkish women 13.1 per cent, for Tunisian women 7 per cent and for Algerian women 6.8 per cent.

Between 1947 and 1970, the active population of Belgium increased by 131,834. Foreigners accounted for 47.7 per cent of the increase. Between 1961 and 1970, nearly 70 per cent of the growth of the active population was accounted for by foreigners. The male active population of Belgium decreased steadily during the entire period: by 3.1 per cent between 1947 and 1961 and by 3.2 per cent between 1961 and 1970. The growth in the number of active Belgians was therefore due to the employment of women. The economic crisis has had no appreciable effect on the demand for foreign workers in Belgium. Since 1974, the number of employment permits issued in respect of foreign workers has been virtually the same as the number of permits issued before that year.

Geographical distribution and its effect on the regions

The immigration policy which was dictated by economic needs —especially, at the beginning, by the needs of the Walloon collieries— accounts for the uneven geographical distribution of foreigners in Belgium. Nearly half the foreign population today is living in the Walloon region: a quarter in Brussels and a quarter in Flanders. This pattern of distribution is very different from that of the geographical distribution of the Belgian population as a whole. On the average, 21 per cent of the 1 million people living in the nineteen communes of the city of Brussels are foreigners. In the Walloon region, foreigners account for 13 per cent of the population; and in Flanders, 4 per cent. As compared with the nationwide average of 8.7 per cent, we find that the density index for Brussels is 2.4, for the Walloon region 1.5 and for Flanders 0.5. It should be noted, however, that in certain provinces of the Walloon region and Flanders the density of foreigners exceeds the regional average. After 1961, the increasing numbers of foreigners entering Belgium tended to converge on Brussels. Foreigners continued to be attracted towards the centre of the country until 1970, but since that year the trend has reversed, so that the foreign population has been decreasing in that area.

Besides an uneven geographical distribution of the foreign population, we observe an uneven regional distribution of the various nationalities. Of the three regions, Brussels has the largest number of Moroccans, Spaniards and Greeks; the Walloon region has the largest number of Luxemburgers, French, Germans, Italians and Poles; Flanders has the largest number of British, Dutch and Turks.

Migration plays an important demographic role in Belgium. Since 1964, the drop in the birth rate has slowed down the natural growth of the population. In 1975, the natural growth rate was zero; it now depends, to an ever-increasing extent, on the birth of children of foreign nationality. The foreign population, however, represents only 8.7 per cent of Belgium's total population. The Belgian population has a birth rate of 11.5 per cent, whereas the birth rate of the foreign population is as high as 21.5 per cent. As a result of the negative natural growth rate, the population of Belgian nationality has decreased in recent years.

Out of 1,000 Belgian males, 218 are under the age of 15 (Table 5), and this figure is less than that recorded for the foreign population. The disparity is even greater in the case of women. Over 50 per cent of the men of foreign nationality are under the age of 24. For Belgian men, the

TABLE 5. Distribution of Belgians and foreigners by sex and age group

Age group	Men		Women	
	Belgian	Foreign	Belgian	Foreign
0–14	218	321	197	348
15–64	662	634	632	587
65+	120	45	171	64
	1 000	1 000	1 000	1 000

TABLE 6. Total active foreign population by age group

Age group	Active foreign population	Total foreign population
0–14	415	334
15–64	565	612
65+	20	54
	1 000	1 000

corresponding age is 34 and for Belgian women it is 39. The *Gastarbeiter* or foreign workers are characterized by an even more youthful age structure. The age structure of workers coming from Greece, Turkey, Portugal, Spain, Yugoslavia, Algeria, Morocco and Tunisia is shown in the Table 6.

It should be noted, however, that one of the aims of Belgium's immigration policy is to promote population growth. In a report on the negative rate of demographic growth in the Walloon region (1962),[6] Sauvy and Delpérée suggested that the number of immigrants to Belgium be increased by 32,000 persons per year. Be that as it may, it is true that, initially, the primary objective of the immigration policy was to supply the country with manpower.

Housing and welfare services

As a consequence of the immigration policy very little has been done to improve social conditions for foreign workers. With the exception of the Belgian collieries which provided miners with accommodation and minimum medical services, few firms have troubled themselves with such aspects of the lives of foreign workers. It is true that the employer is obliged by law to provide living quarters for workers who have come as a group but that rule has the effect of placing the worker in a very precarious situation should he be dismissed. Foreign workers, who come to Belgium with the aim of accumulating a certain sum of money as quickly as possible, usually look for cheap accommodation, often in old, crowded and insanitary buildings. A survey has shown that, on the average, the lodgings of Belgian workers date back to 1930, but those of foreign workers to around 1908. The dwellings of nearly 39 per cent of these immigrants were built before 1900, whereas this is the case for only 17 per cent of Belgians.[7] The National Institute of Statistics has established that in 1970 a Belgian had 26 m² of living space, while a Moroccan had 13 m² and a Turk 12.5 m².

It is especially at the beginning of his stay in Belgium that a foreign worker is badly housed. After a few years, particularly when his family has joined him, he acquires a more spacious dwelling. However, he often experiences difficulty in finding accommodation because rents are high and some landlords harbour racial prejudices.[8]

The Secretary of State for Social Affairs himself admitted, at a press conference, that, as a rule, foreign workers are left to fend for themselves.[9] It is surprising that so little money is made available for immigrants' reception services. The sum allocated to the reception and integration of the 250,000 migrant workers in Brussels, for example, amounts to 7.5 million Belgian francs; in 1977, 2.6 million francs of that sum were expended on psychological and religious assistance services and 1.8 million francs on the travelling expenses of the workers' families.

For many years now, the reception and 'guidance' of foreigners have been left to local volunteer services.[10] Between 1964 and 1970, a few provinces organized reception services. In the absence of a coherent national policy in this field, the personnel of those services do what seems best with the funds made available to them by the provincial governments. In most cases, their work consists in running information centres.

Social mobility

The wage structure

The socio-occupational characteristics of migrant workers leave much to be desired. The wage structure is determined, *inter alia* by the personnel categories in which the workers are placed. Table 7 presents a summary of the data available for the years 1970 and 1977.

Whereas the number of Belgians in the 'employers and self-employed' category decreased, the number of foreigners in that category showed an increase: 7.1 per cent in 1970 and 9.8 in 1977. The increase was particularly noticeable among foreign workers:[11] in 1970, they boasted 1,624 employers or self-employed persons and in 1977 this figure had risen to 4,078, showing an increase of 151 per cent. After spending a few years in Belgium, they try to gain a footing in trade or in the catering field. As a result, every Belgian town with a large foreign population has witnessed the development of districts where all the tradesmen are foreigners.

In 1970, 35.6 per cent of the active Belgian population were registered as manual workers and 41.4 per cent as office workers. These figures contrast with the percentages concerning foreigners: 69.5 per cent of these were manual workers and 21.6 per cent were office workers. Thus, the index representing the ratio between foreign and Belgian workers was 1.95 in the case of manual workers and 0.52 in the case of office workers. The position of the *Gastarbeiter* was marked by even greater disparities: in 1970, 90.1 per cent were manual workers and

TABLE 7. Active foreign population and personnel categories in which foreign workers are placed by sex—1970 and 1977 (percentages)

		Employers and self-employed	Office workers	Manual workers	Helpers and unspecified	Total
Active foreign population						
1970	Male	7.2	18.9	72.8	1.1	100.0
	Female	6.8	30.0	59.2	4.0	100.0
	Both	7.1	21.6	69.5	1.8	100.0
1977	Male	9.6	20.5	69.4	0.5	100.0
	Female	10.3	32.9	52.1	4.7	100.0
	Both	9.8	23.6	65.1	1.5	100.0
Foreign workers (Gastarbeiter)						
1970	Male	2.4	5.0	92.1	0.5	100.0
	Female	4.2	10.1	83.7	2.0	100.0
	Both	2.8	6.2	90.1	0.9	100.0
1977	Male	5.8	7.7	86.3	0.2	100.0
	Female	7.6	18.2	71.1	3.1	100.0
	Both	6.2	10.2	82.7	0.9	100.0
Index of Gastarbeiter *in relation to active foreign population*						
1970	Male	0.3	0.3	1.3	0.5	
	Female	0.6	0.3	1.4	0.5	
	Both	0.4	0.3	1.3	0.5	
1977	Male	0.6	0.4	1.2	0.4	
	Female	0.7	0.6	1.4	0.7	
	Both	0.6	0.4	1.3	0.6	

6.2 per cent were office workers, giving an index of 2.53 and 0.15 respectively. At the time of writing this study, data concerning the Belgians had not yet been made available for the year 1977, but in that year the foreign population was still concentrated in the 'manual workers' category even though there was some evidence of a better balanced distribution. This improvement was a continuation of the trend which emerged during the period 1961–70.

Vocational training

In Belgian industry, 36 per cent of male workers are skilled, 26 per cent are unskilled and 38 per cent are given on-the-job training. The corresponding figures for the *Gastarbeiter* are 9.6 per cent, 38.7 per cent and 51.7 per cent. It is interesting to note that in the case of the Italians, who have been working in Belgium for a long time, 26 per cent are skilled and 28.3 per cent are unskilled.[12] This would seem to indicate that there is a limited possibility of advancement for foreign workers.

The concentration of foreigners in the least skilled categories is one of the reasons why they find themselves at the bottom of the wage scale. In Belgium the pay of an unskilled worker is equal to 79 per cent of the pay of a skilled worker. For women workers, the corresponding figure is 81 per cent.[13] Furthermore, in each category, foreign workers are paid according to the lowest wage rates. Thus, according to a recent study, the average hourly wage of a foreign skilled or unskilled worker is equal to 89 per cent of the wage of a Belgian worker whether skilled or unskilled. A foreign woman worker earns 93 per cent of the wage of her Belgian counterpart if she is skilled and 89 per cent if she is unskilled.[14]

Some foreign workers try to make up the difference by doing overtime or shift work, etc.

The status of migrant workers in the firms employing them

In Belgium, very few studies have been undertaken on the specific situation of foreigners in the firms employing them. Whatever facts are known have been mentioned in earlier paragraphs. Let us recapitulate the main points:

In the firms employing them, foreigners have the same rights and the same duties as Belgians.

The distinction between foreigners and Belgians is most in evidence when their level of qualifications and rates of pay are considered.

Very few firms provide their foreign workers with any specific services. In most cases, foreigners who have been living for some time in Belgium give help to their compatriots. In other cases, it is the children of foreigners who aid their parents, using the knowledge of the host-country's language and institutions which they have acquired in a Belgian school.

On the average, foreigners do not change employers any more frequently than Belgian workers performing the same tasks.[15] It has been established, however, that there is a greater turnover in the secondary labour market than in the primary labour market.[16] Inasmuch as foreigners are heavily concentrated in the secondary sector, their average rate of turnover is higher than that of Belgian workers.

Several Belgian firms do not employ foreign labour but engage other firms to carry out work for which foreigners are usually hired.

Several firms allow their foreign workers to accumulate their days off so as to enable them to return home for their holidays. Some allow them to take extra days off without pay.

The Belgian collieries organize work schedules in such a way as to enable Muslim workers to observe Ramadan.

Unemployment among migrant workers

In Belgium, 8.3 per cent of the active population is accounted for by workers of foreign nationality; 15.3 per cent of the persons who are totally unemployed and receiving unemployment benefit are foreigners.[17] In relation to the corresponding active population, the unemployment rate for foreigners therefore stands at 13.8 per cent as against 6.6 per cent for Belgian nationals.

Given the large number of unemployed workers among foreigners, it is also clear that they lose their jobs more often than do Belgian workers for the number of unemployed foreigners increases every year at a faster rate than that observed for unemployed Belgians. For example, between 30 June 1977 and 30 June 1978, the number of unemployed rose by 12.3 per cent in the case of foreigners as against only 6.4 per cent in the case of Belgians. Far from being an isolated phenomenon, this recurs every year. Nearly half (49 per cent) the number of unemployed foreigners are women, but women account for only 28 per cent of the active population of foreign nationality. This shows that they have a very high rate of unemployment.

Over half (59.1 per cent) the number of foreigners are nationals of an EEC member country, but they account for 64 per cent of the active foreign population. The Italians are an exception, however, for in their case the corresponding figures are 45.9 and 34.7 per cent. Among nationals of countries which are not members of the EEC, the Greeks (18.9 per cent), the Turks (15.5 per cent), the Tunisians (19.9 per cent) and above all the Moroccans (24.1 per cent) have a considerably higher unemployment rate than the average rate for the foreign population.

The occupational characteristic that has contributed to creating this situation is the inadequacy of the qualifications of foreign workers. Unskilled workers are the first victims of unemployment. Thus, 62.8 per cent of the totally unemployed persons receiving unemployment benefit in Belgium have attended only primary school (some completing the course, others not); 82.8 per cent of the unemployed foreigners are in this situation.

It should also be noted that nearly half the foreign population lives in the Walloon region of Belgium, which has a much higher unemployment rate than the national average (+ 32 per cent). The length of time during

TABLE 8. Length of time out of work (percentages)

Period	All unemployed	Foreigners
Less than a year	53.4	39.0
One to two years	17.7	19.7

which unemployed foreigners remain out of work differs from that observed for the unemployed as a whole (see Table 8).

A bill tabled in the House of Representatives on 15 March 1978 proposed that the right to unemployment benefit should be denied to foreigners having been out of work for more than six months during the previous year.

Integration of migrants and their families into the host society

Participation of migrants in political and associative life

The public rights of foreigners

The Belgian Constitution guarantees to all foreigners on Belgian territory the protection of their person and property, except as provided otherwise by law. The protection of the foreigner is the general rule and there can be no departure from that principle unless a special law is passed to that effect. Consequently, a foreigner enjoys all public rights except when a special law expressly reserves certain rights for Belgian citizens (for example, the right to vote) or lays down special rules applicable solely to foreigners (for example, those concerning the right to work).

The right to vote and to stand for election is the prerogative of Belgian nationals. This applies not only to parliamentary elections but also to the election of members of provincial or communal bodies. For many years now, various pressure groups have been demanding that foreigners having resided in Belgium for a certain length of time be granted the right to vote, at least in communal elections.

At the last parliamentary session devoted to the question of amendments to the Constitution (held at the end of 1978), Glinne, who was one of the members participating in the debate, proposed that the right to vote in communal elections be granted to certain categories of foreigners. The proposal was not adopted.

With very rare exceptions (university professorships, certain teaching posts in primary schools), no public office may be held by a foreigner. Such posts are open only to Belgians.

As a general rule, the right of assembly is guaranteed both to Belgians and to foreigners. Up to the present time, no law has been voted to make it obligatory to obtain prior authorization for public meetings held by foreigners in closed premises. Foreigners enjoy the right to freedom of association: they can join associations of their choice and occupy administrative posts therein.

There are exceptions, however: a foreigner cannot serve on the administrative committees of a mutual insurance society or a professional body.

Migrant workers and trade unions

A foreign worker has the right to join the trade union of his choice. The regulations governing the activities of trade-union representatives which are in force on the premises of firms have been established by collective agreements for each sector.

Although most of these collective agreements make no distinction between Belgian and foreign workers in respect of the election or appointment of trade-union delegates, some agreements do, however, specify that the members of the delegation shall be either Belgians or migrant workers who have obtained Work Card A or nationals of EEC countries.

In 1975, the last remaining legal distinctions between Belgian and migrant workers were removed, in so far as the right to vote for and stand for election to the Works Council and the Safety and Health Committee was concerned: migrant workers and Belgian workers have the same rights and are subject to the same conditions.

Pressure groups

Various groups, movements or organizations are endeavouring to improve the lot of migrant workers.

Reception centres have been set up in many towns and communes having large communities of migrant workers, thanks almost entirely to the action taken by the Belgian inhabitants, for the immigrants themselves played only a very minor role.

In most cases, such centres are the fruit of the efforts of private individuals who have only limited funds at their disposal. Some centres, however (in the provinces, in particular), have obtained official recognition and are receiving large subsidies.

The reception centres play an essential role not only in helping migrant workers to adjust to their new surroundings but also in bringing this problem to the notice of public opinion and politicians. The migrants started fairly recently to co-operate with these centres and are now participating in their operations and in the organization of their activities. A year ago, the Brabant Reception Centre began publishing a magazine with the collaboration of migrant workers.

Generally speaking, Belgian trade unions are rather guarded in their relations with immigrants. They are primarily concerned with defending the interests of Belgian workers, and this is particularly apparent when the country is faced with a difficult economic situation: migrant workers then tend to be regarded as competitors. At the same time, it must be admitted that the Belgian unions have shown concern for practical difficulties encountered by foreign workers in their daily life and have done a great deal to improve their lot. This shows that once the decision had been taken to integrate foreign manpower into a particular industry, the unions concerned took a real interest in the problems of the immigrants employed in that industry.

As foreign workers began to feel more at home in Belgium and were joined by their families, they gradually came to realize the importance of participating in union activities, especially since the trade unions themselves made an effort to take account of the different nationalities of the workers selected for training as union delegates.

It was not long before foreign residents' associations began to appear in towns or communes where there were large numbers of migrant workers. These organizations or, to be more exact, these clubs are closely linked with the various nationalities: there are clubs for Turks, Moroccans, Italians, etc.

These clubs are primarily concerned with cultural and social activities: their role is to provide immigrants with opportunities to maintain ties with their home countries and to meet their fellow-countrymen and friends. They serve, therefore, as centres for the social life of migrant workers and play practically no political role. Furthermore, in order to prevent the development of opposition movements, certain governments of emigration countries have tried to induce their nationals to join cultural associations which they have set up in Belgium with this end in view. It goes without saying that such associations or societies are careful not to be drawn into any political activity.

In some Belgian communes, the authorities have set up a Foreigners' Communal Advisory Council; this is an official body composed of foreigners who have been resident for some time in the commune. The members of the Advisory Council are elected by the foreign population of the commune. The communal authorities consult the Foreigners' Advisory Council on all questions concerning the foreign population of the commune.

For various reasons, these foreigners' advisory councils—which have been in existence for some years—are not being very actively developed and the experiment has not been repeated by other communes.

Certain groups, movements or organizations have been led by certain circumstances to play an important role as pressure groups: (a) in the last few years the Belgian League for the Defence of Human Rights has been militating in favour of a better legal status for foreigners; (b) at the beginning of the 1970s the student movement vigorously defended foreign students who were threatened with being sent home (*renvoi*) and this action induced the Minister of Justice to set up a commission to review the legal status of foreigners in Belgium. The work of the commission resulted in the drafting of a bill which is now before Parliament.

Lastly, we must draw attention to the existence in Belgium of the Movement against Racism, Anti-Semitism and Xenophobia (MRAX).

Integration policy

As we have already shown, Belgium has tried to attract foreign workers in order to use their labour 'so as to provide the Belgian economy with the manpower required for its development'. Nevertheless, the government has facilitated and encouraged the immigration of families, and foreign workers can now bring in their families without waiting until a certain period has elapsed. The Belgian collieries have even paid part of the travelling expenses of miners' families. This family immigration policy was also dictated by economic considerations because about 30 per cent of newly arrived miners had been returning home before completing their first contract, for various reasons connected with the absence of the family, the climate, food, the tempo of work, etc. This explains why employers have made efforts to encourage the immigration and establishment of families.[18]

Although Belgium has always endorsed the principle of reuniting families, the government has failed to work out an unambiguous policy for the reception and integration of foreigners. The frontiers have been apparently open as if the aim was to encourage the establishment of foreigners but in reality the authorities have organized a system of rotation for migrant workers.

Conclusion

Belgium has always relied on workers of foreign nationality to solve its labour problems. The need for foreign workers, which initially arose out of a particular economic situation, has now become a structural need.

Ever since the 1930s, Belgian legislation in this field has been dictated by the needs of the labour market and by the imperative duty to protect the interests of Belgian workers. Even though immigrants have been encouraged to bring in their families, the authorities have not sufficiently developed the structures for providing reception, information and integration services.

The steadily growing number of foreigners, their concentration in certain towns and regions and their impact on the Belgian economy have raised questions about the soundness of this policy, its implications and the needs created by their presence. The problems are much more complex, however, than certain bills concerning the expulsion of foreigners or their integration through enfranchisement would lead one to believe.

The authorities have a duty to keep both Belgians and foreigners informed. The Belgians must get to know the foreign workers and the reasons why they choose to live in Belgium, they should learn about the customs of the workers' countries of origin. The foreigners, for their part, should make an effort to understand Belgian ways.

In this spirit, the Belgian institutions should adapt themselves to the task of promoting a better approach to the integration of foreign workers. An effort should also be made to look ahead and consider what immigration problems are likely to arise in the future.

Notes

1. *L'économie belge en 1947*, p. 39, Brussels, Ministère des Affaires Économiques et des Classes Moyennes, 1948.
2. Fédéchar (Doc. st. 41,623 and 43,750).
3. 'Les travailleurs étrangers et leur famille. La migration en Belgique: un problème social', *Contracts '72*, December 1971, pp. 92–3.
4. H. Debbaut, *Vreemde arbeidskrachten in de Belgische economie*, pp. 56–7, Ghent, 1976.
5. No account is taken of sector 00 which may be regarded as a 'remainder' item.
6. A. Sauvy, *Conditions du développement économique et mesures à prendre en vue d'un renouveau général*, Conseil Économique Wallon, 1962.
7. Debbaut, op. cit., p. 152.
8. See, among others, F. Delfosse, *Huisvesting van gastarbeiders*, Brussels, NIH, 1977, and Debbaut, op. cit., pp. 150 et seq.
9. Anciaux, in Debbaut, op. cit., p. 25.
10. Ibid., p. 2.
11. The available statistics give the breakdown for Spaniards, Greeks, Moroccans and Turks.
12. Debbaut, op. cit., pp. 36–7; *Statistisch Tijdschrift* (NIS), No. 5, 1975, p. 658.
13. J. Haex, A. Martens and S. Wolf, *Arbeidsmarkt, discriminatie, gastarbeid*, p. 121, Leuven, 1976.
14. Ibid., pp. 122–3.
15. Debbaut, op. cit., p. 48.
16. Haex et al., op. cit., pp. 161 et seq.
17. Totally unemployed on 30 June 1979.
18. A. Berten, 'De vestiging van gastarbeiders en hun gezin in België', *Arbeidsblad*, No. 12, 1966, pp. 1532–3.

Bibliography

Law

BOLLEN, R. *Explorerend onderzoek naar de rechtspositie van der buitenlandse werknemer inzake sociaal zekerheidsrecht.* Leuven, Instituut voor Sociaal Zekerheidsrecht, 1978.
HERREMAN, J. *De vreemdelingenreglementering.* Heule, UGA, 1974.
Het juridisch statuut van de vreemdeling in België [Proceedings of the 21st Interuniversity Law Congress]. Leuven, Vlaams Rechtsgenootschap, 1969.

MISOTTEN, O. Tewerkstelling van vreemdelingen. In: Professor R. Blanplain (ed.), *Arbeidsrecht.* CAD, n.d.

RIGAUX, F.; GODDING, P. et al. La condition des étrangers en Belgique. *Annales de droit,* Vol. XXX, 1970.

Miscellaneous

ANDRÉ, R. Étude régionale des mouvements migratoires des populations belge et étrangère. *Revue de l'Institut de Sociologie.* Brussels, 1969.

BATTESTI, L.-M. *L'immigration de la main-d'œuvre étrangère et la communauté économique européenne.* Lille, 1973.

BERTEN, A. De vestiging van gastarbeiders en hun gezin. *Arbeidsblad,* No. 12, 1966.

BRACKMAN, C. *Les étrangers en Belgique.* Brussels, 1975.

BRUYERE, J. L'immigration de main-d'œuvre étrangère en 1976, nécessité . . . ou mésaventure? *Pop-Infor,* No. 3, June 1976.

CASTELEIN, T. *Onderwijs-dossier m.b.t. gastarbeiderskinderen die basisonderwijs volgen in Vilvoorde.* Vilvoorde, 1977.

COLIN, P. Statistiek van de in België tewerkgestelde vreemde werknemers op 31-12-1968 en 31-12-1971. *Arbeidsblad,* January–February–March 1973.

COMMISSION DES COMMUNAUTÉS EUROPÉENNES. *Emploi de travailleurs étrangers, 1975.* December 1976. (T/264/76F. s.l.)

DEBBAUT, H. Gastarbeid in België: achtergronden en evolutie. Een op het beleid gerichte sociaal-economische benadering. *Bevolking en gezin,* No. 2, 1977.

——. *Onderzoek naar bewoners en bewoning in het gebied gelegen tussen Sluizeken en Muide in de stad Gent.* Ghent, 1977.

——. *Vreemde arbeidskrachten en economische groei. Theoretische analyse met een praktische toepassing op België.* Ghent, 1977.

——. *Vreemde arbeidskrachten in der Belgische economie.* Ghent, 1976.

DOOGHE, G.; VANDELEYDEN, L. Publieke opinie en vreemdelingen. *Bevolking en Gezin,* No. 1, 1974.

HANOTIAU, B. *Les problèmes de sécurité sociale des travailleurs migrants.* Brussels, 1973.

KING, R. The Evolution of International Labour Migration Movements concerning the E.E.C. *Tijdschrift voor economische en sociale geografie,* No. 2, 1976.

MARTENS, A. *25 jaar wegwerparbeiders. Het Belgisch immigratiebeleid na 1945.* KUL, 1973.

MARTENS, A.; WOLF, S. *Buitenlandse werknemers op de huisvestingsmarkt.* Leuven, 1977.

MEEUS, B. De vreemdelingen te Brussel. *De gids op maatschappelijk gebied,* No. 9, 1974.

PANCIERA, S.; DUCOLI, B. Immigration et marché du travail en Belgique: fonctions structurelles et fluctuations quantitatives de l'immigration en Belgique. Période 1945-1975. *Courrier hebdomadaire du CRISP,* 23 January 1978.

The status of immigrant workers in France

Eric-Jean Thomas

Introduction

Unlike many other European states, France has long been a major immigration country as a result of the potentialities and needs of its economy and a population policy that made it easy for foreigners to gain access to its territory.

Between the two wars, France's foreign population was, for the most part, made up of nationals from neighbouring states, but it also included large numbers of immigrants from more distant countries like Poland.

From the mid-1920s onwards, the General Immigration Society, composed of various employers' associations, organized the recruiting and transportation of workers in many countries. The flow of immigrants was therefore geared, by and large, to the needs of the principal sectors of the French economy. In the early 1930s, the foreign population exceeded the 2 million mark and comprised 808,000 Italians, 507,000 Poles, 351,000 Spaniards and some 250,000 Belgians.

Up to the Second World War, the state pursued a liberal immigration policy and accordingly never played a prominent role in the operation of the immigration control system.

After the Second World War, an important new trend emerged. In the first place, the year 1945 saw the establishment of the National Immigration Office (ONI), whose original purpose was to facilitate immigration with a view to increasing the population while at the same time regulating migratory flows. The Ordinance of 2 November 1945, which instituted the ONI, is still the basic text governing the regulation of immigration to France. The state thus equipped itself with the instruments it needed for developing and implementing a real immigration policy.

In the second place, the traditional migratory flows gradually changed until the foreign population structure in France had been radically transformed. This change was, in fact, the result of the great political upheavals that followed the Second World War: the sealing off of the countries of Eastern Europe from the West had the effect of stopping practically all migratory flows from the socialist countries. Moreover, the decolonization movement which began in the 1950s made workers who had hitherto enjoyed French citizenship into foreigners; at the same time, there was an increase in the number of immigrants from the Third World countries.

Despite the radical change in the law constituted by the Ordinance of 2 November 1945, immigration was not really brought under control—or even simply regulated—until the mid-1970s. In a very short time, the machinery that had been set up and the institutions that had been established ceased to perform their assigned functions owing to the laxity and empiricism that passed for an immigration policy until the summer of 1974 when new measures were taken.

Uncontrolled immigration proceeded apace and by the end of the 1960s about 80 per cent of the migrants were entering the country without complying with the regulations in force. They first found a job and then set about regularizing their situation. The authorities ended by accepting the *fait accompli* and this system of *a posteriori* control became the standard procedure.

In 1970, the regulations began to be more stringently applied as the executive systematically modified the existing texts—by means of statutory instruments—always with a view to making them more restrictive.

Finally, the Council of Ministers decided, on 3 July 1974, that the importation of foreign labour should be temporarily interrupted —except in a few cases, notably those concerning nationals of EEC countries—pending a new definition of the government's immigration policy.

In September 1977, the government also modified the orientation of its family immigration policy and suspended *sine die* the admission of families of immigrants; it then barred them from entering the labour market by a decree which was, however, annulled by the Council of State in December 1978.

As a result of this Draconian policy, the volume of the permanent migratory flow was considerably reduced, dropping from 226,066 in 1973 to 56,693 in 1979.

In the autumn of 1979, the government laid before Parliament two bills concerning the expulsion, entry and residence of foreigners in France. These texts, which were the subject of heated debates between members of Parliament and members of the government, reaffirm, in more precise terms, many provisions already introduced into the regulations by statutory instruments. They are important on two accounts. First, because they are the culmination of efforts to develop a very restrictive immigration policy which seems to have started in the early 1970s; secondly, because they reflect the government's determination to have this restrictive policy ratified by Parliament although some of its legal foundations are ill-defined. The government's attitude has met with a great deal of criticism not only on the part of public opinion but also in the Council of State which has had occasion to annul several texts emanating from the government.

The adoption of these texts by Parliament can be said to mark the end of a period which witnessed the growth of the powers of the administrative authorities in a sphere where conditions are particularly favourable to arbitrary action and the misuse of power. It is desirable that Parliament should prove equal to its task and vote legislation safeguarding the fundamental rights of foreign workers.

Today, with a foreign population of some 3.7 million, France is one of the leading immigration countries in Europe. The immigration policy pursued in France, accordingly has a significance recognized far beyond its national boundaries. Although it does not necessarily serve as an example, French policy has an influence on that of other immigration countries, just as it is itself influenced by changes introduced into the regulations applied by its neighbours.

From the legal standpoint, the French model is characterized by an incredible proliferation of laws and regulations. Far from according immigrants the same political rights as the French, they entangle them in a web of regulations and confer inordinate powers on the administrative authorities.

From the economic standpoint, the immigrant has become an indispensable factor of production in numerous sectors. However, the foreign worker is 'useful' only in certain occupations and at a certain level of qualification. The law then comes to the assistance of the economy by regulating the mobility of immigrants within the economic structures.

Lastly, from the standpoint of social integration, great progress has been made in democratizing the working environment, but the immigrant does not always have opportunities to participate in local or regional community life.

France has created a difficult situation for its foreign workers and the years ahead will certainly witness a tightening of controls and a deterioration of their socio-occupational status.

Immigration policy and regulations

Conditions governing entry into French territory and access to the labour market

In order to enter French territory, foreign workers must be in possession of 'the documents and visas required by international conventions and the regulations in force' (Ordinance of 1945). The Act of 10 January 1980 added new conditions to be fulfilled by foreign workers seeking access to French territory. Henceforth, the migrant will be required to 'produce, unless otherwise provided in international conventions, guarantees of repatriation defined by decrees of the Council of State or, if he intends to exercise a professional activity, to present the prescribed author-izations' (Article 1 of the Law). The same Act stipulates that 'permission to enter French territory can be refused to any foreigner whose presence would be prejudicial to public order'.

It is clear that this Act seeks to put an end to immigration disguised as tourism; at the same time, it reduces the importance and effectiveness of the regularization procedure which is described later in this study. It is legitimate to ask, however, what criterion will be used by the frontier control authorities to enable them to decide that a foreigner is not a tourist but a would-be immigrant.

The wording of the Act makes it clear that the *sine qua non* for obtaining access to the territory is that the migrant shall be in possession of a work permit, this prerequisite being in line with current practice and earlier texts according to which the issue of a residence permit was conditional upon the prior issue of a work permit.

Thus, in France, immigration is controlled at the level of access to the labour market and not at the level of residence permit procedures, as is the case in many countries.

According to the standard procedure, foreign labour is imported into France through the agency of the National Immigration Office. The admission of a foreign worker is subject to the possession of a work contract endorsed by the services of the Ministry of Labour.

In addition, Article R.341–3 of the Labour Code lays down an 'authorization to work' procedure designed to enable foreigners already established in France to take up paid employment.

Lastly, in 1975, the Council of State recognized that a foreigner residing in France by virtue of a valid residence permit, whatever the type, could submit an application for a work permit to the administrative authorities, who could not refuse his request in the absence of relevant legislative provisions.[1]

Ordinary immigration law: importation of foreign labour
by the National Immigration Office (ONI)[2]

The current regulations have three objectives: to protect the labour market, giving priority to French nationals who are looking for work; to institute a system for controlling the movements of foreigners; to define the status of immigrants. In pursuance of the first objective, an equalization procedure has been developed. An employer desiring to recruit a foreign worker must file with the Local Employment Office (ALE) a job vacancy notice containing a description of the type of work he intends to offer to a foreigner. If, after five weeks have elapsed, no one has been found to fill the vacancy, the regular procedure for bringing in a foreign worker can be set in motion. In this way, ordinary immigration law in France aims to ensure that every foreign worker seeking employment in France shall be recruited abroad, even if the work contract drawn up by the employer gives the name of the person to be hired.

At this juncture the administrative authorities can start to exercise their powers of control over the migratory flow for, after the five weeks have elapsed, ALE forwards the file to the competent services of the Ministry of Labour to obtain the visa which is required before the procedure can be carried further. Should the administrative authorities refuse to endorse the work contract submitted for their consideration, the immigration is halted. It is in this way that frontiers have been closed to immigrants since the Council of Ministers took the decision of 3 July 1974.

Consequently, it is the employer, acting independently, who proposes that a foreign worker should be brought to France, but there are two factors which allow immigration to be controlled: the ALE equalization procedure and the Ministry of Labour's power to block the process of approving the work contract.

It is important to note that, despite its technical merits, the equalization procedure is not very effective. The system presupposes that the labour market is perfectly fluid, that is to say that nationals and immigrant workers are interchangeable. In reality, however, this is not the case, for two reasons: in the first place, the jobs offered to foreign workers are usually those which the national work force refuses as being too hard; secondly—and this point is closely linked to the first—it is usual for employers to offer foreigners lower wages than those actually received by French workers. An employer has all the more reason not to offer higher wages because he knows full well that this is the best way of finding the foreign manpower he needs.

Procedure for obtaining authorization to work[3]

This procedure applies to foreigners already established in France, that is to say to those who already have a residence card, provided that—if they possess only a temporary residence card—they were admitted to France as members of a reunited family or have already exercised a paid or unpaid professional activity in France; accordingly, foreign students cannot avail themselves of this procedure.

It is a simplified procedure: there is no medical examination and the employer is not required to deposit a job vacancy notice.

Cases of a general character

The foreigner files the following documents with the *mairie*, police station or, if in Paris, the Préfecture de Police: (a) a work contract or a promise of employment; (b) his residence card. The foreign worker's application will then be examined in the light of the situation of the labour market, which may justify a refusal to grant the desired authorization.

Special cases where authorization is automatically granted[4]

The following persons fall into this category: (a) a foreigner who has had a Privileged Resident's Card for ten years; (b) the spouse of a French national; (c) the spouse of a worker who is a national of an EEC member country; (d) a refugee or stateless person who has resided for three years in France or has one or more children of French nationality; (e) a young foreigner who, at the time of his application, can prove that during the three previous years he has completed two years of an educational course in France, provided that one of his parents has been living in France for over four years. The persons concerned must apply for a work card valid for all occupations and throughout French territory (Card C), following the standard procedure for obtaining authorization to work, except that they are not required to prove that they have a work contract (see section on 'The Work Card System', below).

Regularization procedure

This procedure concerns foreigners who wish to exercise a professional activity after they have entered French territory and who cannot follow the regular procedure for obtaining authorization to work.

Since it is a question of regularizing an illegal situation, this procedure is applicable only in exceptional circumstances. However, the Council of State has recognized and validated the admissibility of such a procedure (we refer to the Da Silva judgement).

When a foreigner in this situation has found a job, his employer must file a vacancy notice pertaining to that job with ALE. If the job is still vacant after five weeks have elapsed, ALE forwards the worker's file to the appropriate police station.

The police thereupon contact the Departmental Labour Board, requesting them to issue the authorization to work. At present, this type of request is stringently screened by the services of the Ministry of Labour.

In the event of a favourable decision, the applicant is given an appointment at an ONI centre for a medical examination. If he is found to be in good health, he is given a work card and is then summoned to the police station to receive a residence permit valid for the same period as the work card.

At present, the only persons who can avail themselves of this provision are highly qualified foreigners and foreigners whose authorization to work is not conditional upon the state of the labour market, i.e. those whose application is handled according to the 'automatic authorization' procedure (see above). Not only do the services of the Ministry of Labour screen applications with the utmost severity, especially as regards their evaluation of the labour market situation, but the Act of 10 January 1980 has also imposed significant limitations on the application of the regularization procedure. Article 6 of that Act stipulates that 'the Minister of the Interior can order, by decree, the expulsion of a foreigner from French territory' when 'the foreigner has stayed on the territory for a period exceeding three months since the date of his entry into France without having obtained an initial residence permit issued in accordance with the regulations in force'. This means that a foreigner who takes steps to regularize his situation can be expelled by virtue of an emergency procedure without prior notification and without having been heard by the special commission which is attached to the prefect's office and is specifically charged with hearing the testimony of foreigners threatened with an expulsion order. Inasmuch as it is necessary to hold a work permit in order to obtain a residence permit, any foreign worker who files an application to regularize his situation falls foul of Article 6 of the Act of 10 January 1980 since he cannot be in possession of a residence permit before he has received a favourable reply from the Ministry of Labour!

TABLE 1. Mode of entry into French territory of permanent immigrant workers (excluding EEC nationals) as recorded by the National Immigration Office

Year	1975	1976	1977	1978	1979
Recruited abroad	2 656	1 691	1 764	1 079	1 006
Regularization	13 013	15 562	12 485	8 942	8 219
Total recorded number of immigrants	15 769	17 253	14 249	10 021	9 225

Source: ONI.

Regulations governing work permits for foreigners (Decree of 21 November 1975)

The work card system[5]

Authorizations to work do not all have the same validity as regards geographical area, duration or occupational field. Moreover, the longer a foreign worker stays in France, the more extensive the rights he enjoys: there are 'rewards for long service'.

There are three kinds of work cards:

The temporary card, known as Card A, entitles the holder to exercise a specified type of paid professional activity in the department(s) designated on the card. It is valid for one year and is renewable. Card A is the one usually issued to a worker who has been recruited abroad or who has regularized his situation.

The ordinary card, known as Card B, entitles the holder to exercise, in the department(s) designated on the card, the professional activity or activities specified thereon. Card B can be issued to a foreigner holding Card A when the validity of the latter expires if he proves that he has been employed for one year by virtue of his possession of Card A. Card B is valid for three years and is renewable. When Card B comes up for renewal, the foreign worker may be called upon to show proof that since the time it was first issued or last renewed he has, in fact, exercised the professional activity or activities specified.

The work card for all paid occupations, known as Card C, entitles the holder to exercise throughout the territory of metropolitan France any paid professional activity of his choice subject to the laws applicable to the exercise of that activity. It is valid for ten years and is renewable. At the time of the renewal of Card C, the worker may be called upon to show proof of having in fact exercised a paid professional activity since the card was first issued or last renewed. Moreover, some categories of foreigners now receive Card C on request, regardless of the labour market situation (see page 46).

The renewal of a work card can only be authorized if the worker holds a job. However, if he is unemployed through no fault of his own, he can obtain a limited extension of the period of validity of his work card. The other factors that are taken into consideration when granting or refusing an application for a work card are as follows: the present and future prospects of employment in the occupation and region concerned, the manner in which the employer complies with the labour regulations, the working conditions and pay offered to the foreign worker and the housing arrangements made by the employer. In the final analysis, therefore, an immigrant worker can never be certain that his work permit will be renewed.

Special systems

Not all foreigners come under the system that has been described above.

First of all, there are certain foreigners who receive preferential treatment owing to their exceptional circumstances. This category includes refugees and stateless persons; in their case, an authorization to work cannot be refused because of the situation prevailing in the labour market. Moreover, refugees in possession of a certificate delivered by the French Office for Refugees and Stateless Persons (OFPRA) are exempt from the obligation to have a work permit.

A second category comprises foreigners who enjoy a special status as a result of agreements existing between their country of origin and France. For example, under the terms of an agreement concluded between France and Portugal on 11 January 1977, the spouses of Portuguese nationals who have been permitted to enter France in accordance with the policy of reuniting families cannot be denied authorization to work because of the labour-market situation. Similarly, by virtue of the Franco-Algerian agreement of 27 December 1978, Algerian nationals are not subject to the jurisdiction of ordinary law. The nationals of African states south of the Sahara formerly under French administration, enjoy a rather distinctive status which is gradually being changed to bring them under the jurisdiction of ordinary law.

Lastly, there is of course a special category in which we find the rules concerning nationals of EEC member states. These rules derive from community law and there is no need to elaborate on them here. Suffice it to say that EEC nationals receive on request a residence card which is valid for five years and that this is the only document they need to reside and work in France.

Regulations governing residence permits

Residence permits[6]

In France, foreigners are divided into three categories depending on the length of their stay and the type of permit they hold: (a) foreigners holding a temporary resident's card (CRT), valid for one year; (b) foreigners holding an ordinary resident's card (CRO), valid for three years; (c) foreigners holding a privileged resident's card (CRP), valid for ten years.

Conditions governing the issue of residence permits

A residence card can be issued only by the Prefect of Police or the prefect of the department where the foreigner resides. A medical certificate is mandatory. The immigrant worker must produce either a work contract endorsed by the competent services of the Ministry of Labour or an authorization issued by the same services.

Special conditions

CRT. This card must be held by tourists residing on French territory for a period exceeding three months, students, temporary workers and, in general, foreigners who come to France for a limited time and do not intend to take up regular residence on French territory.

CRO. This card concerns foreigners who wish to take up residence in France. The application must specify the foreigner's reason for wishing to settle in France.

CRP. This card can be obtained by foreigners who show proof that they have resided in France for at least three years. This period is reduced to one year for the following categories: (a) foreigners who are married to French women and have kept their own nationality; (b) foreigners who are the father or mother of a French child; (c) foreigners holding an ordinary resident's card and living in France with their spouse and children who, as at 1 July 1979, had entered and were residing in France in accordance with the regulations in force.

In addition, foreigners having fought for France or rendered services to the country are not subject to any minimum residence requirement, nor are their spouse, forebears and descendants.

Renewal

In order to obtain authorization for the renewal of any type of residence permit, the holder must satisfy the same conditions as those required when he first applied for the permit.

CRT. This card is renewable. Moreover, before it expires, the holder can apply for a privileged resident's card or an ordinary resident's card. CRTs are not automatically renewed.

CRO. An application for renewal must be filed within the three months preceding the expiration date. An application for a CRP may be filed when the holder of a CRO fulfils the necessary conditions. CROs are not automatically renewed.

CRP. An application for renewal must be filed within the three months preceding the expiration date. CRPs are automatically renewed.

Cancellation

CRT. It can be cancelled at any time when the holder no longer meets the conditions on which it was granted.

CRO. It can be cancelled when its holder is under an expulsion order. It can also be cancelled if it is proved that the holder 'has either left France for a period exceeding six months, save for a motive recognized as valid before the expiry of that period, or has been without work or regular means of support of his own accord, for over six months'.

CRP. Apart from the case where the holder is under an expulsion order, he can only be deprived of the status of privileged resident by a decree issued by the Minister of the Interior after consulting a special commission. A foreigner who forfeits his privileged resident's card is given a temporary resident's card or an ordinary resident's card.

Family immigration

Developments over the last ten years

The developments during this period were mainly connected with the economic situation and changes in the regulations. Until 1969, the flow of immigrants' families was of moderate proportions, averaging around 23,000 families per year. After that year, there was a notable increase in the number of families admitted into France and in 1971 this figure amounted to 39,798, representing 81,496 persons. Immigration proceeded apace until 1974, and the steep upward trend coincided with a period characterized not only by strong economic activity but also by the flexible application of the regulations, as is shown by the fact that, during the early 1970s, about 90 per cent of members of families regularized their situation after their arrival (94.2 per cent in 1971).

From 1975 onwards, there was a progressive decline in immigration. It was during this period that the first laws were drafted with the aim of closing the frontiers to migratory flows. In fact, the immigration of families was halted between July and the end of December 1974 and, on 10 November 1977, the government decided, by decree, to suspend the issuing of work permits to members of immigrant workers' families. However, this text was annulled on 8 December 1978 by the Council of State, on the grounds that foreigners residing in France had the same right as French citizens to lead a normal life, that this right implied, in particular, that foreigners should be able to arrange for their families to join them and that the government could not lay down a blanket rule forbidding the members of foreigners' families to take up jobs. The annulment of that text does not mean, however, that henceforth members of families are assured of obtaining a work permit. It is still possible for the immigration control authorities to refuse to issue work cards inasmuch as the labour market situation can still be given as a reason for turning down applications from the members of foreign workers' families.

TABLE 2. Families and individuals admitted into France—1969–79

Year	Families	Individuals	Year	Families	Individuals
1969	26 617	57 333	1975	27 911	51 824
1970	37 145	80 952	1976	29 071	57 377
1971	39 798	81 496	1977	26 958	52 318
1972	37 660	74 955	1978	21 007	40 120
1973	37 748	72 647	1979	19 863	39 298
1974	35 284	68 038			

Source: ONI.

TABLE 3. Mode of immigration of families—1969–79

Year	Entry through official channels	Regularization	Total number of families	Entry through official channels in relation to total number (%)
1969	4 155	22 462	26 617	15
1970	3 030	34 115	37 145	8
1971	2 333	37 465	39 798	5.8
1972	3 339	34 321	37 660	8.9
1973	4 030	33 718	37 748	10.6
1974	5 479	29 805	35 284	15.5
1975	5 253	22 658	27 911	18.8
1976	10 981	18 090	29 071	37.7
1977	12 001	14 957	26 958	44.5
1978	≃ 11 197	≃ 9 810	21 007	53.3
1979	≃ 11 282	≃ 8 580	19 863	56.8

Source: ONI.

It is therefore not surprising that there has been a sharp decline in the number of families admitted into France. Between 1974 and 1979, the number of families fell from 35,284 to 19,863, representing a drop in the number of individuals from 68,038 to 39,298. At the same time, there was a marked increase in the number of families immigrating through official channels which, in 1980, accounted for 56.8 per cent of the total number of admissions as against 5.8 per cent in 1971.

In France, the right of families to be reunited was established by decree in 1976.[7] Article 1 of the decree stipulates that:

the spouse and the children under the age of 18 of a foreign national holding a residence permit who wish to join that person shall be denied neither access to French territory nor a residence permit except on one of the four following grounds:

1) the head of the family has not completed one year of legal residence in France or does not have regular and adequate means of support;

2) housing conditions are not suitable;

3) the results of the medical examination which the family is required to undergo are unsatisfactory;

4) reasons of public order justify a refusal to allow the family to enter France.

The above list is exhaustive; Article 1 of the decree therefore establishes a right to immigrate for the families of foreigners. As in the case of immigrant workers, ONI has a monopoly in bringing their families to France. The details of the admission procedures were set out in the circular of 19 July 1976. It should be noted, however, that these texts are not applicable to Algerian nationals whose situation is still governed by the bilateral agreements concluded by France and Algeria. Moreover, compliance with the provisions in question is optional for EEC nationals as well as for nationals of ten or so African countries.

Basic rules and prescribed procedures

As in most immigration countries, the decision to admit the family depends on the situation of the worker. In practice, this means that the latter must have been in possession of valid residence and work permits for at least one year, which is considered to be the length of time needed by a migrant in order to become adjusted to his new environment. In addition, he must be earning a regular income in a permanent job.

In so far as housing is concerned, it must meet the same standards as those considered reasonable for the family of a French worker in the same category.

One of the features of French law in this domain is implicit in the definition it gives of a family. In the first place, the admission of the members of the family must be exclusively motivated 'by the social desirability of reuniting the family'. This means that they should not be seeking to immigrate in order to find employment. The corollary of this definition is that the whole family should come to France. It is not possible for an immigrant worker to bring in only his spouse while their children are left behind in the country of origin. In principle, collateral relatives and forebears are not covered by the procedure for reuniting families.

A worker whose family is admitted into France through ONI channels pays an inclusive fee, in return for which the ONI assumes responsibility for the travelling arrangements and medical examinations of the family. Moreover, as soon as the family arrives in France, it receives an 'establishment allowance' amounting to the equivalent of three months' rent. These advantages are offered to families in order to induce them to follow the ONI procedure, and thus discourage illicit immigration.

Aid to return home

In the belief that the return of immigrants to their country of origin is 'one of the possible outlets of the migratory chain', the government set up, in June 1977, a system for aiding them to return home.

The purpose of such aid is to facilitate the resettlement of those immigrants who wish to return home. It is based on the idea that an immigrant worker will surrender such rights as he may have acquired in France in return for a lump sum to be used to enable him to re-establish himself in his country of origin. He and his family will then have relinquished their right to reside and work on French territory.

Since September 1977 this system has applied 'to all immigrant workers who can prove that they have been gainfully employed in France for a minimum of five years'.

A worker filing an application for aid to return home must hold valid residence and work permits. He can be: (a) out of work and receiving unemployment benefit; (b) out of work and receiving no unemployment benefit; or (c) in paid employment. If he is in either of the last two categories, he must show proof that he has been gainfully employed in France for a period of five years.

The spouse and the children under the age of 18 of the beneficiary can obtain aid to return home, the amount of which is calculated according to different scales, provided that they hold: (a) a work card; or (b) a residence card or a residence certificate identifying the possessor as a 'paid worker'. This type of aid is not accorded to: (a) refugees or stateless persons; (b) spouses of French nationals; or (c) spouses of nationals of an EEC member state.

TABLE 4. Distribution of aid to immigrants returning home in 1978 by principal nationalities

Country	Files handled			Persons concerned
	Unemployed	In paid employment	Total	
Algeria	1 185	820	2 005	2 512
Morocco	1 393	1 744	3 137	4 435
Portugal	2 263	13 098	15 361	31 898
Spain	1 396	6 419	7 815	21 666
Tunisia	2 042	2 036	4 078	5 607
Turkey	588	1 300	1 888	2 554
Yugoslavia	269	1 433	1 702	3 482

Source: Ministry of Labour and Participation.

Once an immigrant's application for aid to return home has been accepted, the beneficiary has two months in which to leave the country with his family. His air fare and that of his spouse are paid in full, and the children receive a transport allowance which varies according to the age of the child. The lump sum due to the returning immigrant is deposited in his country of origin. It amounts to 10,000 French francs for the head of the family, but it is fixed at 5,000 francs for a working spouse who cannot show proof of five years of gainful employment, and at the same amount for children.

To make sure that the recipient of aid and his family will not come back to France to take up paid employment, a special card index has been constituted. It is kept up to date by ONI and contains the names of all immigrants who have received aid to return home. Henceforth it is mandatory to consult this card index before applying the procedure for regularizing the situation of migrant workers or for recruiting them abroad.

A critical appraisal of the regulations in force

Despite some recent improvements, the French immigration control system reveals a number of inconsistencies. The changes introduced since 1975 show how ill-defined French policy has been in this field and also reflect the extensive powers of the administrative authorities. This situation has led to the development of a set of *ad hoc* rules that lack cohesion and whose real scope and significance have seldom been seriously assessed.

Improvements on the former system

The improvements that have been made primarily concern the work permits and their correlation with residence permits. Prior to the Decree of 21 November 1975, the type of work permit issued to an immigrant worker was determined by the length of the applicant's stay in France and the type of residence card he held. Thus, in order to obtain a permanent work card valid for all occupations, it was necessary to have held a privileged resident's card for ten years. At present, there is no interdependence between the conditions for obtaining residence permits and work permits. A work permit is issued solely with reference to the type of permit already held by the worker at the time of application. For example, card B 'can be issued to a foreigner holding a card A which is about to expire'.

In addition, the number of work cards has been reduced from seven to three, and this measure has undoubtedly simplified and unified the prescribed procedures.

Moreover, in an effort to streamline administrative procedures, a 'single counter' system has been introduced. This means that, henceforth, an immigrant worker can obtain both the work permit and the residence permit from the same administrative department. So that the 'single counter' system may work smoothly, the periods of validity of the different work and residence permits have been synchronized. For example, Work Card A is valid for the same period as the temporary resident's card, and Card B for the same period as the ordinary resident's card. However, the rules applying to Card C and those applying to the privileged resident's card have not been completely harmonized.

Nevertheless, it is now possible to obtain Card C after only four years' residence, whereas it was previously necessary to wait thirteen years; this is a great change.

However valuable these few reforms may be, they must not be allowed to divert attention from certain inadequacies and inconsistencies of French immigration policy.

Inadequacies and inconsistencies

The reform introduced in the autumn of 1977

The way in which these reforms were handled is typical of the methods used by the administrative authorities and of their consequences. The reforms in question were concerned mainly with the immigration of families and the aid offered to immigrants returning home. As already stated earlier in this study, the restrictions on the immigration of families and the issuing of work permits which had been introduced by decree in 1977 were annulled by the Council of State in the following year. As regards the aid offered to immigrants returning home, the situation is even more typical. On 27 April 1977, the government announced the decision to set up this system which was formally brought into being with the publication of a circular in June of the same year. That circular was annulled on 24 December 1978 by the Council of State, on the grounds that it was not within the competence of the Minister of Labour to enact such measures through a circular. The government made it known, however, that it was determined to pursue its policy, notwithstanding the judgements pronounced by the Council of State.

It is also noteworthy that the legal grounds for the 'aid to return home' system are regarded as tenuous by many observers.

In the first place, aid to return home should be accompanied, as a matter of principle, by training facilities for immigrants willing to return home, so as to equip those workers who so desire with qualifications in an occupational field which will enable them to make an effective contribution to the economic development of their country[8] of origin. The idea of this training for immigrants returning home was adopted in December 1975. Up to now, however, only a few hundred migrant workers have been able to benefit from such training owing to the lack of funds allocated for this purpose.

In the second place, the system of offering departure bonuses like the aid to return home is legally unsound. In the opinion of Professor J.-J. Dupeyroux, the system actually defrauds the law inasmuch as it, in fact, enables employers to avoid dismissing immigrant workers on economic grounds, thereby depriving the workers of unemployment benefits, which amount in that case to 90 per cent of the wage they had been earning. This new system therefore makes it possible to circumvent the application of the law concerning dismissals and the payment of the social benefits due to unemployed persons.[9] The migrants and their families who return home renounce all their rights in France and are so 'listed'; accordingly, they will never be able to come back to settle in France.

The duality of permits

Although the conditions for issuing permits are no longer interdependent, the procedures themselves are very closely linked. In order to obtain a residence permit, the applicant must produce a work contract endorsed by the services of the Ministry of Labour. This endorsement is likewise needed in order to obtain a work permit. Thus, the procedures for obtaining work and residence permits are interlocked. This seems logical when the different types of work and residence permits have the same period of validity. However, there is a fundamental inconsistency in the case of Card C and the Privileged Resident's Card. An application for the renewal of the latter is automatically granted, while Card C is renewable on certain conditions. Consequently, the situation of the labour market can always be given as a reason for refusing to issue a Card C to a person holding a Privileged Resident's Card, so that, even though he automatically has the right to reside in France, he can be denied access to the labour market. In short, the automatic renewal of the Privileged Resident's Card in no way protects the interests of a foreign worker who may have resided for fourteen years in France but may be compelled to leave French territory because, from the official standpoint, he has no better guarantees of employment than the holder of a Work Card A. This possibility does not seem to be the result of a lack of co-ordination between the various legal texts, for it coincides with the abolition of permits having permanent validity. In this way, the situation of foreign workers has been made even more precarious, and this is hardly conducive to their integration into French life. A foreigner remains a complete foreigner, even after fourteen years of residence in the country. Lastly, it should be noted that a decree of 15 January 1976 authorizes the cancellation of an ordinary resident's card when the holder has been without work *of his own accord,* for over six months. Formerly, the ordinary resident's card could only be confiscated if this action was taken in conformity with the expulsion procedures; persons holding this card thus enjoyed some degree of protection, whereas today the expression 'of his own accord' is sufficiently vague to lend itself to many different interpretations.

Discretionary power

The precarious situation of immigrant workers is largely due to the discretionary powers enjoyed by the administrative authorities. It is clear, however, that these powers are not unlimited even though, as we have already pointed out, the administrative authorities tend to misuse them. The rule that a minimum degree of control shall be exercised over acts of discretionary power ensures that the judge hearing an action *ultra vires* may scrutinize, to some extent, a decision of the administrative authorities.

It is important to note, however, that such scrutiny concerns only procedural and jurisdictional rules, the material accuracy and the legality of the grounds for the decision. The judge does not scrutinize the 'legal definition of actions'. This means that, in so far as the discretionary powers of the administrative authorities are concerned, the judge is not empowered to determine whether the incriminatory actions—or the actions that have simply been taken into consideration—justify the decision of the administrative authorities.

It seems that a distinction can be drawn between acts of discretionary power which have general implications and are the object of the watchful attention of associations for the protection and defence of immigrants, and acts of discretionary power which are directed against an individual. There can be no doubt that the *de facto* exercise of discretionary power is much more prevalent in the latter case since the obstacles already existing between the French population and the judiciary are magnified as a natural consequence of the social exclusion of immigrants.

Diversity of the relevant laws

One of the most serious problems is, unquestionably, the sheer diversity of the relevant laws, their lack of consistency and the practice of modifying the laws by means of implementary circulars and, consequently, by a method that is not in keeping with the correct standard procedures. While the regulations concerning work cards are relatively clear, those concerning residence permits are extremely confused, since two different legal texts have to be consulted in order to know how the law stands on this matter. Yet it is only a question of ordinary law. As regards the special systems, their multiplicity has the effect of making the subject particularly arduous and complicated in a field where—having regard to the persons concerned—the utmost clarity would be desirable.

However, the greatest defect of this method of enacting regulations is that it keeps the persons concerned in ignorance of their situation and leaves them defenceless. Any regulations issued by means of administrative circulars are very liable to change inasmuch as they can be superseded within a few months or even a few weeks by another circular,[10] modifying the previous text. Moreover, in the absence of any rules regarding the publication of circulars, most of them are not published at all and even remain confidential. Lastly, the fact that the texts are drafted solely on the initiative of a minister, and usually without consulting the parties engaged in labour negotiations, is not conducive to their homogeneity, nor does it enhance their legal or even constitutional value, as is shown by certain decisions or opinions on this subject which have been delivered by the Council of State.[11]

The place and role of migrants in economic structures

The size and nature of the foreign population in France

The migrants' place and role in the country's economic structures depend primarily on factors having to do with the foreign population itself. The latter can be perceived in terms of stocks (state of the population at a given moment) or in terms of flows (seasonal balances of

TABLE 5. Foreign population by nationality—1980 (estimate)

Nationality	Active	Non-active	Total
Italians	175 800	290 100	465 900
Other EEC nationals	66 200	86 800	153 000
Spaniards	184 500	322 800	507 300
Portuguese	385 000	438 000	823 000
Yugoslavs	43 100	30 900	74 000
Turks	36 300	21 600	57 900
Poles	19 300	77 900	97 200
Moroccans	181 400	118 500	299 900
Algerians	361 000	431 000	792 000
Tunisians	73 700	73 400	147 100
Other Africans	50 700	41 900	92 600
Other nationalities	65 800	124 300	190 100
TOTAL	1 642 800	2 057 200	3 700 000

Source: Ministry of Labour and Participation.

entries and departures). In view of the fact that the statistical instruments available in France do not lend themselves very well to a study of flows, we shall use here the statistics which relate to the state of the population, while noting that they are of unequal value and significance. They vary considerably according to the population groups studied and the methods used in the gathering, processing or handling of the data.

In these circumstances, an interministerial working group was set up in 1979 with the aim, *inter alia*, of providing the most reliable evaluation it was able to make of the foreign population living in France. Whenever possible, the figures calculated by that working group have been given in the present study.

The working group estimated that the situation on 1 January 1980 was as shown in Table 5.

The foreign population and population growth in France

Foreign immigration affects the French population in many ways. There are direct effects (growth of the population in absolute terms) and secondary effects (modification of the population structure).

Direct effects of immigration

Between 1950 and 1970, the average annual figure for net migration movements in France represented 6 per cent of the French population existing in 1960. This average was largely due to foreign immigration inasmuch as movements of nationals during the same period usually showed a negative balance.

The role of immigration in population growth varies considerably from region to region. It can be said that many foreigners have been attracted to the most densely populated regions of France, where their communities have made a marked impact in terms of numbers. Thus, between 1962 and 1968, immigration accounted for 35 per cent of the growth of the population in the Paris region, 21 per cent in the Rhône–Alpes region and 8 per cent in the Provence–Côte d'Azur region.[12]

Lastly, the naturalization of immigrants has the effect of appreciably increasing the French population. The 1975 census showed that, since 1946, 1,392,000 persons, or 2.8 per cent of the French population, had acquired French citizenship.

The secondary effects of immigration

The change in the structure of the population is even more important than the change in its size. The French population is ageing as a result of the relative increase in the number of old people, and immigration plays an important rejuvenating role, partly because of the arrival of

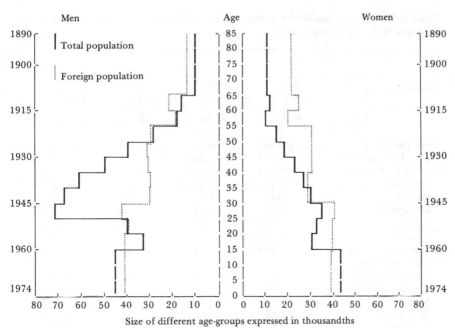

N.B. The construction of the pyramid does not begin at age '0', for the data on that age-group were lacking at the time of the census.

FIG. 1. Population pyramid according to 1975 census.[13] (N.B. The construction of the pyramid does not begin at age 'o', for the data on that age-group were lacking at the time of the census.)

young foreigners and partly because of the change in the structure of the foreign population itself. The last-mentioned factor is the consequence of the policy of reuniting families and the ensuing births. According to the 1975 census, 25 per cent of the foreign population were under the age of 15, as compared with 17 per cent in 1962. Furthermore, the median age of foreigners dropped from 36 in 1962 to 30 in 1975. As for births, they doubled between 1960 and 1973, rising from 3 to 6 per cent of the total number of births recorded in France during that period.

The effects of these figures must be weighted, however, inasmuch as they refer to population stocks whereas migrations should be viewed mainly in terms of flows.

The active foreign population[14]

According to the 1975 census, the active foreign population comprised 1,584,340 persons at that time. Its structure differs from that of the French working population and also from that of the total labour force

TABLE 6. Total active population in employment by sex, nationality and economic activity according to the 1975 census: men

Nationality	Agriculture, forestry, fishing	Agro-food industries	Energy production and supply	Intermediate goods industry	Capital goods industry
French by birth	1 372 605	366 705	234 015	1 133 365	1 274 845
French by acquisition	24 730	8 590	11 495	53 875	43 775
Foreigners: Europe	78 125	25 195	16 555	192 945	167 935
Spaniards	17 680	2 905	535	17 415	16 110
Italians	9 975	2 455	3 100	28 085	16 750
Portuguese	10 515	4 985	590	36 295	26 050
Poles	1 560	470	970	3 475	1 985
Swiss	1 005	385	15	660	815
Yugoslavs	695	490	160	4 625	7 210
EEC nationals (excl. Italians)	5 055	1 165	1 260	4 660	5 050
Foreigners: Africa					
Algerians	3 065	6 750	4 090	56 790	42 355
Moroccans	22 685	2 245	5 160	20 205	27 325
Tunisians	3 350	1 190	145	7 410	7 480
Foreigners: Asia					
Turks	1 500	600	90	6 115	4 985
Other nationalities	1 040	1 555	440	7 220	11 820
Total population	1 475 460	400 490	262 065	1 380 185	1 486 555

Source: M. L. Samman, *Les étrangers au recensement de 1975*, Paris, La Documentation Française.

in France. The main characteristics of the active foreign population are as follows:

Whereas the French working population comprises 41 per cent of the total population of French nationality, the active foreign population comprises 46 per cent of the total foreign population.

Foreign workers account for 7.3 per cent of the total labour force whereas the total foreign population accounts for only 6.5 per cent of the total population of France.

The percentage of active foreign women in relation to the foreign female population is inferior to that of active French women in the French female population, the figures being 21.5 per cent and 30.75 per cent respectively.

However, the percentage of active foreign men in relation to the foreign male population is superior to that of active French men in the French male population, the figures being 62.4 per cent and 52.1 per cent respectively (see Tables 6 and 7).

Consumer goods industry	Building, civil and rural engineering	Commerce	Transport and tele-communications	Marketable services	Rental, leasing, credit, insurance, financing	Non-marketable services	Total
684 475	1 333 615	1 176 780	939 545	1 390 470	271 010	1 478 230	11 855 660
28 085	66 395	38 980	19 130	45 235	5 395	32 145	377 830
84 760	401 165	66 405	33 990	113 740	6 205	47 635	1 234 655
10 230	46 635	8 500	3 160	13 195	725	4 700	141 790
9 000	58 690	8 335	3 390	12 935	755	3 285	154 755
18 215	118 965	8 255	4 310	14 885	740	4 370	248 175
1 345	2 040	830	320	1 335	70	815	15 215
670	755	1 155	370	1 450	155	1 250	8 685
3 075	6 390	1 325	835	2 620	95	815	26 335
3 350	3 780	4 920	1 695	6 735	650	6 155	44 475
17 740	96 135	15 330	11 460	29 735	1 075	10 380	294 895
6 460	33 690	5 375	3 495	8 170	420	2 390	137 620
4 430	21 475	5 330	1 895	7 435	385	2 220	62 745
4 140	9 635	845	290	745	50	285	29 260
6 105	4 975	6 205	2 770	14 500	1 085	10 970	68 685
797 320	1 801 175	1 282 165	992 665	1 549 445	282 610	1 558 010	13 288 145

Permanent immigration flows

In 1979, the total number of entries stood at its lowest level since 1975 (see Table 8). It had fallen by 88.7 per cent as compared with 1973, which was the last year of 'uncontrolled' immigration. This trend is even more striking when we know that the figures take into account the refugees and 'quasi-refugees' who streamed in from South-East Asia: they alone accounted for nearly half the total number of new immigrants.

As for family immigration, it has declined slightly but continues to account for about 70 per cent of total permanent immigration.

Distribution of the foreign population by region

More than half the foreign population is concentrated in three regions. The Paris region comprises 33.6 per cent of the foreign population which represents 7.1 per cent of the total population of this region. The Rhône–Alpes region comprises 12.9 per cent of the foreign population which represents 3.8 per cent of the total population of the region.

TABLE 7. Total active population in employment by sex, nationality and economic activity according to the 1975 census: women

Nationality	Agriculture, forestry, fishing	Agro-food industries	Energy production and supply	Intermediate goods industry	Capital goods industry
French by birth	614 980	188 620	38 345	313 540	417 865
French by acquisition	9 805	5 820	665	13 285	14 765
Foreigners: Europe	8 435	8 350	540	21 555	22 030
Spaniards	1 545	1 240	75	2 615	2 760
Italians	1 615	1 020	75	3 510	2 815
Portuguese	2 690	4 220	150	10 110	10 155
Poles	500	210	40	530	435
Swiss	130	15	10	140	105
Yugoslavs	195	435	30	1 425	1 895
EEC nationals (excl. Italians)	895	220	30	565	745
Foreigners: Africa					
Algerians	110	440	50	1 145	1 245
Moroccans	315	210	40	540	685
Tunisians	45	95	5	310	355
Foreigners: Asia					
Turks	50	60	0	135	135
Other nationalities	145	185	35	530	700
Total population	633 220	202 790	39 750	348 380	454 660

Source: M. L. Samman, *Les étrangers au recensement de 1975*, Paris, La Documentation Française.

Lastly, the Provence–Côte d'Azur region comprises 9.1 per cent of the foreign population which represents 7.6 per cent of the total population of the region. It should be added that the Nord–Pas de Calais region, which comprises 5.9 per cent of the foreign population is still an important immigration region even though its power to attract workers is on the decline.

TABLE 8. Permanent immigration flows (1975–79)

Year	1975	1976	1977	1978	1979
Entry of permanent workers	25 591	26 949	22 756	18 356	17 395
Entry of members of families[1]	51 822	53 371	52 315	40 120	39 298
Total permanent immigration	77 413	84 320	75 071	58 475	56 693

1. Not including members of families of EEC nationals, concerning whom no information is available.
Source: ONI, Ministry of Labour and Participation, and Ministry of the Interior.

Consumer goods industry	Building, civil and rural engineering	Commerce	Transport and tele-communications	Marketable services	Rental, leasing, credit, insurance, financing	Non-marketable services	Total
721 810	97 240	1 011 035	270 200	1 506 110	269 595	1 725 240	7 174 580
29 330	3 370	37 045	5 410	49 705	6 165	49 025	224 590
44 635	4 285	23 495	3 570	53 770	3 725	82 195	276 585
6 595	570	4 480	555	9 080	635	24 310	54 460
7 615	740	4 845	515	6 515	695	6 835	36 995
18 305	1 445	5 910	925	18 470	1 070	30 045	103 495
1 080	45	515	60	1 310	60	1 765	6 550
190	25	300	75	795	30	820	2 635
2 980	150	720	95	2 275	70	1 590	11 860
1 130	130	1 780	365	3 900	320	5 080	15 160
2 330	575	1 710	270	3 555	215	2 035	13 680
965	230	695	150	1 905	100	2 445	8 280
990	140	875	125	1 005	180	930	5 055
550	65	90	0	70	0	95	1 250
1 905	170	1 575	435	4 890	350	6 245	17 165
795 775	104 895	1 071 575	279 180	1 609 585	279 485	1 858 460	7 675 755

Distribution by economic sector and the effects of this distribution on the sectors

Principal sectors employing foreign labour

As is shown in Tables 6 and 7, the building, civil and agricultural engineering sector employs by far the greatest number of foreigners—405,450; it is followed by the intermediate goods industry sector with 214,490, the capital goods industry sector with 189,965 and, lastly, the marketable services sector with 167,510. It is important to note here that the distribution by sex, within each of these sectors, is not evenly balanced. This reflects the nature of the work, for some jobs demand more physical stamina than others. Thus, women account for 63.3 per cent of the foreign workers employed in the non-marketable services sector whereas they account for only 1 per cent of the foreign workers employed in the building, civil and rural engineering sector.

The most recent immigration flows are quite different from traditional flows. In the first place, the geographic origin of migrants is

TABLE 9. Distribution of new permanent workers by economic activity (1975–77)

Sector of activity	1975		1976		1977	
	Number	%	Number	%	Number	%
Fishing, agriculture, forestry	1 364	5.3	1 258	4.7	637	2.8
Fuel, ore extraction	1 484	5.8	320	3.0	564	2.5
Metallurgy	512	2.0	452	4.7	455	2.0
Mechanical and electrical engineering	1 484	5.8	2 940	10.9	2 654	11.7
Glass, tiles	202	0.8	239	0.9	174	0.7
Building and public works	3 656	14.3	4 008	14.9	2 643	11.6
Chemical industry, rubber	265	1.0	398	1.5	361	1.6
Agricultural and food industries	321	1.3	307	1.1	359	1.6
Textiles, weaving apparel, leathers and furs	797	3.1	1 225	4.5	1 090	4.8
Wood industry, furniture	284	1.1	378	1.4	323	1.4
Other industries	949	3.7	1 224	4.5	1 216	5.3
Commerce	6 131	24.0	6 214	23.1	5 498	24.2
Health, domestic services	3 532	13.8	3 189	11.8	2 393	10.5
Other tertiary activities	4 610	18.0	4 297	16.0	4 389	19.3
TOTAL	25 591	100.0	26 949	100.0	22 756	100.0

Source: Ministry of Labour and Participation.

changing. Since immigration was halted, Europeans (EEC) and Asians (refugees) account for most of the entries into France. In the second place—as a direct consequence of the fact just mentioned—the new migrants are, as a rule, more highly qualified than their predecessors. Thirdly, the persistent slump is having the effect of reducing the demand for labour in sectors such as building and public works which have always been major employers of foreign workers. Thus, it can be said, although it is a simplification, that the two major sectors which have cut back on the employment of foreign workers are building and public works and health and domestic services, whereas the mechanical and electrical engineering industries, as well as commerce, are hiring an increasingly large proportion of the number of new immigrants. In the case of commerce, it should be noted that the trend got under way at the beginning of the seventies and has not slackened. This sector is undoubtedly the one which is least affected by the decrease in immigration (see Table 9), for it has benefited considerably from the influx of refugees from South-East Asia.

Causes and effects of this sectoral distribution

Apart from causes of a general and structural nature, which, it must be added, are not peculiar to France, there are causes which pertain specifically to each of the sectors considered.

There can be no doubt that the post-war immigration flows were encouraged because of a severe shortage of national manpower in the 1950s. The immigration flows were therefore proportionate to a demand for labour on the domestic market. The strong migratory currents had the effect of changing the distribution of the national labour force, since French workers could then choose to move into sectors that were less subject to economic fluctuations and were characterized by high productivity.

It is often asserted that the replacement of labour by capital is a key factor in the process of modernizing industries and that, as a result, when sectors employing a high proportion of foreign labour become modernized, they necessarily witness a decrease in the size of the migrant work force. A question which is of some interest, but seems difficult to answer at the present juncture, is as follows: In what way does the presence of immigrant workers in a given form—or even in an economic sector—help to accelerate the substitution of capital for labour? In other words, it would be desirable to know more about the role the migrants play in the process of economic development. That question raises many problems, however, and, at the present time, economic theory has no definitive conclusions to offer.

Anicet Le Pors put it this way:

The search for a relationship between immigration and the development of the productive instruments comes up against great difficulties. Even if economic theory suggests that this relationship exists, it operates only through a chain of factors (relative costs of capital and labour, growth of demand, the structure and size of markets, etc.) which are themselves influenced by immigration in various ways depending on the country, the region, the sector or the firm concerned.[15]

In his study on immigration and economic development in France, Anicet Le Pors showed that two sectors with dissimilar capitalistic structures—building and public works, and the car industry—were impelled to use foreign labour for substantially the same reasons, and that the effects of this policy depended mainly on the structure of the productive instruments considered. Thus, in the building and public works sector, a process of substituting capital for labour, accompanied by only slight increases in productivity and the need to make profitable use of costly equipment, contributed significantly to the deterioration of working conditions and made it more and more necessary to use foreign workers. In the car industry, where capital expenditure is high, the modernization of the productive instruments contributed to the down-grading of jobs directly linked to the splitting up of operations and made it necessary to hire enormous numbers of foreign workers.[16]

We must therefore proceed with the utmost circumspection when analysing the causes and effects of the employment of foreign workers. In particular, the relationship between capital and labour must be studied with great care.

Employment of foreigners

Professional qualifications and the wage structure

As we saw from our survey of the distribution of workers by sector, immigrant workers occupy the lowest-grade jobs: 17 per cent of all unskilled workers and labourers in France are foreigners and this figure

TABLE 10. Total active population by sex, nationality and socio-occupational category according to the 1975 census: men

Nationality	Farmers	Farm workers	Proprietors of industrial and commercial concerns	Members of the professions and senior executives	Middle-grade executives
French by birth	1 057 365	257 860	1 044 770	1 059 500	1 451 485
French by acquisition	14 580	9 625	45 845	28 445	33 715
Foreigners: Europe	12 435	64 325	44 435	32 725	30 310
Spaniards	2 225	15 625	6 210	1 645	3 420
Italians	4 960	4 880	13 140	2 605	5 145
Portuguese	180	9 205	2 160	540	1 570
Poles	425	1 125	615	575	675
Swiss	815	180	1 150	1 645	925
Yugoslavs	45	710	720	430	735
EEC nationals (excl. Italians)	3 245	1 845	3 660	9 955	4 720
Foreigners: Africa					
Algerians	80	2 520	8 190	885	2 765
Moroccans	95	22 800	2 345	1 190	1 350
Tunisians	45	3 225	2 575	1 285	2 110
Foreigners: Asia					
Turcs	20	1 485	260	210	215
Other nationalities	300	725	3 410	11 760	6 680
TOTAL POPULATION	1 084 380	331 810	1 138 050	1 120 670	1 515 510

Source: M. L. Samman, *Les étrangers au recensement de 1975*, Paris, La Documentation Française.

represents 49 per cent of the foreign working population. Furthermore, 23 per cent are skilled workers, foremen or apprentices. These percentages vary, of course, from sector to sector and some sectors like building and public works or the car industry employ a very large proportion of unskilled workers. The level of qualifications of the foreign population also varies from nationality to nationality, as may be seen from Tables 10 and 11. Immigrants from the Maghrib include a particularly large number of unskilled workers: for example, 67 per cent of the Algerians are classified as *ouvriers spécialisés*[17] or labourers. The same is true of the Turks, for 71 per cent are in this category. Among workers from Europe, the Portuguese are found to be the least skilled: 55 per cent of them fall into the *ouvriers spécialisés* or labourers' category.

However, their low level of qualifications is less important as a factor of discrimination than their low wages and the large gap between their wages and those of French workers. A survey of the wages of foreigners

Office staff	Foremen, skilled workers apprentices	Ouvriers spécialisés and labourers	Miners, merchant marine and fishing workers	Services personnel	Artists, clergy, army and police	Total
1 305 790	2 655 380	2 406 960	85 360	238 830	403 510	11 966 810
31 600	107 115	89 020	8 375	10 105	6 320	380 835
48 845	340 230	658 905	15 975	26 010	11 835	1 286 030
5 525	51 770	54 075	615	4 290	1 000	146 400
5 815	62 800	52 385	3 155	3 555	1 050	159 690
5 520	86 745	142 380	675	3 385	320	252 680
725	3 920	6 005	865	435	380	15 845
680	1 155	1 165	5	225	970	8 865
935	10 545	14 210	160	685	305	29 480
3 075	7 000	7 300	925	1 160	2 960	45 835
12 310	61 920	215 105	3 820	5 780	335	313 710
3 820	22 245	81 430	5 270	1 910	225	142 680
3 715	16 535	35 845	105	1 455	145	67 040
340	5 770	21 300	90	80	50	29 820
6 435	9 825	27 625	270	3 100	4 105	74 235
1 386 325	3 102 725	3 154 385	109 710	274 945	423 665	13 642 675

TABLE 11. Total active population by sex, nationality and socio-occupational category according to the 1975 census: women

Nationality	Farmers	Farm workers	Proprietors of industrial and commercial concerns	Members of the professions and senior executives	Middle-grade executives
French by birth	556 095	36 930	543 495	322 205	1 213 690
French by acquisition	7 700	1 515	22 230	10 565	25 105
Foreigners: Europe	2 690	5 225	5 150	5 845	10 645
Spaniards	240	1 220	745	310	965
Italians	1 165	600	1 175	275	1 125
Portuguese	55	2 365	375	170	715
Poles	220	270	185	170	320
Swiss	115	15	150	180	515
Yugoslavs	40	170	170	110	240
EEC nationals (excl. Italians)	770	75	830	2 050	2 875
Foreignerss: Africa					
Algerians	15	70	490	95	565
Maroccans	0	290	185	100	280
Tunisians	0	35	175	55	260
Foreigners: Asia					
Turks	0	45	35	35	50
Other nationalities	70	70	635	2 295	2 705
TOTAL POPULATION	566 485	43 670	570 975	338 615	1 249 440

Source: M. L. Samman, Les étrangers au recensement de 1975, Table 12 A.

in 1972[18] showed that there was a difference of 16.5 per cent between the average annual income of foreign workers and that of wage-earners as a whole, and a difference of 17.4 per cent between the income of foreign workers and that of French wage-earners alone.

These figures highlight a crucial aspect of the relationship between the economic structures of the host country and the migratory phenomenon. One of the reasons for migration—and for perpetuating it—is the existence of a great demand for unskilled labour. The French economic system (and this applies to immigration countries as a whole) stands in need of unskilled workers to do the hard and poorly paid jobs. The interministerial study conducted by Anicet Le Pors shows very clearly how much certain sectors depend on such manpower. It would therefore be unrealistic to think that there are short-term or medium-term prospects of witnessing an improvement of skills and working conditions together with an upgrading of the occupations and jobs open to foreign workers. This pessimistic view is supported by several reasons.

Office staff	Foremen, skilled workers apprentices	*Ouvriers spécialisés* and labourers	Miners, merchant marine and fishing workers	Services personnel	Artists, clergy, army and police	Total
2 354 095	391 925	1 231 325	1 885	850 645	89 725	6 132 185
63 115	18 630	55 470	55	34 840	2 435	241 680
37 165	22 560	117 905	70	82 860	8 175	298 310
6 030	3 735	16 930	15	25 595	1 765	57 590
7 790	4 090	15 270	0	6 675	1 380	39 745
6 350	7 050	57 435	25	33 335	175	108 050
485	565	2 615	5	1 735	440	7 030
505	70	245	0	345	625	2 765
815	1 865	6 895	0	2 355	70	12 730
3 965	480	1 610	5	1 920	1 710	16 290
4 360	1 665	7 395	10	2 700	15	17 380
1 230	665	3 965	5	2 835	20	9 575
1 540	740	2 005	0	1 065	25	5 940
65	305	770	0	65	25	1 385
4 030	1 330	2 770	5	4 015	1 905	19 830
2 454 375	433 135	1 404 700	2 010	968 545	100 335	7 592 215

It is only after a worker has immigrated that his proficiency can be improved by means of vocational training. This presupposes that the worker has found a job matching the level of the qualifications which he possessed at the time of his arrival in the host country, but this is not by any means what happens in reality. The worker is also presumed to be interested in a kind of training which, in the final analysis, is designed to meet only the needs of the host country. Lastly, as G. Tapinos has noted, the migrant 'seeks, above all, to ensure his *social* advancement when he returns home. He has a better chance of improving his social status by accumulating financial capital than by acquiring a "human" capital of technical qualifications'.[19] In other words, the migrant is more interested—on a short-term or medium-term basis—in doing overtime work than in devoting his spare time to a vocational training course.

No marked improvement in working conditions, which presupposes a restructuring of firms, seems likely to occur in the absence of a policy of substituting French labour for foreign labour. Nevertheless, in certain sectors—notably in the car industry—some minor improvements could be introduced without jeopardizing the economic structure of firms (part-time work, reorganization of work schedules). It is clear, however, that the extreme pressures on French industry to be competitive will compel firms to continue using foreign labour while preserving their present production structure.

As regards the upgrading of jobs, the problem arises in practically the same terms as the problem of improving working conditions, inasmuch as it necessarily involves wage increases.

In the final analysis, the French economy has a structural requirement for large inputs of foreign manpower. It can therefore be argued that the present wage structure and the general proficiency level of the foreign population are precisely tailored to meet the demands of the labour market and the imperative need to keep French industry competitive.

To be sure, legal structures have been set up to make it easier for migrant workers to gain promotion by providing them with vocational training, but there is no denying that only an infinitesimal percentage of foreign workers derive any benefit from it. In firms employing more than nine wage earners, for example, fewer than 1 per cent of foreign workers receive vocational training, whereas it is estimated that over 10 per cent of French workers employed in firms subject to the law on vocational training take advantage of the opportunity.

Unemployment among foreigners

Whereas, in the 1960s, the rate of unemployment among foreigners was generally lower than the national rate, there was a marked reversal of this trend at the beginning of the 1970s, and the higher rate persisted until the middle of 1978. The second half of the year 1978 witnessed a return to the situation prevailing in the 1960s, when the number of foreign job-seekers increased at a slower rate than that of French job-seekers.

To explain this development, several hypotheses can be advanced.

It seems obvious that the decline in the rate of unemployment among foreigners during the 1960s coincided with a period of expanding economic activity when there was a need for unskilled manpower, so that the prevailing conditions were conducive to the hiring of migrant workers. The slump which occurred at the beginning of the 1970s revealed that these workers were extremely vulnerable to economic fluctuations, and their situation was further aggravated by the serious difficulties experienced by many sectors employing a high percentage of foreigners.

In terms of nationalities, it was the Algerians who were especially hard hit by unemployment. In 1977, the Algerians, who represented about 20 per cent of the total foreign population, accounted for over

35 per cent of the job-seekers among the foreign population. In terms of socio-occupational categories, it was the most highly skilled workers who were most affected. Between 1974 and 1975, the rate of increase of unemployment among skilled workers was almost three times greater than that observed among labourers (242.2 per cent and 88.8 per cent respectively).

It is interesting to note that, contrary to appearances, there is no inconsistency or conflict between an analysis of the unemployment trend in terms of nationalities and an analysis of that trend of socio-occupational categories. It is true that the least skilled national groups have the highest unemployment rate, but this is probably because they are also the groups

TABLE 12. French and foreign job-seekers at the end of each quarter (1973–79)

		French job-seekers	Foreign job-seekers	Percentage of foreigners in relation to total number
1972:	31 December	376 822	36 288	
1973:	31 March	342 008	35 727	9.5
	30 June	297 458	32 054	9.7
	30 September	385 421	33 778	8.1
	31 December	421 158	39 488	8.6
1974:	31 March	398 154	40 778	9.3
	30 June	344 993	33 677	8.9
	30 September	491 803	42 506	8.0
	31 December	655 791	67 638	9.3
1975:	31 March	667 526	87 284	11.6
	30 June	649 495	88 810	12.0
	30 September	850 557	95 234	10.1
	31 December	903 929	105 753	10.5
1976:	31 March	835 551	102 684	10.9
	30 June	726 973	86 016	10.6
	30 September	872 957	82 395	8.6
	31 December	941 210	95 679	9.2
1977:	31 March	914 020	106 543	10.4
	30 June	863 073	104 623	10.8
	30 September	1 062 532	112 550	9.6
	31 December	1 029 367	115 523	10.1
1978:	31 March	954 638	118 478	11.0
	30 June	923 675	115 584	12.5
	30 September	1 160 117	124 466	10.7
	31 December	1 195 107	133 201	10.0
1979:	31 March	1 170 156	142 858	10.9
	30 June	1 100 231	132 736	10.8
	30 September	1 291 502	132 377	9.3
	31 December	1 332 208	136 664	9.3
1980:	31 March	1 272 728	139 592	9.9

Source: Minister of Labour and Participation.

which are most inclined to remain in France after they have lost their jobs. For the very reason that they are unskilled, they have little hope of finding a job in their own country, but better prospects of quickly finding a new job in France. It must be borne in mind that the unemployment rate among foreigners is an indicator not only of a cessation of productive activity, but also of their tendency to return home.

Precisely because of the ambiguous significance of the unemployment rate, it is not easy to interpret the recent reversal of the unemployment trend among immigrant workers which has been observed since the second half of 1978. Whereas between March 1977 and March 1978 the number of French job-seekers had increased by 5.1 per cent and that of foreign job-seekers by 11.2 per cent, between 31 December 1978 and 31 December 1979, the number of French job-seekers increased by 11.5 per cent and that of foreign job-seekers by 2.6 per cent. Whatever their shortcomings, the statistics on the recent socio-occupational distribution of job-seekers show that, in so far as nationalities are concerned, the foreign communities which have been established in France the longest have benefited most from this trend. In contrast, there has been a great increase in the number of job-seekers among nationals from the countries of South-East Asia.

Great caution is advisable when analysing this new unemployment trend among foreign workers. An improvement in the unemployment rate does not necessarily mean that the situation of foreigners on the labour market has improved. In the first place, immigrant workers who have lost their jobs are likely to be reluctant to register as job-seekers because they are in a precarious situation from the administrative point of view (see above). In the second place, this drop in the rate of unemployment among foreigners may in fact reflect a reduction of the foreign population living on French territory. Lastly, it may be explained by a lower level of mobility among foreign workers who, because of the economic crisis, prefer to keep a poorly paid or disagreeable job than to start looking for another job which they are not even sure to find.

A number of hypotheses have been advanced concerning the ways in which the French labour market is affected by the existence of an unemployed foreign population, and it is often suggested that foreigners are responsible for the growth of unemployment and other ills as well.

The existence of an unemployed foreign population may, of course, exert pressure on wages, especially as immigrant workers are ready to accept lower wages than French workers.[20] However, it does not follow that the immigrant and French work forces are in competition with each other, since immigrants occupy jobs which are generally refused by the French population. For this reason, a mass exodus of foreigners would not have the effect of making a large number of jobs available for French nationals unless such jobs were upgraded. Many other parameters should be taken into consideration when attempting to forecast the side effects of a mass exodus of immigrant workers. The hypothesis of such an exodus was the subject of a macro-economic study based on a physico-financial econometric model used in the preparation of economic development plans.[21] On the assumption that the active immigrant population is reduced by 150,000 persons over a five-year period during which the process of substituting capital for labour is accelerated, the study indicated that the results of an exodus would be as follows: (a) a reduction of 10,000 in the number of unemployed and a higher rate of productive activity, so that the active population would be increased by 7,000 persons; (b) a decrease of 4,000 in the number of unemployed immigrants and the creation of about 13,000 jobs; (c) the abolition of 133,000 jobs; and (d) a probable fall-off in foreign trade.

According to Anicet Le Pors, the last two points show that, far from helping to solve the problems of the French economy, a large-scale cutback in immigration would trigger a series of disastrous consequences for the future pattern of employment and economic growth.

At the same time, it is important, when gauging the significance of such evaluations, to bear in mind that they are based on projections which simulate medium-term economic developments but which cannot take into account all the parameters entering into the study of phenomena connected with migratory movements.

Integration of migrants and their families into the host society

Rights of foreigners in France

As a general rule, foreigners living anywhere on French territory have the same rights as French nationals. The rule is a theoretical one, of course, and the foreigners' life is quite different from that of French citizens, particularly in the field of rights and freedoms and the exercise thereof.

As in many countries, the first obstacle to the application of the principle of equality of rights between foreigners and French nationals consists in the discriminatory attitudes displayed by the latter. Even though this problem lies outside the scope of the present study, it is worth recalling that the Act of 1 July 1972 provides penalties for any discrimination based on a person's origin or his affiliation or non-affiliation with a particular ethnic group, nation, race or religion.

However, the rights and freedoms of foreigners are also restricted by law in certain domains.

The right of association

While France recognizes the principle of freedom of association, it is not applied to foreigners. A statutory order issued in 1939—at a time when xenophobia was rife—lays down strict regulations governing the creation of foreign associations, for which authorization must first be obtained from the Ministry of the Interior. Foreign associations are defined as 'groups displaying the characteristics of an association, whose headquarters are abroad or which, if their headquarters are in France, are, in fact, run by foreigners, or include foreigners among their office-holders, or have a membership of which at least one-quarter is composed of foreigners'.

The authorization granted by the minister may be only temporary and, in any case, it is never definitive.

Lastly, only privileged residents or ordinary residents can become office-holders or permanent members of such associations.

The right to participate in public affairs

Unlike many other European countries—Belgium, Luxembourg and Sweden, for example—France has not developed institutions to promote the participation of foreigners in the political life of the country and, in particular, at the commune level, as is the case in the countries just mentioned. It should be noted, however, that the rights granted to foreigners are not really perceived as political rights and that a definite distinction is generally drawn between political rights in the strict sense of the term, and the various rights that might be described as 'participatory'. The participation of foreigners in the life of the commune is a case in point. But there are also many activities unconnected with the commune in which foreigners can participate to a certain extent.

Political activity in the strict sense of the term

It is a principle of customary law in France that foreigners are under an obligation to observe political neutrality. The principle is a matter of custom for, although it is a long-standing practice of the Ministry of the Interior to refer to it on frequent occasions, it is not sanctioned by statute law. Moreover, in our view, a distinction should be made between the public expression of a political opinion and its 'individual' expression through such means as membership of a political association. While the latter does not seem to fall into the category of activities conflicting with the foreigner's obligation to observe political neutrality, the former is consistently repressed by the authorities and often constitutes grounds for an expulsion order. To be sure, there is no hard and fast dividing line and it cannot be said that there is any sphere within which the foreigner can engage in political activity without risking harassment by the authorities.

Associative life

Apart from the restrictions applicable to foreign associations and the obligation to observe political neutrality, foreigners are free to join any non-profit associations, those commonly referred to as 'associations under the Act of 1901'. Moreover, certain provisions authorize foreigners to participate in the activities of associations or committees concerned with the management or improvement of certain public services. Such bodies include parent–teacher associations,[22] governing boards of secondary schools[23]—which extend the right to vote and to stand for election to foreign parents—or the boards of higher educational institutions.[24] Foreigners also have voting rights in a number of other bodies, such as chambers of agriculture or industrial conciliation boards.[25] It would be a mistake, however, to overestimate the importance of the role that foreigners are likely to play through the channels of such bodies. Furthermore, the political debate which arouses most controversy concerns the participation of foreigners in local affairs at commune level.

The participation of foreigners in local affairs at commune level

While demands are seldom voiced in favour of enabling immigrants to play a role in national affairs, it is quite a different matter in the case of local affairs, which are considered to have fewer political implications than the former and are of more direct concern to immigrant workers. For this reason, the psychological or legal barriers which loom up in connection with national elections do not seem to be insuperable to groups campaigning for greater civil and political rights for migrants. The participation of foreigners in local affairs is therefore one of the major demands of the numerous associations which offer protection and support to immigrants. However, there is no clear definition of the form to be taken by such participation and though several proposals have been made, no general agreement has been reached among the representatives of the principal institutions involved, and a number of obstacles have arisen.

Along what lines have efforts been made up to now? To tell the truth, it is much more a question of showing a receptive attitude towards the needs of immigrants than of setting up machinery for their participation. The initiative in respect of measures responding to the needs of immigrants always lies with municipal councils, which sometimes consult immigrant workers' aid associations and, on rare occasions, the workers themselves. There is no denying that one of the factors hindering efforts to promote the direct participation of foreigners in local affairs is their mistrust of the administration, and this would be true even if they had to deal with commissions created specifically to solve their problems. Another impediment consists in the contradictions that may exist between the action which the municipality wishes to promote and what the immigrants want it to do for them. It is probable, for example, that an immigrant is inclined, in the light of his own experience, to perceive his interests in short-run terms and seek the immediate satisfaction of his needs, whereas the municipality will adopt a general approach with the aim of easing the problems of the foreign community as a whole. The failure of the Management Board of the Office for Immigrant Workers of the Dauphiné seems to be attributable to these factors.[26]

For the above reasons, municipalities very often set up commissions which take action within the local government framework whenever public service missions are delegated to them. Either a specialized commission is set up or the regular municipal commissions are charged with studying the specific problems of the foreign community. In most cases, the latter solution is adopted.[27] It must be said, however, that this type of action concerns only a very small number of communes.

Lastly, some municipalities prefer to act through immigrant workers' aid associations: either an association is set up by the municipality itself, or an existing association becomes the principal intermediary between the municipality and the immigrants. It sometimes happens that the latter system is combined with the former.

It should be noted that the effort to promote the participation of immigrant workers in local affairs usually consists in setting up a purely French service to attend to the needs of the foreign community and seldom results in a system ensuring the direct representation of foreigners or giving them a voice in the decision-making process. The same approach was adopted at departmental level: a circular of 27 April 1973 created departmental advisory committees for social action to deal with the specific problems of immigrant workers.[28] These committees are composed exclusively of representatives of the public services concerned with social affairs (social security, health and welfare, public education, etc.) and representatives of trade unions.[29]

The participation of foreign workers in the affairs of the firms employing them

Two laws have paved the way for the representation of foreigners on worker participation bodies. The legal obstacles have been greatly reduced and it can now be said that the remaining difficulties are of a sociological rather than legal nature. In other words, they have more to do with the social exclusion of foreign workers and their mistrust of institutions than with a legal disability.

Firms in France operate a three-level system ensuring that the employees have a say in the firm's affairs.

Employees' delegates. Their role is to bring the individual or collective complaints of the employees to the notice of the management. Moreover, in firms employing fewer than fifty persons, the delegates run the social services of the establishment and can offer suggestions concerning the organization and productivity of the firm. An Act dated 27 June 1972 considerably extended the voting and eligibility rights of foreign workers, but it was the Act of 11 July 1975 which really secured the foreigner's right to stand for election as employees' delegate, since it provided that the only condition to be met by a candidate for election was that he should be able 'to express himself in French'. Furthermore, the Supreme Court of Appeal recognized that persons speaking only a foreign language could be elected when a tacit agreement—comparable to an internal management/personnel agreement—had previously authorized the choice of an employees' delegate who did not speak French.[30] That decision primarily concerns firms employing a high percentage of foreign workers and in particular those located in frontier zones. As regards the right to vote, there are no nationality or language conditions.

Members of works committees. The works committees perform various functions. In the first place, they manage the firm's social services. This is the field in which they have the widest powers. Secondly, they play an advisory role in matters concerning the organization and productivity of the firm. Thirdly, they have some say in the firm's economic management. The works committee is therefore an extremely important body whose powers affect the workers' daily life. Foreigners may stand for election and have the right to vote under the same conditions as those applying to employees' delegates. However, the Supreme Court of Appeal has ruled that the Law of 1975 shall be strictly applied as regards the need to be able 'to express themselves in French'.[31]

Trade-union delegates. The Act of 27 December 1968 recognized the right to engage in trade-union activity inside firms. To that end, unions appoint delegates who carry out their duties within the union's section in the firm employing them. The Act of 11 July 1975 removed the discriminatory conditions which prevented foreigners from serving in that capacity. At present, the same conditions apply both to foreigners and to French citizens. It is also possible for a foreign worker who is a union member to become an office-holder in the administrative and policy-making bodies of the union, provided that he has worked in France for at least five years and has not infringed the provisions of the Election Act. That condition is not applicable to nationals of EEC countries. Lastly, the number of foreigners serving on the policy-making or administrative bodies of a union must not exceed one-third of the total number of union members serving in a similar capacity. It must be made clear, however, that the Supreme Court of Appeal has ruled that a trade-union delegate 'must be able to express himself in French'.[32]

There can be no doubt, therefore, that the firm is one of the areas of community life where, in theory, de jure equality between French nationals and foreigners is most firmly established.[33] But, in practice, de facto equality is far from being assured, as is shown by a survey carried out in a firm at the end of 1975.[34] This valuable study throws light on certain aspects of the discrimination which is in fact practised against foreign workers. The most important points are as follows: (a) in general, immigrant workers, including those with a record of five or six years of service in the same firm, are paid the lowest wages; (b) they are called to account for breaking factory rules more often than French workers; (c) French workers show their hostility whenever they find themselves in competition with immigrant workers; (d) immigrants are ill at ease in factory unions and are not willing to accept responsibilities.

Admittedly, this study is not based on a representative sample, but it shows quite clearly that there is a wide gap between the rights of immigrant workers as recognized by law and those which they are likely to exercise in reality.

Conclusion

The two principles that guided French law-makers working in this field at the end of the Second World War have left a deep mark on the country's immigration policy. It was necessary, on the one hand, to promote immigration in the interests of population growth, and on the other hand, to regulate the migratory flow. Thus, unlike most European countries, France lost no time in developing a coherent system of rules and regulations.

Until the 1970s, this policy tended to be implemented less and less rigidly, with the result that France became a country wide open to immigration; subsequently, however, the control regulations were tightened up and France finally closed its doors to migrant workers. In this sense, France can be said to be comparable with many other countries. The fact remains, however, that the idea of immigration acting as a factor in population growth has never quite disappeared and this is borne out, for example, by French law governing nationalities and the large number of naturalizations among second-generation immigrants.[35]

The official immigration policy is very ambivalent. While numerous measures have been taken to promote the integration of migrants (literacy programmes, courses in the mother tongue, opportunities—though admittedly limited—to preserve traditional cultures, housing facilities), the government now wishes to restrict the entry of families and has set up machinery to encourage immigrants to return home. It goes without saying that, in theory, migrants are free to choose whether or not to return home. However, it is permissible to feel doubtful about the real reasons for a migrant's decision when we bear in mind that the workers concerned are hard hit by the slump and come up against various forms of discrimination.

At the same time, French policy regarding the admission of refugees is a particularly liberal one and this has resulted in a different type of migratory flow. Political migration (refugees) is tending to take the place of economic migration (migrant workers). Nevertheless, regardless of the nature or origin of the migratory flow, a migrant remains a foreigner in the full sense of the word, and this is all the more true because of the presence among the refugees of a minority enjoying the privileged status of political refugees.

It is an undeniable fact that, instead of working towards the formulation of a legal status for foreigners that would enlarge and more effectively secure the rights of immigrant workers, the most recent French legislation places the main emphasis on the obligations of foreigners and confers even wider powers on the administrative authorities.

Notes

1. Decision of the Council of State, 13 January 1975, D. Da Silva, p. 784.
2. Art. L. 341–9, *Code du travail*.
3. Art. R. 341–3, *Code du travail*.
4. Art. R. 341–7, *Code du travail*.
5. *Le dossier de l'immigration*, 6th ed., Paris, Ministère du Travail et de la Participation, Secrétariat d'État à la Condition des Travailleurs Immigrés, June 1980.
6. Ord. No. 45–2658 of 2 November 1945, as amended by the Decree of 15 January 1976.
7. Decree No. 76–383 of 29 April 1976; its provisions were carried over by Act No. 80–9 of 10 January 1980 (Art. 5–1).
8. Note issued by the Office of the Secretary of State Responsible for Immigrant Workers, 27 September 1977.
9. J.-J. Dupeyroux, 'Les primes au départ, démissions négociées ou licenciements déguisés?', *Le Monde*, 9 November 1977.
10. For example, the Circular of 17 July 1977 provided that spouses admitted within the framework of the family immigration system could avail themselves of the regularization procedure, whereas the Decree of 11 November 1977 took away that prerogative.
11. It is interesting to note that, in October 1977, the Council of State delivered an unfavourable decision on the family immigration reform prepared by the Secretary of State. Despite that decision, the latter signed the Decree of 10 November 1977, which was annulled by the Council of State on 8 December 1978.
12. M. L. Samman, 'Les migrations internationales récentes', *Revue française des affaires sociales*, April–June 1978, p. 36.
13. Ibid., p. 57.
14. See, inter alia, A. Lebon, 'La présence étrangère en France', *Droit social*, May 1976, pp. 11–16, and G. Tapinos, *L'immigration étrangère en France*, pp. 120 et seq., Paris, PUF, 1975.
15. A. Le Pors, *Immigration et développement économique et social*, p. 140, Paris, La Documentation Française, 1977, 364 pp.
16. Ibid., pp. 143 et seq.
17. Oddly enough, this expression is used in French terminology to mean an unskilled worker.
18. E. Vlassenko and S. Volkoff, 'Les salaires des étrangers en 1972', *Économie et statistique*, No. 70, September 1975.
19. Tapinos, op. cit., p. 78.
20. Ibid., pp. 164 et seq.
21. Le Pors, op. cit., pp. 167 et seq.
22. Decree of 28 December 1976, Art. 4.
23. Decree 1305 of 18 December 1976, Art. 14.
24. Act of 12 November 1968, Art. 14.

25. See *Colloque sur la participation des ressortissants étrangers aux élections municipales dans les pays de la CEE* (René Chapus's report on France), p. 40; the boards in question are labour courts.
26. For more details, see 'En France, une municipalité et les travailleurs immigrés: Grenoble', *Hommes et migrations/Migrants-formation*, pp. 65–70 (special issue).
27. See BELC-Migrants, *Les travailleurs migrants et leur représentation dans la vie communale en France*, 1975, 12 pp.
28. Circular PSM No. 0673 of 27 April 1973 (Ministry of Labour).
29. On the whole question dealt with in this paragraph, see Catherine Wihtol de Wenden, *Les immigrés dans la cité*, Paris, Ministère du Travail/La Documentation Française, 1978, 136 pp.
30. Decision delivered by the Social Affairs Division, Supreme Court of Appeal, on 28 April 1977 (Cass. Soc. 28 avr. 1977 D. 1977 I.R. 282).
31. Ibid.
32. Cass. Soc. 20 oct. 1976 D. 1976 I.R. 300.
33. See Anne-Françoise Beylier, 'L'action législative et réglementaire récente concernant les étrangers', *Revue française des affaires sociales*, April–June 1978, pp. 147–57 (special issue).
34. F. Gugenheim, 'Les relations entre Français et immigrés. Observation en entreprise', *Recherches sur les migrations*, November–December 1976, pp. 1–11.
35. In 1973/74, children accounted for one-third of the total number of naturalizations which amounted to 50,679. Moreover, of the 40,000 foreign children born in France every year, some 8,000 register as French citizens before attaining their majority (18 years).

Bibliography

ABOU SADA, G.; GALOO, F.; JACOB, P.; TRICART, J. P. *La condition de la seconde génération d'immigrés*. Migrations/Études, 1977.

BENOÎT, Jean. Renvoyer les immigrés? *Le Monde*, 4 October 1977.

BEYLIER, A.-F. L'action législative et réglementaire récente concernant les étrangers. *Revue française des affaires sociales*, April–June 1978. (Special issue.)

CHAPUS, R. *Colloque sur la participation des ressortissants étrangers aux élections municipales dans les pays de la CEE.*

CHAZALETTE; MICHAUD, P. La deuxième génération d'immigrants dans la région Rhône-Alpes. *Migrations*, March 1977.

DE COURSAC, M. La formation des travailleurs immigrés: Vers une nouvelle politique. *Droit social*, May 1976.

DUPEYROUX, J.-J. Les primes au départ, démissions négociées ou licenciements déguisés? *Le Monde*, 9 November 1977.

GRANOTIER, B. *Les travailleurs immigrés en France*. Paris, Maspero, 1976.

GUGENHEIM, F. Les relations entre Français et immigrés. Observation en entreprise. *Recherches sur les migrations*, November–December 1976.

LEBON, A. La présence étrangère en France. *Droit social*, May 1976.

LE PORS, A. *Immigration et développement économique et social*. Paris, La Documentation Française, 1977.

MAILLAT, D. *Structures des salaires et immigration*. Paris, Dunod, 1968.

MALEWSKA PEYRE, H. L'identité et les jeunes immigrés. *Migrants-formation*, October 1978.

SAMMAN, M. L. *Les étrangers au recensement de 1975*. Paris, La Documentation Française.

———. Les migrations internationales récentes. *Revue française des affaires sociales*, April–June 1978.

TAPINOS, G. *L'immigration étrangère en France*. Paris, PUF, 1975.

VLASSENKO, E.; VOLKOFF, S. Les salaires des étrangers en 1972. *Économie et statistique*, No. 70, 1975.

WIHTOL DE WENDEN, C. *Les immigrés dans la cité*. Paris, Ministère du Travail/La Documentation Française, 1978.

WISNIEWSKI, J. *Nouvel atlas de l'immigration*. Hommes et Migrations, Paris, 1977.

The status
of immigrant workers
in the Netherlands

Chris Smolders

Foreword

The problem of overpopulation is one of the major concerns of the Netherlands authorities. In an effort to find a solution to this problem, a special committee was set up to study population growth data and submit a report of its findings to the government. The committee, Interdepartementale Commissie Bevolkingsbeleid, established in 1977, is responsible for recommending measures designed to help stabilize the population in the years ahead.

Special attention has been devoted to the question of immigrant workers. The committee postulated that the Netherlands should avoid moving towards the adoption of an immigration policy. On several occasions in the past, the government had enlarged on the idea that the Netherlands should not be regarded as an immigration country. However, there is much opposition to this official position; it is pointed out that a large number of immigrants are living in the Netherlands and that the majority have obviously come into the country with a view to settling there. That is unquestionably true.

Without going into the details of the controversy for the moment, it may be as well to state explicitly that the use of the term 'immigration' does not imply in the present monograph that the writer has adopted one position or another in the current debate. The word 'immigrant' will be used here to designate any foreigner who has come to live in the Netherlands no matter whether he plans to find temporary employment

---

Chris Smolders is Secretary of the Interdepartementale Commissie Beleid Buitenlandse Werknemers (Interdepartmental Committee Responsible for Foreign Workers).

and eventually return to his own country or intends to establish himself permanently on Netherlands territory.

Furthermore, it should be noted that Parliament recently promulgated a new Act concerning the admission of foreign workers to the domestic labour market (Wet Arbeid Buitenlandse Werknemers); it came into force on 1 November 1979. In many instances, it will be useful to compare the old and the new laws.

The main feature of the new Act is that it introduces stricter regulations concerning access to the labour market for potential immigrants to the Netherlands.

Immigration policy and regulations

Recruiting procedures

Since the Netherlands is in a very special situation as regards immigration, this problem must be placed in its general context. First and foremost, something must be said about the historical factors which explain the presence of several competing groups of migrants on the national territory.

The principal ways in which immigrants have obtained authorization to stay in the Netherlands are as follows:

Admission on an individual basis of migrants coming from 'third party' countries (that is to say, countries other than those which are members of the EEC or from part of the Netherlands West Indies).

Recruitment of workers in certain countries with a surplus labour force (Turkey, Morocco, Spain, Portugal, Yugoslavia and Tunisia). Despite the conclusion of a recruiting agreement between the Netherlands and Greece, no recruitment office was ever established in the last-mentioned country.

Regularization of the situation of migrants living illegally in the Netherlands.

Admission of nationals of the Netherlands West Indies.

Let us look more closely at each of these four cases in turn.

Admission on an individual basis of migrants coming from 'third party' countries

Any immigrant from a 'third party' country as well as his employer—for practical reasons—can apply for a work permit. The permit can be refused if other workers are already available on the labour market who are willing and able to accept the job being offered. Before a decision is taken, other factors are taken into consideration, such as age, qualifications or the wage to be paid. Foreign workers residing legally on Netherlands territory are registered as persons already available for work on the labour market.

Permits are issued in the name of the Ministry of Social Affairs (labour). The permit so issued may be accompanied by restrictions. However, the only restriction which is imposed in practice concerns the period of validity. A permit is usually valid for twelve months. As a general rule, a foreign worker who has held a permit of this kind for five years running is given a permanent permit that will never expire.

An appeal can be lodged with the Ministry of Social Affairs in the following eventualities: if a permit is refused or cancelled; if a permit is issued for less than twelve months; if an application for the renewal of a permit is refused at the time of its expiry; if a permit is renewed for less than twelve months. In the event of an appeal against a categorical refusal, a mixed commission composed of representatives of employers and trade unions and chaired by a neutral party advises the minister and helps him to arrive at his final decision. If the foreigner and/or his employer is not satisfied with the final decision, the appeal can be taken higher and the case will then be heard by the supreme administrative court (the Council of State). An appeal of this kind is founded on a general right to appeal any administrative decision (Administratieve Rechtspraak Overheidsbeschikkingen, 1975). The decision of the Council of State is final and binding on all courts as well as on the administrative authorities.

Recruitment of workers in certain countries with a surplus labour force

This is a procedure for opening the labour market to a special category of migrants coming from 'third party' countries. At the end of the 1950s, the Netherlands experienced an acute shortage of manpower, especially in sectors requiring unskilled workers. At that time, there was a large influx of immigrants from the Mediterranean Basin who had decided spontaneously to seek work in northern Europe. In view of the pressing need for manpower, the stability of the labour market was not affected by this development. However, the foreign workers themselves suffered some adverse effects, mainly as regards their housing and working conditions. In an effort to eliminate the undesirable consequences of uncontrolled immigration, recruiting agreements were concluded with a number of countries (Spain, 1961; Portugal, 1963; Turkey, 1964; Morocco, 1969; Yugoslavia, 1970; and Tunisia, 1971; the agreement signed with Greece in 1965 was never implemented). By and large, the provisions of the agreements were based on the same principles:
Priority was to be given to the recruitment of workers belonging to the above-mentioned 'recruitment' countries.

Because deplorably bad accommodation had been offered to migrants in the 1950s, the recruitment of a group of would-be immigrants was to be authorized only after the Netherlands authorities had approved the housing earmarked for their occupation. This was a sound principle, but only in theory. In practice, many immigrant workers chose, for personal reasons, to leave the premises assigned to them, while others were unable, after changing their initial jobs, to keep the lodgings provided for them by the employee who had recruited them.

As for working conditions and all related matters (wages, holidays, social security, job security, etc.), they were to be as good as those enjoyed by Dutch nationals. Work contracts were subject to the approval of the Dutch authorities, who had prepared a model, and had also drawn up certain rules concerning bilingualism.

To be eligible for recruitment, a worker had to meet certain criteria: he had to be in good health, have a clean police record (political offences being disregarded), be between 18 and 35 years old in the case of an unskilled worker, or between 18 and 45 in the case of a skilled worker, and show that he was capable of doing the job that had to be filled.

Although these recruitment agreements were not legally enforceable, employers found that it was in their interests to comply with them. However, the implicit assumption that the workers would return to their home countries after one or two years of employment in the Netherlands was not at all borne out by subsequent experience.

*Regularization of the situation of migrants living illegally
in the Netherlands*

In May 1975, the Ministry of Justice (which is responsible for regulating the admission of foreigners) and the Ministry of Social Affairs (which is responsible for regulating the labour market) jointly defined the conditions to be met by persons wishing to regularize their situation. They were required to: (a) be in possession of a valid passport; (b) furnish proof of having entered Netherlands territory before 1 November 1974 and of having resided on Netherlands territory since that date; (c) produce a certificate of good conduct (*antecedentenverklaring*); (d) undergo an examination of the respiratory tract (TB check-up); (e) show that they had been gainfully employed and that they were not unemployed of their own accord; (f) be in the appropriate age-group; and (g) be entitled to a work permit under the laws in force.

Since the wording of the last two points listed above could be understood in different ways, it was supplemented by certain guidelines. Regional employment offices (Gewestelijk Arbeidsbureau) were informed that the points in question should not be interpreted too strictly. Accordingly, no work permit was refused on the grounds that the applicant failed to meet one or another of these two requirements.

The total result of this operation was that the situation of some 15,000 migrants was regularized. Most of these workers came from recruitment countries and they accounted for quite a significant number of the 100,000 work permits issued to nationals of those countries.

Admission of nationals of the Netherlands West Indies

Up to 25 November 1975, the migratory flows from the Netherlands West Indies were not regarded as being part of international migratory movements. This was explained by the fact that, even though the Netherlands West Indies were independent in so far as their domestic affairs were concerned, they were still part of the Kingdom of the Netherlands at the beginning of the 1970s. At that time, the insignificant flows characteristic of the traditional pattern of immigration from the South American territories (Suriname) began to increase. This development gave rise to talks between governmental advisory committees, on the one hand, and organizations representing people from Suriname, on the other hand, with a view to determining whether measures based on the principle of 'positive discrimination' should be taken to improve the employment and housing opportunities open to Dutch nationals from the West Indies. These talks gradually became linked with the discussions which were opened on the subject of the independence of Suriname.

There was some fear that, after Suriname acceded to independence, certain ethnic groups would take control of the new republic. The situation was especially complicated because two major ethnic groups were strong enough to seize power and the minorities threw in their lot with one or the other. As a result, the migratory flows towards the Netherlands took on new proportions. As soon as the Dutch authorities had announced the forthcoming independence of Suriname and at the very moment when they were beginning to set up reception facilities, enormous numbers of immigrants arrived all at once.

The reception centres gave priority to the allocation of housing and financial aid (for the purchase of furniture and clothing, among other things) and also helped immigrants to find jobs. When the independence of Suriname was proclaimed in November 1975, an agreement concerning nationality rights was signed (Toescheidingsovereenkomst, 1975). By that time, some 150,000 immigrants had been added to the Surinamese community in the Netherlands, which had previously numbered about 450,000 persons.

Although Suriname nationals must obtain a work permit, this cannot be withheld if the applicant has a job.

Immigration control mechanisms

The pattern of immigration differs from one category of migrants to another and the responsibility for operating the necessary control system is vested in the Ministry of Justice. The relevant regulations are based on the Aliens Act (Vreemdelingenwet, 1965) and the related implementary Decree (Vreemdelingenbesluit, 1966) which amplifies its provisions, taking into account the international agreements concluded in this field. The Circular on Aliens (Vreemdelingencirculaire) defines the procedures for applying all these rules. This circular has been published and it can be cited in any appeal proceedings instituted against a decision of the administrative authorities.

The regulation of movements of persons entering the territory of the Netherlands is the subject of a Benelux convention (Overeenkomst tussen het Koninkrijk der Nederlanden, het Koninkrijk België en het Groother-togdom Luxemburg inzake Verlegging van de Personencontrole naar de Buitengrenzen van het Beneluxgebied, 1960). That agreement, which provides implicitly for open frontiers, makes it very difficult to exercise effective control over entries into Netherlands territory.

Consequently, the regulation of immigration consists less in operating a frontier control system than in checking, *a posteriori*, on the legality of a migrant's presence in the country. Because of the large number of illicit workers, this is a major problem.

In theory, foreign workers from 'third party' countries, those from recruitment countries and those who have regularized their situation all enjoy the same status. The validity of their residence permits is checked by means of *a posteriori* control mechanisms. For the first five years of residence, the period of validity of the permit is limited to twelve months. After five years' residence, foreigners can apply for a permanent residence permit. The registration of a residence permit can serve, if necessary, as proof of entitlement when, for example, a foreigner has lost his residence card.

Nationals of EEC countries are required to hold a special residence permit, in conformity with Community Regulations and, in particular, with Directive 68/360. In so far as the regulation of immigration is concerned, this permit has hardly any value. It is valid for five years. However, if a national of an EEC country seems to have entered Netherlands territory for a reason other than the intention to seek or take up regular employment, the validity of the permit issued to him may be limited to one year.

Before Suriname became independent, no measures were taken to regulate the immigration of people from that country. The opinions of experts vary as to whether such measures were technically impracticable or politically inexpedient. As noted earlier, it is extremely difficult, in practice, to stop the migratory flow from Suriname because of the very broad wording of the provisions governing the immigration of Surinamese nationals.

If an application for a residence permit is refused, the applicant can lodge an appeal with the Minister of Justice. The Aliens Act provided for the creation of a consultative committee to be responsible for advising the minister. Unlike the advisory commission which deals with refusals to issue work permits and is composed exclusively of representatives of employers and workers and an independent chairman, the consultative committee in question comprises representatives of practically all the principal institutions involved. An appeal against the refusal of a residence permit can be taken as far as the Council of State.

The issuing of permits

In the Netherlands, a foreign worker from either a 'third party' country or a recruitment country must hold both a work permit and a residence permit. Certain distinctions exist according to whether the foreign worker was officially recruited in a recruitment country, was recruited in a 'third party' country (an extremely rare occurrence) or was admitted to the labour market in an individual capacity. All these cases are covered in the Work Permits Act (Wet Arbeidsvergunning Vreemdelingen).

There is, of course, a close connection between work permits and residence permits. For example, workers recruited abroad are given a provisional residence permit by the diplomatic mission of the Netherlands established in their country of origin, which authorizes them to enter Netherlands territory. This provisional permit is granted only if the applicant can prove that he is sure of obtaining a work permit.

After they have arrived in the Netherlands, such foreigners are given a work permit by the regional employment office.

This procedure does not apply only to nationals of recruitment countries. All nationals of 'third party' countries (except Austria, Finland, Iceland, Monaco, Norway, Sweden, Switzerland and the United States) must be in possession of a provisional residence permit before entering Netherlands territory if they intend to stay there longer than three months.

Applications for a work permit can be filed either by the worker or by his employer with the local employment office. If it is the worker who applies, the employer must support his application with a job description. This procedure is applicable regardless of the way in which the worker has entered the Netherlands (as the member of a group of workers recruited abroad or as an individual who has to apply personally for authorization to work) and no matter what reasons he may have for seeking employment.

An employer wishing to recruit workers abroad must obtain authorization from the Ministry of Social Affairs (Employment Board).

In the case of a worker to be recruited in a country having a recruitment agreement with the Netherlands, the employer must file an application with the local employment office of the region where the worker is to be employed. The application must be filed no later than eight days after the worker's arrival.

When an employer wishes to recruit workers in a country which does not have a recruitment agreement with the Netherlands, he must show proof that only workers of the nationality concerned meet his recruitment requirements.

Workers recruited in a country having a recruitment agreement with the Netherlands will be given a work permit issued by the local employment office on the basis of a list communicated by the Employment Board which contains the names of those foreigners whose recruitment it has authorized.

In the eventuality of a worker applying after his recruitment for a work permit and a residence permit, they are issued, in practice, without further formalities inasmuch as the desirability of his recruitment has already been the subject of negotiations (not only with employers but also with trade-union representatives).

On the other hand, the issuing of permits is anything but a simple formality when workers have to apply for them independently, without reference to the prescribed recruitment procedure. In their case, a work permit will only be issued if the following conditions are fulfilled: (a) the present situation and future prospects of the national labour market must not be such as to make it undesirable to employ the migrant worker; (b) the nationals of most countries who are not living in their country of origin must be in possession of a valid residence permit authorizing them to reside in the country where they submit their application and issued at least twelve months earlier; (c) decent accommodation must have been placed at the worker's disposal in the Netherlands; (d) unskilled workers must be between 18 and 35 years old; (e) skilled workers must be between 18 and 45 years old; (f) the applicants must have undergone a TB check-up.

Work permits can be refused if the issuing thereof is deemed contrary to the interests of the labour market or if the vacant jobs can be filled by workers already available on the national territory (even if it is necessary to organize vocational training programmes for this purpose).

Applications for work permits filed by workers who have not been recruited abroad must be transmitted to the Employment Board by the local employment office, together with a recommendation for rejecting it whenever: (a) the labour market situation does not justify the issuing of the permit; (b) the applicant fails to submit the requisite documents (proving, for example, that the members of his family are living in the Netherlands) by the fourteenth day after the date on which he filed the application, in spite of receiving several reminders from the authorities;

(c) the applicant does not meet the age requirements; (d) the applicant fails to provide adequate information on his housing conditions in spite of receiving several requests to that effect; (e) the applicant fails to produce a work contract or the latter is not complete.

In the Netherlands, a distinction is made between a temporary (ordinary) work permit and a permanent work permit.

The temporary work permit mentions the name of the employer and the type of work authorized. It must be renewed every year. A new permit is required every time the worker changes jobs or when he has been unemployed for a certain length of time. It should also be noted that a foreign worker can register as a job-seeker and be classified as such as long as his work permit remains valid. He is then entitled to unemployment benefits.

After five consecutive years of employment, a permanent work permit is issued; it is valid for all types of jobs.

Even though the same rules apply in principle both to the issue and to the renewal of a work permit, it must be emphasized that an application for its renewal which is submitted on account of a change of employment is very seldom refused.

In view of the close connection existing between work permits and residence permits, it is difficult to study them quite separately. However, a few specific points may be mentioned.

In the Netherlands, there is only one type of residence permit, which is valid for one year throughout the national territory. It is renewable for consecutive periods of one year. After five years, the holder is usually granted an establishment permit.

An application for the granting or renewal of a residence permit can be refused on the grounds that acceptance would be contrary to the public interest. Apart from cases where there is a threat to public order, public health or public safety, a residence permit can be withheld when the applicant has not obtained a work permit.

The validity of a residence permit does not depend upon the validity of a work permit previously issued. However, the authorities can refuse to renew a residence permit if the applicant has stopped working. On the other hand, if he has become unemployed through no fault of his own, the residence permit is renewed for one year. This rule enables the person concerned to look for a new job and apply for a new work permit.

After five years, a foreigner can apply for Dutch nationality. Such an application is seldom refused, but it is quite exceptional for a national of a recuitment country to seek to acquire Dutch nationality. A request for Dutch nationality is granted by a special Act which mentions the name of the person on whom it is conferred.

The relationship between work permits and residence permits

In view of the connection which exists between these two permits and which has long been recognized by the government, it is necessary for the Ministry of Social Affairs (labour) and the Ministry of Justice (foreigners) to work closely together.

At the end of 1979, a new Act was promulgated. In order to understand its implications, it may be helpful to compare it with the earlier system.

Formerly, the law laid down the principle that the residence permit had primacy over the work permit. Article 4 of the Work Permits Act (Wet Arbeidsvergunningen Vreemdelingen) stipulates that a work permit shall be refused when a residence permit has not been granted. Moreover, a residence permit shall not be granted if the applicant has no means of support in the Netherlands (such means being mainly derived from gainful employment). The strict application of this rule might trap a foreigner in a vicious circle of successive refusals. The two ministries concerned have co-operated in doing whatever was possible to counteract the effects of these provisions, but some persons have nevertheless suffered from their disastrous consequences.

The new provisions governing the residence of foreigners are designed to improve the situation. Thus, an amendment to the regulations regarding the admission of foreigners to the national territory stipulates that a residence permit shall not be refused solely on the grounds that the foreigner has no means of support, at least as long as he is waiting for a decision on his application for a work permit.

The new provisions on the employment of foreigners replace the work permit by an employment permit authorizing an employer to hire a foreigner.

However, as in the past, the Act provides that a work permit shall be refused when a residence permit has not been granted to a foreign applicant. Furthermore, a work permit shall be cancelled if the holder's application for renewal of his residence permit has been turned down.

An application for a work permit is not taken into consideration until a foreigner has submitted his application for a residence permit. Once this is done, the application for a work permit is examined separately.

Stopping or reducing the immigration flow: the government's reasons and present policy

The government's policy regarding access to the labour market was defined in a Note to Parliament concerning Foreign Workers dated

14 January 1970 (Parliamentary Document No. 10504/2) and in follow-up notes.

These notes were signed by several members of the government. Proceeding from the assumption that it was necessary to reduce the immigration of workers, they concluded that it was necessary to restrict immigration in general. The second note to Parliament (Parliamentary Document No. 10504/9) outlined a restrictive immigration policy. Most of the ideas contained in this note have been incorporated into the new Act, except for the idea of providing immigrants with aid to return home, which encountered stiff opposition both in Parliament and among the associations formed to defend the interests of immigrant workers.

The main features of the new Act (Wet Arbeid Buitenlandse Werknemers) are as follows:

The basic principle is that the admission of migrant workers (newly recruited abroad) shall be authorized only if no other alternative exists.

The new permit shall be an employment permit issued to the employer.

In the event that a foreigner has been gainfully employed in the Netherlands for a period of three years, no permit need be obtained by the employer. This provision highlights the fact that a worker has usually been integrated into the Dutch labour market by the end of that period. At that stage, it is virtually impossible to expel a foreign worker from Netherlands territory for reasons connected with the employment policy. This privilege is also accorded to a foreigner who is unemployed through no fault of his own (redundancy or sickness).

A ceiling can be set for the work permits issued to each firm. This should enable the authorities responsible for regulating the labour market to keep a check on the total number of foreign workers employed.

Family immigration policy

Admission of members of the family: conditions and restrictions

In application of the principle of reuniting families, one wife is admitted to the Netherlands (not several, in the case of workers belonging to polygamous communities), as well as children under age, provided that they live with the immigrant worker and are dependent on him for support.

The general conditions governing family immigration can be summarized as follows:

The nationals of recruitment countries must have lived and worked in the Netherlands for the twelve months preceding the application for admission of the family. This period is 24 months in the case of nationals of 'third party' countries. The worker must, moreover, be assured of employment during the 12 months ahead.

Accommodation must be available for occupation by the family.

For members of the family over the age of 18, a good-conduct certificate must be supplied.

A TB check-up is mandatory. It is important to note, however, that the results of this medical examination cannot be given as a reason for refusing to allow the family to be reunited.

The reuniting of families can take several forms:

Reuniting a normal family. This concerns the wife and the children under the age of 21. Children who are not the offspring of the parents in question may be allowed to immigrate if they were part of the family unit in the country of origin.

Reuniting an extended family. This notion can include members of the family who, in the country of origin, formed part of the family and are dependent on the immigrant worker for support. Unmarried daughters who have attained their majority, and also forebears, can be placed in this category.

Reuniting part of a family. This may concern the wife and some of the children. A case in point may arise, for example, when one of the children wants to come to the Netherlands in order to pursue his studies.

Reuniting a family by authorizing the husband to enter the Netherlands. The basic idea is that a married man living elsewhere than in the Netherlands should have the same right as a woman to be reunited with his family when his wife is living and working in the Netherlands; however, certain additional conditions must be met: (a) the marriage must have been contracted at least twelve months prior to arrival in the Netherlands, the object being to avoid marriages of convenience; and (b) the wife must be capable of supporting her family: this means that she must be earning no less than the minimum statutory wage.

Although, as a general rule, only one wife has the right to be admitted with her children, exceptions can be made.

The regulations concerning the reuniting of families include a very special provision which authorizes the admission of foreigners who have a 'stable' relationship with a Dutch national or with a refugee having legally entered the Netherlands. Admission is granted solely for the period during which the relationship exists. The Dutch partner bears full responsibility for the person so admitted, including if necessary the cost of his or her return journey to the country of origin.

Employment opportunities open to members of the family

The Dutch authorities consider that it is not possible to permit members of an immigrant worker's family to enter the Netherlands and yet deny them the right to work. This liberal point of view is expressed in legal terms in the new Act on the Employment of Migrant Workers (Articles 3 and 8).

As already mentioned above, the new Act has replaced the permanent work permit by a 'declaration' issued by the authorities responsible for regulating the labour market when a foreign worker has been gainfully employed for three years. The Employment Act expressly stipulates that the declaration which exempts the employer of an immigrant worker having worked for three years from the obligation to obtain an employment permit shall also be issued in respect of the wife or the children under age who make up the family of an immigrant worker living in the Netherlands (Article 3, 2b).

Table 1 shows a very marked decrease in the number of foreign workers admitted to the labour market.

Although there was a slight decrease in the number of migrants in 1976, there was an increase in the number of residents that had come

TABLE 1. Recruitment trend in respect of workers from recruitment countries, 1969–77 (by nationality)

Nationality	1969	1970	1971	1972	1973	1974	1975	1976	1977
Yugoslavs	1 965	3 142	4 482	1 139	1 100	1 005	581	10	79
Portuguese	—	—	220	56	281	270	16	—	—
Spaniards	4 369	6 402	5 897	1 886	2 503	2 172	245	1	3
Turks	4 022	4 702	4 699	689	1 838	1 480	28	—	17
Moroccans	401	2 305	1 249	84	23	166	49	3	—
Tunisians	—	—	218	127	419	38	1	—	—
TOTAL	10 757	16 551	16 765	3 981	6 164	5 131	920	14	99

Source: Ministry of Social Affairs.

TABLE 2. Immigration and emigration of foreign workers in 1977, by nationality of recruitment country

Nationality	Immigration	Emigration	Balance
Portuguese	598	262	336
Spaniards	834	2 619	—1 785
Yugoslavs	780	1 027	—247
Greeks	210	283	—73
Turks	10 565	3 748	—6 817
Moroccans	5 881	825	5 056
Tunisians	173	65	108
TOTAL	19 041	8 829	—10 212

Source: CBS (Central Bureau of Statistics).

from the seven recruitment countries, as shown in Table 3. The increase was mainly due to the influx of Turks and Moroccans, and the most marked decrease was recorded for the Spaniards.

Table 4 shows that the total number of work permits issued rose in 1978. However, it should be noted that there was a marked decrease in the number of ordinary work permits. The number of ordinary work permits held by foreign workers from recruitment countries fell off by about 5,000 units, but at the same time the number of permanent work permits showed an increase of that order. This indicates that immigrant workers from recruitment countries tend to prolong their stay in the

TABLE 3. Foreign residents and foreign workers, by nationality of recruitment country (in thousands)

Nationality	1975		1976	
	Residents	Workers	Residents	Workers
Portuguese	8.5	4.9	8.8	4.9
Spaniards	29.5	17.6	27.8	15.9
Yugoslavs	13.5	9.9	13.0	9.5
Greeks	4.1	2.2	4.1	2.2
Turks	72.9	37.6	79.5	38.2
Moroccans	39.9	28.2	44.4	29.1
Tunisians	1.3	0.9	1.4	0.9
TOTAL	169.7	101.3	179.0	100.7

Sources: Ministry of Justice and CBS.

TABLE 4. Total number of work permits and ordinary work permits issued, by nationality of recruitment country (in thousands)

Nationality	1975		1976		1977		1978	
	Total	Ordi-nary	Total	Ordi-nary	Total	Ordi-nary	Total	Ordi-nary
Portuguese	4.9	2.7	5.0	2.2	5.2	1.7	5.4	1.5
Spaniards	18.3	8.0	17.5	4.9	17.5	2.6	17.6	1.6
Yugoslavs	9.1	7.9	7.3	4.8	8.0	2.6	8.1	1.9
Greeks	1.9	0.8	1.9	0.5	1.9	0.3	2.0	0.2
Turks	38.4	22.8	39.2	17.5	42.4	14.3	45.1	12.3
Moroccans	27.3	11.7	27.9	7.8	29.2	6.3	31.0	6.0
Tunisians	1.0	0.8	1.0	0.7	1.1	0.5	1.1	0.3
TOTAL	100.9	54.7	99.8	38.4	105.3	28.3	110.3	23.8
Others	18.2	12.1	19.0	11.4	21.0	10.8	23.0	11.0

Source: Ministry of Social Affairs.

Netherlands and remain longer than five years, for they are then able to obtain a permanent work permit. Since 1978, the same trend has been observed, but it is less pronounced.

The place and role of migrants in economic structures

Study of key sectors

Distribution of immigrants by sector

Caution is advisable when interpreting the figures shown in Table 5, since they concern only workers holding a temporary work permit. No comparable statistics are available in respect of workers holding a permanent work permit and this is regrettable inasmuch as their number is growing and even exceeds the number of workers holding a temporary permit. At the end of September 1978, there were 93,868 permanent permits as against 37,016 temporary permits.

In interpreting these figures, it may be useful to compare the latest data available on a few key sectors with the data gathered in 1969 and 1972. Although there is some dissimilarity between the entries found in the tables concerning 1969 and 1972 respectively, the figures can be usefully compared.

TABLE 5. Distribution of workers holding an ordinary work permit (temporary) by economic sector (November 1978)

Economic sector	Number of ordinary work permits	Economic sector	Number of ordinary work permits
Agriculture/fishing	1 681	Shipbuilding	1 626
Industry:		Others	2 659
Food	4 615	Construction	1 597
Textiles	2 168	Commerce	1 944
Wood/furniture	866	Restaurants/hotels	5 265
Chemicals	1 135	Medical services	1 267
Rubber	949	Transport	861
Glass/pottery	1 167	Culture, social work	1 024
Steel	4 202	Others	4 700
Mechanical engineering	973	TOTAL	39 641
Electronics	942		

In September 1969, the number of temporary permits totalled 83,480. This figure had risen to 120,026 by January 1972. Towards the close of 1975, it dropped to 66,800, but then it rose again and by the end of 1977 it had climbed to 93,100. Today, this figure has fallen back to 37,016.

A survey carried out by the Central Planning Bureau in 1972 revealed a heavy concentration of foreign workers in all branches of industry. This was confirmed by the 1977 Population Census.

Table 6 shows quite clearly that, throughout the period in question, migrant workers were distributed in even proportions among the various industrial sectors. It is reasonable to assume that foreign workers holding a permanent work permit are more or less proportionately distributed among the same sectors. However, this can only be a short-term assumption, for long-term forecasts must take into account the fact that migrants' children who have been brought up in the Netherlands tend to look for the same kind of job as Dutch children and may therefore move into other sectors. Moreover, migrants who have lived in the country long enough to learn the language are sometimes upgraded and this may induce them to seek work in other directions.

The explanation offered by the Central Planning Bureau for the concentration of immigrant workers in all branches of industry is closely connected with the analysis of the geographical distribution of workers which will be examined later in this chapter.

However, as regards the ways in which the employment of migrant workers may affect the labour market at a time of stress, the Central Planning Bureau thought that the following conclusions could be drawn:

The employment of foreign workers may help to relieve tension in some areas. This can have a desirable effect at works level but not at national level, for the action taken in order to establish the necessary infrastructures is itself a source of new tensions.

Consequently, the downward pressure on wages and prices is less noticeable than might be expected.

This downward pressure makes it necessary to cut back capital expenditure on producer goods or prolong the life of old machinery, with

TABLE 6. Distribution of workers holding an ordinary work permit (temporary) among certain branches of industry

	Sept. 1969	Jan. 1972	Nov. 1977	March 1978
Food	7 300	10 693	4 615	4 354
Textiles	5 470	6 920	2 168	1 838
Steel	17 700	26 279	4 202	4 559
Shipbuilding	—	—	1 626	1 536
Chemicals	2 600	3 337	1 135	1 116

the possible consequence that action to restructure the weakest sectors of economic activity is deferred.

The advantages that are likely to accrue to the active population are negligible while firms can expect much larger profits.

The economy as a whole benefits from immigration even though the latter puts a strain on the labour market. Therefore, immigration is viewed as desirable by employers but not from the standpoint of the labour market situation.

The positive effect of immigration on the economy is weakened when families are reunited (in the eventuality that no newly arrived members of the family work).

Preference should be given to increasing the internal labour supply (women) since this option would not affect the total size of the population and, at the same time, would augment the volume of per capita production.

The possibility of hiring foreign labour may stimulate capital expenditure and thereby feed inflation.

Lastly, the study of the Central Planning Bureau emphasized that a structural need for foreign labour would result in a steady growth of the population of the Netherlands, which would be undesirable and extremely costly, especially if family immigration were to expand on a large scale.

No comparable study has been undertaken by the Central Planning Bureau since then. It is clear, however, that the hypotheses advanced by the bureau have proved correct, particularly after the considerable expansion of family immigration during the economic recession.

In the next two years, provided there is no further immigration, no more than 5,000 children of foreign workers will come on to the Dutch labour market. In the long run, however, the problem will become much more serious, for about 50,000 foreign children under the age of 16 are now living the Netherlands and no one can say how many more will be coming into the country in the future.

Geographical distribution of immigrants

As in the case of the question dealt with above, the statistics available concern only workers holding an ordinary work permit. Here too, therefore, it is necessary to proceed cautiously when interpreting the data.

Roughly 63 per cent of migrants holding an ordinary work permit are working in the western part of the country.

Some 35 per cent are working in Amsterdam, Rotterdam and The Hague.

The geographical distribution of immigrants is linked, like their distribution by economic sector, to the economic needs of the country

TABLE 7. Geographical distribution of foreign workers holding
an ordinary work permit (November 1977)

Place of work	Number of ordinary work permits
North	799
Centre/East	7 157
West	24 594
South	6 612
TOTAL	39 162

Source: Ministry of Social Affairs.

and is not the result of any governmental policy. The authorities
responsible for regulating the labour market have in fact recruited
foreign workers for the regions—and hence for the sectors—that were
in need of manpower.

Housing and welfare services

The municipal authorities are responsible for housing and the allocation
of accommodation in accordance with statutory regulations.

In this regard, a clear distinction must be made between various
categories of foreign workers inasmuch as their rights to housing may
vary quite considerably.

Foreign workers recruited abroad
At the time of their recruitment, the future employer is obliged to
provide accommodation which has already been inspected by the
employment authorities. The same procedure for the inspection of
housing was prescribed in the case of migrant workers who had taken
steps to regularize their situation; however, it was stipulated that poor
housing conditions could not be given as a reason for refusing to issue
a work permit, but that they were to be reported to the local employment
authorities.

The minimum housing standards are based on two sets of regulations
(Woonketenbesluit, 1965, and Besluit tot Wijziging van het Veiligheit-
besluit voor Fabrieken en Werkplaatsen, 1960), which place particular
emphasis on sleeping arrangements (area, proper ventilation, etc.),
sanitation, kitchen facilities and safety conditions.

Immigrants from the West Indies
Special reception facilities have been provided for this category of
foreigner.

Immigrants living in the Netherlands

As immigrants now tend to stay longer in the Netherlands, they are more demanding in matters concerning housing. Those who live alone insist on conditions meeting higher standards than those established by law as the minimum at the time of their recruitment. The reuniting of families contributes to this trend, especially as family immigration is authorized only if the family is assured of satisfactory accommodation.

Everyone recognizes the fact that immigrants are poorly housed, particularly when they come from the recruitment countries and hold unskilled jobs or only the lowest-grade skilled jobs. Accordingly, the Dutch authorities responsible for developing an integrated immigration policy endeavoured, in a note drafted for internal distribution, to establish why foreigners tended to settle in the poorest quarters of towns. The following explanations were ..c anced: (a) houses are bought at low prices in the oldest quarters of towns in order to be converted into boarding houses for foreigners; (b) as a result, the former residents move away; (c) this process is accelerated as other houses in the same neighbourhood are bought by the immigrants themselves; (d) immigrants like to live near their friends; (e) immigrants are not as discriminating as the Dutch about the quality of housing since they compare their living conditions in the Netherlands with those experienced in their own countries.

The note also cites a number of specific shortcomings, as follows: there is a lack of adequate accommodation for reunited families; the housing conditions are not such as to ensure the smooth integration of immigrant families into Dutch society; the housing conditions of unmarried immigrant workers are, on the whole, quite unacceptable.

However, after this note has listed the reasons for the poor housing conditions of immigrants, it does not go on to suggest any ways of improving the situation.

Social mobility

The wage structure and its development

Despite the dearth of exhaustive information on this subject, a few general observations may be made.

The opinion is widely held that immigrant workers are underpaid and relegated as a group to the lowest grades of the wage scale. The accuracy of that view can be judged only be examining the whole wage structure. In the first place, it should be noted that in the Netherlands there is a guaranteed minimum wage which is adjusted upwards at regular intervals. Moreover, many sectors of economic activity are governed by agreements concluded as the result of collective bargaining between employers and union representatives which prohibit the payment of lower wages to immigrants. When the first work permit of an immigrant is applied for—either in the case of a foreigner recruited from abroad or in the case of a migrant admitted on an individual basis—the authorities responsible for regulating the labour market make sure that the wage offered to the foreign worker is not lower than the one that should be paid to a Dutch worker.

Although a foreign worker is not paid less than his Dutch counterpart, it is true that he is relegated to the lowest grades of the wage scale.

A regional survey conducted in July 1975 by the Regional Commission for Foreign Workers in the Province of North Holland showed that 75 per cent of migrant workers had unskilled jobs in their country of origin. At the time of the survey, only 36 per cent held unskilled jobs, 32 per cent held semi-skilled jobs and 32 per cent held skilled jobs. The figures reported in that survey in respect of unskilled jobs have been corroborated by other statistical data, as is shown in Table 8.

It emerges from Table 8 that certain nationalities account for a particularly large number of workers holding unskilled jobs. In relation to the total number, the percentages are as high as 50 per cent in the case of Turks, and 47 per cent in the case of Moroccans.

It should be noted that, given the rising trend in the statutory minimum wage paid in the Netherlands, advancement in terms of socio-occupational categories does not necessarily imply an advancement in terms of wages.

The status of foreign workers in the firms employing them and the employers' attitude towards them vary considerably from one place

TABLE 8. Number of foreign workers holding an ordinary work permit and employed on an unskilled job as compared with the total number of foreign workers, by nationality

Nationality	Unskilled jobs	Total number of foreign workers
Portuguese	608	1 704
Spanish	1 449	2 760
Yugoslavs	593	2 660
Greeks	114	300
Turks	7 401	14 506
Moroccans	2 890	6 299
Tunisians	407	1 588
Others	1 150	10 824
TOTAL	14 612	49 641

Source: Ministry of Social Affairs.

to another. However, there can be no doubt about the general attitude of employers. It becomes sufficiently clear from reading a series of interviews published, in 1974, in the weekly bulletin of the Union of Dutch Companies (Verbond van Nederlandse Ondernemingen). These interviews with certain executives of leading Dutch firms revealed that employers in the Netherlands disapproved of the government's policy of restricting immigration immediately. In another context, however, company managers as a whole expressed a desire to free themselves of their dependence on foreign labour. Their preference for the national work force is regularly confirmed at the level of regional employment offices.

Unemployment among foreign workers

Until the onset of the economic recession, unemployment among foreign workers was not a problem for the Netherlands. It was only then that the number of jobless immigrants began to grow. Although no official explanation has been given for this trend, it is quite possibly connected with the employers' preference for the national work force. Furthermore, any worker who has a reasonably good command of the Dutch language can probably be regarded as part of the national work force.

Table 9 presents the available statistics on unemployment among foreigners. As this shows, the total number of unemployed foreign workers increased, but there were great differences between the figures

TABLE 9. Unemployment among foreigners, by nationality

Nationality	31 March 1976	24 December 1978
Portuguese	240	575
Spaniards	550	480
Yugoslavs	350	405
Greeks	170	170
Turks	4 320	4 645
Moroccans	3 370	2 490
Tunisians	140	100
TOTAL	9 140	8 865
Italians	720	735
Others	3 180	5 575
TOTAL	13 040	15 175
Incl.		
Men	10 020	10 115
Women	3 020	5 060

Source: Ministry of Social Affairs.

TABLE 10. Length of period of unemployment as at 30 October 1977

	< 1 month		1 to 6 months		7 to 12 months		13 to 30 months		Total
	%	Total	%	Total	%	Total	%	Total	
Dutch	14.2	26 959	41.9	79 661	15.5	29 587	28.4	54 083	190 290
Surinam + Netherlands West Indies	11.2	1 053	36.1	3 393	18.3	1 724	34.3	3 220	9 390
Common Market	18.8	592	44.2	1 394	15.6	492	21.4	673	3 151
Recruitment countries	22.8	1 904	46.9	3 921	14.9	1 247	15.5	1 294	8 366
Others	14.3	396	41.7	1 154	16.0	442	28.0	774	2 766
TOTAL	14.4	30 904	41.8	89 523	15.6	33 492	28.1	60 044	213 963

Source: Ministry of Social Affairs.

for the various nationalities. For example, while the number of unemployed Portuguese workers increased by over 100 per cent, there was a decrease in unemployment among Spaniards. The rate of unemployment among Spanish workers is extremely low, in fact, since it does not exceed 2.7 per cent.

A study carried out by the Ministry of Social Affairs in October 1977 made it possible to compare certain groups of workers as regards duration of unemployment. It emerges quite clearly from this study that foreigners from the recruitment countries had a very high rate of unemployment, but also that they did not remain out of work for very long. The percentage of migrants from recruitment countries remaining unemployed for long periods of time was relatively small: only 15.5 per cent were out of work for periods ranging from 13 to 30 months. The corresponding rate for Dutch nationals was almost twice as high: 28.4 per cent.

The explanation for this situation may perhaps be found in the regulations governing residence permits. An unemployed foreign worker can remain in the Netherlands until his residence permit expires. When it runs out, he is granted a new residence permit, valid for a period of twelve months, to enable him to continue looking for a job. If he fails to find one by the end of the extra year, he must leave the Netherlands. However, this explanation is not wholly satisfactory inasmuch as an increasing number of foreign workers hold a permanent work and establishment permit which protects them from expulsion.

For purposes of comparison with other countries, it should be made clear that the active population of the Netherlands amounts to about 4,870,000 persons, of whom 2.2 per cent have come from the recruitment countries, and that the total number of unemployed workers stood at 220,000 in 1978.

Integration of migrants and their families into the host society

The participation of immigrants in political and community life

The foreigner's right of association

Nothing in Dutch law forbids or restricts a foreigner's right of association. Article 9 of the Constitution recognizes the right to form an association and to join a trade union, but this right is the prerogative of residents. These constitutional provisions are amplified in the Act on Dutch Nationality and Residence (Wet op het Nederlanderschap en

Ingezetenschap). A resident is defined as a person who has been living in the Netherlands for the previous 18 months.

As regards the Aliens Act, it lays down a code of conduct which forbids them to act in a way likely to prove prejudicial to the security of the Netherlands or to public order. In some cases, the enforcement of this rule may result in a ban on political activities directed against a country with which the Netherlands has friendly relations. However, even in the case of such political activities, Dutch policy is very flexible. For example, no repressive measures have ever been taken against the associations formed to fight against (or to support) the Moroccan regime, which are very active in the Netherlands.

The representation of foreigners on official bodies

A notable attempt was made in the Netherlands to create a special body representing foreigners—the Utrecht Council of Migrants (Migran-tenraad). Although this very original experiment was short-lived, it is worth while to recall its basic features.

By a decision dated 13 April 1972, the Utrecht City Council set up the Council of Migrants, which was to represent foreigners living in the city of Utrecht. The main functions assigned to the council were as follows: (a) to play an advisory role in the shaping of all decisions which affect the lives of immigrants; (b) to serve as a forum for discussions among the different nationalities; (c) to operate an independent information service and make its voice heard in all fields of activity concerning foreigners.

In addition, the council was expected to play a role at national level in matters concerning not only immigration policy but also church affairs, trade unions, etc.

Elections to the council were to be free and democratic. However, the rules regarding the number of candidates for each nationality were never clearly defined.

The Council of Migrants was never taken seriously at national level and throughout its short existence it was always at odds with the regional institutions that seek to aid immigrant workers.

Lastly, it should be noted that in a few towns immigrants' advisory councils have been established under Article 61 of the Municipalities Act (Gemeentewet). Their advisory role is limited to local affairs.

The right to vote

Pressure groups and even Members of Parliament have repeatedly proposed that foreigners be given the right to vote in local elections. For this reason, the government promised, during the 1974 parliamentary debate on notes concerning immigrant workers, that this question would be studied with a view to deciding |whether such a reform could be included in the proposed revision of the Constitution. That promise led to the introduction of a bill declaring that the draft for a new Constitution should be amended in such a way as to make it possible for the legislature to formulate rules enabling foreign residents both to vote and to stand for election (Parliamentary Document No. 13 991, Nos. 1–4). The practical value of that bill lay in the fact that it created the conditions that would enable this reform to be tackled in future within a legislative framework.

The ensuing debate, which was conducted through written communications, enabled the government to define its position on this subject: the bill did not imply that the foreigners' right to vote should be introduced without further discussion.

The government also made it clear it was too early to open the discussion on the bill and that the necessary criteria had not yet been defined. However, one of the criteria would probably be a certain period of residence in the Netherlands.

Mode of integration of foreigners

Inasmuch as the Netherlands has never regarded itself as an immigration country, it has always considered immigrant workers as temporary residents. The practical implications of that attitude vary widely from one ministry to another.

A new trend is now emerging in favour of a policy of integration, which reflects the new views held in various ministries and also by members of the associations responsible for providing reception facilities and aid for migrants. However, opinions on this subject are very divided in the Netherlands, as was shown by the proceedings of a conference organized by the Dutch Centre for Foreigners (Nederlands Centrum Buitenlanders—NCB) in April 1978, at which the participants failed to reach a consensus on an integration policy.

Many groups of migrants are opposed to the idea of all-out integration. Strong evidence of this attitude is provided by the naturalization statistics at present available, and yet the Netherlands authorities have a very liberal policy in this regard. To acquire Dutch nationality, the applicant must be permanently established in the Netherlands—this excludes persons, like students, who are only temporary residents—and he must be well integrated into Dutch society. This implies that he should have a reasonably good, but not necessarily perfect, command of the Dutch language.

The number of naturalizations is appreciably increasing; it exceeded 4,500 in 1977 and rose to 5,000 in 1978. Out of this total, fewer than fifteen applications were rejected.

However, only 8 per cent of all naturalizations were accounted for by migrants from the recruitment countries. This figure attests to their manifest lack of interest in this mode of integration.

Whatever the points of view expressed by the authorities, the Netherlands cannot be said to practise a *Gastarbeiter* policy, in the sense of a policy of segregating migrants. It would certainly be more correct to say that, in reality, nobody has advanced any clear and convincing ideas as to how the problem of immigration should be approached. Everyone agrees on the need for some form of integration, but when it comes to discussing just how far such integration should go it becomes clear that there are wide differences of opinion. A fresh interministerial debate on this subject will probably be held quite soon. Discussions are already under way at the Dutch Centre for Foreigners (NCB); the future will tell whether the different opinions are reconcilable.

Immigrant workers' aid associations

A network of regional non-profit associations (Stichtingen Buitenlandse Werknemers) exists: these associations are financed by the Ministry of Culture, Leisure and Social Welfare. They were established by private initiative and at first they received little or no financial assistance from the government.

At the present time, eighteen such associations are in existence, each of them having its own specific approach and objectives. So long as their activities are in accord with their statutes, there is no interference from the government, and even though their opinions may be radically different from those of the government, they run no danger of losing their state subsidies.

These associations are linked to each other by the fact that they pursue their objectives in accordance with guidelines laid down by the Dutch Centre for Foreigners (NCB). The latter is a state-financed national association. No hierarchical relationship exists between the NCB and the various regional associations, but, in practice, they accept some kind of chain of command, based on the principle of co-operation.

The regional associations are directly responsible for regional and local activities such as the management of local reception centres for migrants. These associations deal in fact with the whole range of problems concerning immigrant workers, although they are more particularly concerned with helping those who come from the recruitment countries. They make no distinction in their work between legal and illicit immigrants.

Contacts between the regional associations and the government are best established through NCB channels. It should be noted that the centre has very close ties with the Working Group for Legal Aid to Migrant Workers (Werkgroep Rechsbijstand in Vreemdelongensaken). Many of the actions brought against the authorities for refusing to issue residence permits are instituted by members of this working group.

Information pamphlets for migrants are produced either by the NCB or by one of the ministries. There are no set rules as to which body should publish them. Documentation is now available in one or several languages—not necessarily those of the recruitment countries—on the following subjects: health, social security, schools, unemployment, taxes, housing, buying homes, etc. Moreover, officially recruited migrants (but not members of families) are supplied with information on the Netherlands before they leave their country of origin. Even though there is no statistical evidence to confirm the impression, it seems that the dissemination of information of this kind has hardly any influence on a worker's decision to emigrate.

Migrants from the West Indies (Suriname) were not supplied with any of this information material before they left their country. It was only after the migratory flow had taken on major proportions that special reception facilities were provided for these immigrants; in particular, they were given priority as regards the allocation of available housing, they were granted loans for the purchase of clothing and furniture, and special arrangements were made for the children's education and for the breadwinner's access to the labour market.

Lastly, mention should be made of the proposal to establish, under the auspices of the Ministry of the Interior, a body responsible for co-ordinating all questions concerning minorities. This body has not yet come into being, however.

Conclusion

The immigration of workers to the Netherlands was dictated by economic factors. Migrants therefore tended to establish themselves in the country for increasingly long periods. This trend was contrary to the aspirations of the migrants and to the government's policy. For the moment it is impossible to say whether the policy of restricting immigration has been successful or not. Any assessment is particularly hazardous because some firms which have not recruited workers abroad may have hired foreign labour indirectly through other firms which, for certain economic reasons, were in a position to apply for authorization to recruit their manpower abroad. This is a distinct possibility, since the social mobility of foreign workers shows that they move on to better jobs and leave the worst paid ones to the newcomers.

The system of work and residence permits has operated satisfactorily inasmuch as it has ensured that a mass of available manpower has not drifted to and fro on Netherlands territory. Had there not been such a system, the criticisms voiced by those people who allege that migrant workers represent a stock of cheap labour would undoubtedly have seemed still more convincing.

Economic factors have played an important role in determining the trend in the demand for labour, but they have not entered into the decisions which have been taken in regard to the reuniting of families, the provision of reception facilities for migrants and the education of their children. It is clear today that the majority of immigrants are going to stay in the Netherlands. Accordingly, a new approach to the whole problem of integration is urgently needed. The ministers concerned will have to take a definite political stand on this issue. In this context, a new body has recently been established to be responsible for co-ordinating governmental policy on minorities. However, as this is an area where political positions change very quickly, there is no telling what the future holds.

Bibliography

Governmental and parliamentary documents

Nota Buitenlandse Werknemers: Tweede Kamer 10504, nr. 2, Zitting 1969–70: *Nota Buitenlandse Werknemers*; nr. 4, Zitting 1969–70: *Verslag van een openbare hoorzitting*; nr. 5, Zitting 1970–71: *Voorlopig verslag*. Nr. 9, Zitting 1973–74: *Memorie van Antwoord*; nr. 11, Zitting 1973–74: *Eindverslag*; nr. 12, Zitting 1974–75: *Nota naar aanleiding van het eindverslag*.

Nota Buitenlandse Werknemers, Handelingen, Zitting 1974–75, Tweede Kamer der Staten-Generaal, 15–17 october 1974.

Wet Arbeidsvergunning Vreemdelingen. *Staatsblad*, 72/64, 20 februari 1964.

Wet Arbeidsvergunning Vreemdelingen. Memorie van Toelichting, Tweede Kamer 7258, Zitting 1963.

Wet Arbeid Buitenlandse Werknemers. *Staatsblad* 3/(1958), 25 januari 1979.

Wet Arbeid Buitenlandse Werknemers. Memorie van Toelichting, Tweede Kamer 13682, Zitting 1975–76.

MINISTERIE VAN JUSTITIE. HOOFDAFDELING VREEMDELINGENZAKEN EN GRENSBEWAKING. *Vreemdelingenwetgeving*. 's-Gravenhage, Staatsuitgeverij, 1966.

Vreemdelingencirculaire. 's-Gravenhage, Ministerie van Justitie, Directie Vreemdelingenzaken.

Motie 'Molleman', Tweede Kamer 14915, nr. 13, Zitting 1977–78.

Notitie inzake het Nederlandse Vreemdelingenbeleid, Tweede Kamer 15649, nr. 2, Zitting 1978–79.

Wet Arob. Administratieve rechtspraak overheidsbeschikkingen. Editie Schuurman en Jordens, p. 154, par. 1. Zwolle, Tjeenk Willink, 1977.

Overeenkomst tussen het Koninkrijk der Nederlanden, het Koninkrijk België en het Groothertogdom Luxemburg inzake verlegging van de personencontrole naar de buitengrenzen van het Benelux-gebied. *Tractatenblad*, 1960.

Verklaring dat er grond bestaat een voorstel in overweging te nemen tot verandering in de Grondwet, strekkende tot opneming van een bepaling inzake de mogelijkheid kiesrecht voor de gemeenteraad te verlenen aan ingezetenen die geen Nederlander zijn. Tweede Kamer 13991, nrs. 1–4: *Ontwerp van wet*, Zitting 1975–76; nr. 6: *Memorie van Antwoord*, Zitting 1976–77; nr. 7: *Eindverslag*, Zitting 1977–78.

Overeenkomst tussen het Koninkrijk der Nederlanden en de Republiek Suriname inzake het verblijf en de vestiging van wederzijdse onderdanen. *Tractatenblad*, nr. 133, 1975.

Handleiding—Toescheidingsovereenkomst (Trb. 1975/132) inzake nationaliteiten gesloten tussen het Koninkrijk der Nederlanden en de Republiek Suriname. 's-Gravenhage, Staatsuitgeverij.

Wervingsovereenkomsten. *Tractatenblad*, 1967, nr. 24: Griekenland; 1969, nr. 87: Marokko; 1964, nr. 16; Portugal; 1961; nr. 59: Spanje; 1971, nr. 82: Tunesië; 1964, nr. 142: Turkije; 1970, nr. 50: Zuid-Slavië.

CENTRAAL BUREAU VOOR DE STATISTIEK. *Hoofdadeling statistiek van onderwijs en wetenschappen. Leerlingen met Buitenlandse nationaliteit bij het gewoon lager onderwijs, 16 januari 1976–16 januari 1977*.

MINISTERIE VAN SOCIAALE ZAKEN. Gegevens Vreemde Arbeidskrachten. *Statistisch kwartaaloverzicht*.

Wet op het Nederlanderschap en het ingezetenenschap—*Staatsblad*, nr. 268, 1892.

Richtlijnen voor naturalisatie. *Staatscourant*, nr. 81, 1977. 81.

Reports and surveys

SOCIAAL ECONOMISCHE RAAD. *Advies over de werving en tewerkstelling van buitenlandse werknemers*. 's-Gravenhage, Uitgave Sociaal-Economische Raad, maart 1974.

COMMISSIE BELEID BUITENLANDSE WERKNEMERS. WERKGROEP HUISVESTING. *Rapport inzake de huisvesting van buitenlandse werknemers*. Rijswijk, juni 1979.

Bevolking en Welzijn in Nederland. Rapport van de Staatscommissie Bevolkingsvraagstuk. 's-Gravenhage, Staatsuitgeverij, 1977.

PROVINCIE NOORD-HOLLAND. Provinciale Commissie voor de Buitenlandse Werknemers. *Positie van de mediterrane werknemer in de Noordhollandse samenleving*. Haarlem, juli 1975.

Rapport van de werkgroep buitenlandse vrouwen. Rijswijk, Ministerie van Cultuur, Recreatie en Maatschappelijk Werk, januari 1977.

Overlegorgaan medische verzorging buitenlandse werknemers. 's-Gravenhage, Ministerie van Volksgezondheid en Milieuhygiëne, Staatsuitgeverij, 1977. (Jaarverslag 1975–76, nr. 11.)

REGIONALE RAAD VOOR DE ARBEIDSMARKT NOORD-HOLLAND. *Positie van de mediterrane werknemer in het Noordhollandse bedrijfsleven*, februari 1975.

ADVIESCOMMISSIE ONDERZOEK CULTURELE MINDERHEDEN (ACOM). *Advies onderzoek minderheden*. 's-Gravenhage, Staatsuitgeverij, mei 1979.

CENTRAAL PLANBUREAU. *Economische effecten voor Nederland van de werving van buitenlandse werknemers*. 's-Gravenhage, maart 1972.

Concept. Alfabetisering van volwassenen en verder. Achtste advies van de Commissie Open School, vierde advies van de Commissie Plaatselijke Educatieve Netwerken, juli 1978.

Handboek Buitenlandse Werknemers. Documentaire uitgaven. Alphen aan den Rijn, Samson.

HEIJKE, J. A. M. *Sociaal-economische aspecten van gastarbeid*. Rotterdam, Stichting Het Nederlands Economisch Instituut, Afdeling Arbeidsmarktonderzoek, 1979.

VAN DEN BERG-ELDERING, Lotty. *Marokkaanse gezinnen in Nederland*. Alphen aan den Rijn, Samson, 1978.

DREWE, P.; HEIJKE, J. A. M. Immigratie uit Middellandse Zeelanden. *Tijdschrift voor maatschappijvraagstukken en welzijnswerk*. Alpen aan den Rijn, 1973, pp. 375–88.

VERVOERSBOND, C. N. V. *Leven en werken in Nederland. Een sociologisch onderzoek onder de Turkse werknemers in dienst bij de N.S.* Utrecht, mei 1976.

MIK, G. Het buitenlandse werknemersbeleid; dilemma tussen bevolkingspolitiek en economische werkelijkheid (Ned.). *Sociaal maandblad arbeid*, vol. 29, nr. 10, 1974, p. 602–8.

SPAANS, K. Politieke rechten van gastarbeiders. *Ars aequi*, vol. 24, nr. 7, 1975, pp. 487–99.

Allochtone minderheden in Nederland. *Beleid en maatschappij*, vol. 2, nr. 12, 1975, pp. 326–64: ENTZINGER, H. B. Nederland immigratieland. Enkele overwegingen bij het overheidsbeleid inzake allochtone minderheden; BIERVLIET, W. E.; BOVENKERK, F.; KOEBBEN, A. J. F. Surinaamse immigratie: overheidsbeleid en de rol van het sociale onderzoek; VAN PRAAG, C. S. Molukse jongeren in botsing met de Nederlandse maatschappij; de gevolgen van een beleid; BAELDE-VAN HUGTE, G. C. H.; ESTER, P.; HULSEBOSCH-HEERING, E.; ZEGERS, L. Wat doen we met de buitenlanders. Een evaluatie van het overheidsbeleid t.a.v. buitenlandse werknemers; BOVENKERK, F. Literatuur; Nederland als multi-raciale samenleving, een biografie.

GROENENDIJK, C. A.; SWART, A. H. J. De tewerkstelling van buitenlandse werknemers (Ned.). *Nederlands juristenblad*, vol. 51, nr. 10, 1976, pp. 317–43.

BOUMANS, J. H. T. H. Nota buitenlandse werknemers en ontwerp. Wet arbeid buitenlandse werknemers (Ned.). *Sociaal maandblad arbeid*, vol. 32, nr. 4, 1977, pp. 262–72.

STROBAND, D. U. Gastarbeid en overheidsbeleid; enkele achtergronden (Ned.). *Maatschappijbelangen*, vol. 138, nr. 10, 1974, pp. 775–83.

PENNINX, R.; VAN VELZEN, L. *Kast-vorming in Nederland. Buitenlandse arbeiders in de Nederlandse economie, ontwikkelingen en beleid.* Den Haag, Uitg. door NUFFIC/ IMWOO, 1976, 39 pp. (Aanvullende studie in het kader van het Remplod project. Ontwikkeling van de arbeidsmigratie naar Nederland in de periode 1955–76. Plaats van de buitenlandse arbeider in de beroepsstructuur en het loonstelsel. Verdeling buitenlandse arbeiders over de bedrijfstakken. Geografische spreiding in Nederland.)

KOK, H. ICBBW voert geen beleid/interview met W. A. Renardel de Lavalette. *Motief*, vol. 4, nr. 5, 1978, pp. 12–13.

Local government

GEMEENTERAAD ROTTERDAM. *Nota inzake de problematiek rond de vestiging van buitenlandse werknemers in Rotterdam.* (Verzameling 1972, volgnrs. 279E.)

GEMEENTE LEIDEN. *Nota buitenlandse werknemers Leiden, een benadering vanuit het probleem 'gezinsgereniging',* Leiden, januari 1977.

RAAD DER EUROPESE GEMEENTEN. *Gemeentelijk beleid inzake migranten. Inventarisatie en aanbevelingen.* Maastricht, 1977.

GEMEENTERAAD UTRECHT. *Initiatief voorstel instelling migrantenraad.* (Gedrukte verzameling, 1972, nr. 1065 A.Z.)

Miscellaneous

Nederlands Centrum Buitenlanders. Doel en Werkwijze. (Brochure NCB Utrecht.)

VAN DER VEEN, J.; KRUYT, A. *Oriëntatie in de vreemdelingenwetgeving derde druk,* december 1977. (NCB publikatie, nr. 3.)

Studiedagen, integratie en welzijnsbeleid mediterrane migranten, 19 en 20 april 1978. (NCB documentatie, nr. 10.)

NCB. *Inventarisatie van lesmateriaal 'Nederlands als vreemde taal' voor volwassen buitenlanders.* Utrecht, mei 1976.

Stichting buitenlanders/peregrinus. *Peregrinus bulletin,* themanummer. Beverwijk, januari 1979.

RAAD VOOR MAATSCHAPPELIJKE OPBOUW TE NIJMEGEN. *Onderzoek naar huisvesting, onderwijs, gezondheidszorg van de buitenlandse werknemer.*

Stichting Welzijn Buitenlandse Werknemers Zeeland. (Jaarverslag 1976.)

Misschien denken ze bij de gemeente dat we schapen zijn. *Verslag naar aanleiding van de commissie artikel 61 ter behartiging van belangen van buitenlandse werknemers in Gouda, december 1978.*

Gesprekken over gastarbeiders. VNO. Overdrukken uit *Onderneming,* weekblad van het verbond van Nederlandse ondernemingen. 's-Gravenhage, augustus 1974.

Etnische Minderheden en de Amsterdamse woningdistributie. Vakgroep vergelijkende sociaal-economische studiën. Utrecht, september 1977.

Rasdiscriminatie in Nederland. Discriminatie op de Amsterdamse arbeidsmarkt. Utrecht, Vakgroep vergelijkende sociaal-economische studiën, augustus 1976.

Nederland en de zelfstandigheid van Suriname en de Nederlandse Antillen. Een standpuntbepaling, voorbereid door een werkgroep van D'66, de PPR en de PvdA, 1973.

RIJKSUNIVERSITEIT GRONINGEN. ANDRAGOGISCH INSTITUUT. *Gastarbeid en welzijnswerk.* Een onderzoek naar het functioneren van de Stichting Welzijn Buitenlandse Werknemers, in samenwerking met werkgroepen en organisatie van buitenlandse arbeiders. Groningen, october 1978.

The status of immigrant workers in the Federal Republic of Germany

Elmar Hönekopp and Hans Ullman

Immigration policy and regulations

Introduction

The features of international migratory movements in the 1960s and 1970s were so specific that it became necessary to revise policies concerning foreigners:[1] today the dividing line between 'traditional immigration' and 'temporary immigration' has disappeared, together with the distinction which once existed between 'emigration' and the act of 'going abroad to look for work'. This is a particularly urgent matter because international labour markets are expanding and national frontiers are being progressively opened up by the regulations authorizing the free movement of workers. Lastly, the very purpose of migration has been called into question by the increasing mobility of workers.

Like many other European countries, the Federal Republic of Germany has never promised foreign workers that they would have a right to settle permanently in the country, and simply regards them as 'guests', as *Gastarbeiter*. The Federal Republic of Germany does not consider itself to be an immigration country and so *Gastarbeiter* are admitted only according to the needs of the labour market. Consequently, foreigners cannot claim any innate or previously acquired right to enter the country.

As compared with the situation in the other European countries, immigration to the Federal Republic is a fairly recent development. Until the erection of the Berlin Wall in 1961, the country was able to meet its

Elmar Hönekopp and Hans Ullman are research workers at the Institut fur Arbeitsmarkt-und Berufsforschung (Institute for Labour Market Research).

manpower requirements by employing workers from the German Democratic Republic. Thereafter, increasing numbers of foreign workers were attracted to the German labour market on account of its insatiable demand for manpower and the Federal Republic concluded recruitment agreements with most of the Mediterranean countries which were the main source of supply of foreign manpower.

From the outset, the recruitment and employment of foreign workers were handled by a centralized administrative service. In 1972, immigration declined as a result of the steep increase in the recruitment tax (*Anwerbepauschale*) levied on firms and the reduction in the number of visas issued. In November 1973, the German authorities put a stop to the admission of foreign workers (*Anwerbestopp*).

The government's policy on foreign workers is still based on the principle that the Federal Republic of Germany is not an immigration country. However, as will be explained below, the government is seeking, for humanitarian and economic reasons, to bring about a kind of 'temporary integration' of the foreign population. 'Temporary integration' may be nothing more than a political catchword, but it does underscore the provisional nature of all policies concerning foreigners: the desire to remedy short-term difficulties is the primary consideration and all the measures taken are in the nature of *ad hoc* solutions to social problems which have gradually taken on a political dimension.

This state of affairs betrays a lack of foresight and an inability to tackle such problems either conceptually or in a concrete manner. Nevertheless, these problems have not yet caused much commotion. It must be said, for example, that up to now the emigration countries have accepted the fact that the Federal Republic is exporting its unemployment without facing a serious loss of prestige at international level.

Features of the immigration policy

Residence permits and the permanent resident's permit (*Aufenthaltsberechtigung*)

The fundamental principle of German immigration policy is that no alien has the right to reside in the country without a residence permit. The policy of the department responsible for controlling the movements of foreigners (Ausländer behorde) is based on the following texts: (a) the Aliens Act (Ausländergesetz); (b) the Decree on the Implementation of the Ausländergesetz (Durchfuhrungsverordnung zum Ausländergesetz); (c) General Administrative Regulations for the Execution of the Ausländergesetz (Allgemeine Verwaltungsvorschrift zur Ausfuhrung des Ausländergesetz);[2] (d) the regulations of the European Community; (e) bilateral and multilateral agreements (e.g.

establishment conventions signed with Greece, Spain and Turkey and also such instruments as the European Social Charter and the European Convention on Human Rights).

The latest amendments to the Ausländergesetz and its implementary decree were made on 1 October 1978.

Application for a residence permit

A residence permit may be granted, before or after the applicant has entered German territory, for a limited or unlimited period and for a given region. Foreigners who intend to exercise a remunerated activity must apply for a residence permit in the form of a visa. As a rule, the latter is issued by the German Consulate abroad after it has been approved by the immigration authorities in the Federal Republic of Germany. At the present time, it is virtually impossible for a foreigner to obtain a visa to enter German territory. The most recent federal instructions on this question (issued in November 1978) stipulate that a visa shall not be issued to a Greek, Yugoslav, Portuguese, Spanish or Turkish national unless his spouse is a German citizen.[3] However, they also state that a visa shall be granted to foreign workers returning to the Federal Republic after they have discharged their military service obligations in their country of origin.

Persons of the nationalities mentioned above who desire to stay in the country for more than three months must apply to the competent authorities for a residence permit. In practice, this primarily concerns the members of a family with one of the parents living and working there. Foreign workers' children under the age of 16 are not required to hold a residence permit, but their names must be registered with the administrative authorities.

Residence permits of limited duration

The first residence permit issued to a foreign worker (who must hold an ordinary work permit—see below) is valid for a period limited to one year; it is renewable for two-year periods. The same holds good for the spouse and children living under the same roof as the worker, but they need not hold a work permit.

Residence permits of unlimited duration

As in the case of permits of limited duration, the foreigner has no right to a permit of unlimited duration. However, the administrative authorities can use their discretionary powers and under certain conditions, explicitly prescribed by law, they may issue a permit of this kind. The conditions are as follows: (a) the foreign worker must have completed at least five years of continuous and legal residence in the Federal Republic of Germany (an interruption of a few days is disregarded); (b) the applicant must hold a special work permit; (c) he must be able to express himself orally in simple German; (d) he—and the members of his family who are living with him—must be decently housed; (e) the children who are living in the Federal Republic must be enrolled in one of the classes of the compulsory education system.

It must be said that the last three conditions are not very clear. The ability 'to express himself orally in simple German' is interpreted as follows: the foreigner must be capable of answering a few simple questions concerning his application for a residence permit of unlimited duration; there is no written test; German school certificates can also be produced. As regards housing, each occupant over the age of 6 must have 12 m² of living space, and each occupant under the age of 6 must have 8 m²; exceptions to this rule may be made if the accommodation is particularly comfortable. Lastly, the applicant must produce certificates proving that his children are attending one of the classes of the compulsory education system; enrolment in a vocational training college is also accepted. In addition, the applicant is required to furnish a certificate attesting that his children have been registered with the administrative authorities.

The spouse of a foreign worker must fulfil the same conditions except for the work-permit requirement. If the worker already possesses a residence permit of unlimited duration, the spouse is only required to comply with the condition concerning familiarity with the German language. Moreover, in the event of the spouse having acquired a sufficiently advanced knowledge of the language, the spouse can apply for the residence permit of unlimited duration before completing the prescribed five-year residence period; in that case, a written test must be taken.

In so far as the children are concerned, they are covered by special rules if they have already completed five years of residence in the country at the time of the application. They are immediately supplied with a permit of unlimited duration if they can express themselves orally in simple German, if they are decently housed and if they are regularly attending one of the classes of the compulsory education system. The condition concerning continuous and legal residence is applicable only to children who, being over the age of 16, are obliged to hold a residence permit. However, an interval of three months between the date of the sixteenth birthday and the date of the first application for a permit is not considered to be a break in the five-year residence period required of applicants for a residence permit of unlimited duration. Under no circumstances is the permit granted automatically.

Lastly, it should be made clear that all residence permits can carry some restrictions, such as territorial limitations.

The permanent resident's permit
From the legal standpoint, this is the most comprehensive residence permit. In addition to the conditions listed above, the applicant must

have completed at least eight years of continuous and legal residence in the country, he must take an oral and written examination proving his command of the German language and he must have become sufficiently well adapted to the German economic and social structures to meet the relevant criteria defined by the federal authorities. Residence is not subject to any time or territorial limitations, but it may carry certain obligations. The permit cannot be cancelled. The only action that may be taken against the holder is to expel him from the country if he is guilty of certain serious offences. An application for the privileged resident's permit is, in fact, the first step towards naturalization. A foreigner who has obtained this permit enjoys considerable freedom from the supervision of the authorities responsible for controlling the movements of aliens. His position on the labour market and in the country's economic life is therefore comparable to that of the German population.

It should be noted that all the procedures described in this section fall within the competence of the authority (Ausländeramt) responsible for controlling the movements of aliens in the district where the foreign applicant habitually resides.

Work permits

Paragraph 19 of the Employment Promotion Act (Arbeitsförderungs-gesetz—AFG) stipulates that workers who are not German nationals must obtain a permit from the Federal Labour Department (Bundes-anstalt für Arbeit),[4] unless otherwise provided in international agreements.[5] Permits are of two types: a general work permit and a special work permit, which are governed by the Decree on Work Permits (Arbeitserlaubnisverordnung).[6]

The general work permit
This permit is granted 'in the light of the situation and trends of the labour market'.[7] The foreign worker has no automatic right to a work permit and every application is examined separately. The manpower services apply their own criteria when taking the decision, bearing in mind the labour market and employment policy and the specific merits of each case. The basic objective is to ensure that no labour shortages occur and, at the same time, that inadequately qualified workers are not recruited. This means that the job security of German workers must not be threatened by the employment of foreign workers. Accordingly, in periods of underemployment, no work permits will be issued to newly arrived foreigners (regulations of Autumn 1974) or to foreigners who, though resident in the Federal Republic for some time, wish to take a job for the first time (this point will be discussed more fully below in the context of the 'deadline' regulations—Stichtagsregelung).

A new work permit is issued to a foreign worker who has lost his job only if the new job he contemplates cannot be filled by a German worker. Applications for extensions of work permits are examined in the light of the same criterion.

Any application for a work permit is refused in the following circumstances: when the worker has broken the rules laid down by the AFG; when the job has been proposed by an illegal employment agency; when the working conditions offered to the foreigner are inferior to those offered to German workers.

The work permit carries many restrictions: it is valid for only one employer and for one specific occupation to be exercised, as a general rule, in the district under the jurisdiction of the competent employment office. It is usually valid for a period limited to two years, but it may have a shorter or longer period of validity and, in the case of a worker who has been continuously and legally self-employed for the previous two years, it may be valid for as long as three years.[8]

The special work permit

This permit is granted without reference to the situation and trends of the labour market. It is valid for any occupation and any employer and, as a general rule, for the entire territory of the republic and West Berlin; however, some geographical restrictions may sometimes be imposed. It is valid for a period of five years. To be eligible for a special work permit, a foreign worker must fulfil the following conditions: (a) he must have been gainfully employed, continuously and legally, during the last five years; or (b) he must have a spouse of German nationality whose habitual place of residence is in the Federal Republic.

The most recent amendments to the Decree on Work Permits dated October 1978 rescinded the provision that previously enabled the spouse of an immigrant worker to obtain a special work permit if the latter fulfilled all the conditions for obtaining this type of permit and could prove that he had completed five years of continuous residence in the country.

However, the spouses of Greek and Spanish nationals continue to benefit from the more favourable provisions contained in the bilateral agreements on residence signed by the Federal Republic with Greece and Spain. As for the spouses of Turkish nationals, they benefit from the special provisions set forth in Article 7 of the Decree of the EEC-Turkey Association Council.

On the other hand, this derivative right was not taken away from the children of an immigrant worker. They can accordingly obtain a special work permit provided that they have been continuously and legally resident in the country during the five years preceding their eighteenth birthday. Moreover, even if the child does not exercise this right immediately after reaching the age of 18, he or she can do so at some future date provided that he or she continues to be legally resident in the country, as was previously the case. Lastly, an interruption of residence caused by the obligation to perform military service in the country of origin is in no way prejudicial to the exercise of this derivative right to obtain a special work permit.

It is important to note that the Decree on Work Permits also provides that a foreign worker who has obtained a privileged resident's permit after completing the prescribed eight-year period of residence shall be entitled to a special work permit of unlimited duration.

The relationship between residence permits and work permits

A work permit is issued to a foreigner only if he is legally resident in the Federal Republic in accordance with the current residence regulations.

Authorization to reside in the country is not required of children under the age of 16, stateless persons and persons benefiting from the special provisions of international agreements.

When a foreigner applies for a residence permit, he is presumed to have obtained it, pending the final decision of the competent authorities.

Before a residence permit is granted, the issuing authorities must contact the employment office to ascertain whether a work permit is likely to be granted and, if so, for what period of validity.

A work permit expires at the same time as the holder's residence permit or in the event that the migrant worker remains abroad for over three months. The purpose of this provision is to enable the authorities to check up periodically on the necessity of the foreign worker's presence on German territory. The permit will be extended if the foreigner's presence on German territory is not contrary to the interests of the state, but it can be cancelled if this is justified for reasons of public order. It rests with the administrative authorities to establish the factual circumstances on which their decision is based. The authorities therefore enjoy broad discretionary powers and the immigrants are placed in an insecure legal situation which has often been publicly condemned.

Immigration policy as an instrument for regulating the labour market

A few examples of employment policy priorities

The recruiting procedure[9]
An examination of the recruitment machinery in operation until 1973 throws light not only on the priorities of the labour market, but also on the distribution of foreign workers by economic sector. Furthermore, it reveals the role played in this field by the Federal Labour Department (Bundesanstalt für Arbeit) and the employment offices.

The prospective German employer initiated the recruitment procedure by notifying the competent employment office of his desire to hire foreign labour, specifying his requirements as regards the number of workers, their level of qualification and their nationality. After ascertaining that no German workers were available for the jobs offered, the employment office forwarded the employer's request to the Bundesanstalt für Arbeit at Nuremberg. This federal department was in charge of the well-known 'German commissions' established in the recruitment countries. The commissions operated in Athens, Belgrade, Lisbon, Madrid and Istanbul and served as intermediaries for the local administrative authorities who assumed the sole responsibility for recruiting manpower under the terms of bilateral agreements. They also checked on the health and levels of qualification of the proposed candidates and took care of the formalities connected with employment contracts, work permits and residence permits.

A foreigner so recruited could enter the Federal Republic armed with an employment contract with a particular employer which was valid for one year. The workers were provided with an identity card (*Legitimationskarte*) and were transported as a group.

The German commissions also examined employers' requests which gave the names of workers to be recruited individually.

The consequence of this procedure was that, until 1973, the hiring of foreigners depended entirely on economic policy decisions taken by employers. Similarly, it was the manpower needs of employers that determined the distribution of foreign workers by region and by economic sector. Moreover, while foreign workers who had been employed for some time in the country could change employers and regions if they found a better job, newly arrived immigrants could not do so since they were bound by contract to a particular employer for one year. Lastly, it is clear that the recruitment of foreign labour enabled certain firms that offered low wages or poor working conditions to find the personnel they needed.

The decision to stop recruitment

In the face of the deteriorating economic situation, the government of the Federal Republic decided to stop recruitment in November 1973. Accordingly, bilateral agreements notwithstanding, nationals of recruitment countries can no longer enter the Federal Republic to find work. On the other hand, nationals of Common Market member countries continue to benefit from the provisions of Community law ensuring the free movement of workers.

However, members of the family of an immigrant worker can still join their parents in the Federal Republic but, as a general rule, they can only obtain a residence permit; they are not granted a work permit.

Removal of controls over the regional distribution of workers[10]

In an effort to tackle the problems created by the concentration of great numbers of immigrant workers in certain regions, and especially the excessive strain placed on their social infrastructure, the government of the Federal Republic developed the concept of *Plafondierung* and applied it from April 1975 to April 1977. The idea behind this policy was to adjust the number of foreign workers admitted into certain regions to the absorption capacity of their social structures. The criterion adopted was the proportion of foreigners in districts (*Kreise*) or in towns not attached to districts (*kreisfreie Städte*) which should not exceed 12 per cent of the population. It is difficult to see how it came to be established that this percentage represented a strain on the social infrastructure. Be that as it may, the government came to the conclusion that the absorption capacity of some regions might be saturated with a foreign community representing less than 12 per cent of the total population. At *Länder* level, the competent authorities could then declare that the regions in question were overcrowded, but this was in fact an arbitrary decision based on nothing more than intuition.[11]

If this approach was to prove effective, the mobility of workers within the confines of the Federal Republic had to be curbed. To that end, the work and residence permits of the workers carried restrictions as to their establishment in certain regions. The same restrictions (*Sperrvermerke*) were entered on the permits of the members of the worker's household, except in the case of a German spouse.

Nevertheless, the immigration of the family of a worker who was already established in one of these regions was allowed when he could prove that he had found appropriate accommodation.

These restrictions were applicable neither to EEC nationals nor to foreign workers holding a residence permit and a work permit of unlimited duration to which no conditions were attached. Nor were they applicable to foreigners who had entered the country with a visa.

The ban on residing and working in the regions concerned remained in effect for one year. At the expiry of that period, the question was reviewed and a decision was taken on whether the ban should be extended or not.

The procedure described above was discontinued on 1 April 1977 on the grounds that it could no longer be applied to Turkish workers—by virtue of the agreement on Turkey's association with the EEC—nor to Greek and Spanish workers—by virtue of the bilateral agreements concluded by their countries with the Federal Republic of Germany. Since these restrictive regulations then concerned only a small minority of immigrant workers, they were abandoned.

Family immigration[12]

A foreign worker cannot obtain residence permits for members of his family unless he has worked in the Federal Republic for at least three years and can offer them satisfactory accommodation. However, children under the age of 16 are not required to have residence permits.

These regulations do not apply to nationals of EEC member countries; they can send for their families without having to observe the three-year rule.

Residence permits are mandatory both for the worker's descendants and for his forebears.

The basic principle is that the immigration of the family of a national of a recruitment country should be authorized only if all the necessary conditions exist to ensure that the worker and his family can be integrated without any particular difficulties. In reality, however, since all foreigners are obliged to be decently housed, the arrival of the family depends much more on the state of the property market than on the application of the regulations themselves.

Since 1974, it has not been possible for a member of an immigrant worker's family to enter German territory in order to take up paid employment. However, in 1976, the 'deadline' regulations (*Stichtagsregelung*) were drawn up. They made it possible for a spouse and children of a foreign worker to obtain a work permit (which is also required in order to be allowed to attend vocational training colleges) provided that they had entered the country prior to 30 November 1974. As the result of strong pressure exerted by immigrant workers' aid associations and political groups, the deadline was extended to 31 December 1976 for the children of foreign workers. However, this concession did not mark the end of a heated debate. The government finally decided therefore, to rescind this rule and to issue work permits both to spouses and to children but after a waiting period of two years for children and four years for spouses. The waiting period for children can be shortened if they have taken language courses or pre-vocational training courses: a child can even hope to obtain his work permit immediately after completing his pre-vocational course. In the case of a spouse, the waiting period can be reduced only under the most exceptional circumstances; for example, a work permit may be granted when there is an acute shortage of labour in some sector of activity, such as hotel or restaurant services. This goes to show that economic factors play a much more important role than humanitarian or social values in the shaping of immigration policy.[13]

It may be added that considerations of an economic nature explain why German employers recently recommended that the children of immigrant workers be given the opportunity to follow vocational training courses; they are concerned about the predicted shortage of skilled workers in the years ahead.

The conceptualization of German immigration policy:
recent developments

The changes in the regulations regarding foreigners that have been described above are based mainly on the 'Proposals of the Federal and Lander Commission [Bund-Länder-Kommission] for Developing a Comprehensive Foreign Employment Policy', dated 28 February 1977. These proposals covered questions relating to integration (in the sense of improvements to the residence permit system), more appropriate work permits, language courses, housing conditions, family immigration, etc. The main points on which the government of the Federal Republic of Germany declared its position are as follows: (a) the Federal Republic of Germany is not an immigration country; (b) the ban on recruitment is to remain in force for a long time; (c) in future, foreign workers will be employed for longer periods; (d) immigrants should be encouraged and helped to return home; their countries of origin have an important role to play in this matter; (e) foreign workers and their families living in the Federal Republic should have a secure legal and social status and the opportunity to become integrated into society;[14] (f) future foreign employment policies should take into account the problems of the second generation which is growing up in the country in special circumstances.[15]

Pursuant to a memorandum from the Federal Government's Aliens Commissioner (Regierungsbeauftragter), the government promulgated a set of decrees, dated 19 March 1980, bearing on the special problems of the second and third generation of migrants.[15] Henceforth, a young person who has grown up in the Federal Republic will be eligible for naturalization after completing a six-year period of residence. Moreover, he will be entitled to a work permit: (a) if he has reached a level equivalent to the school-leaving certificate of a main school after completing the upper primary course or of a secondary school or of a vocational training college; (b) if he has had one year of elementary vocational training; or (c) if he has signed a training contract.

In addition, these decrees deal with the health and education of young foreigners, together with other problems of particular concern to foreigners, such as housing conditions.

However, there are some inconsistencies in the government's position. In particular, it is incongruous to assert that the Federal Republic is not an immigration country when the present trend is in the opposite direction. On the one hand, the government is proposing to promote the temporary integration of foreigners and, on the other, it has established the principle that immigrants should be encouraged to return home. Recently, Antje Huber, Federal Minister for Youth, Family and Health, summed up this policy by saying that the innate and cultural identity of foreign children should be respected but that, at the same time, an effort should be made to integrate them into

German society, the ultimate goal being 'neither Germanization nor ghettoization'.[16]

Everything that is being done today to tackle the social problems of foreigners and integrate them into German society has to contend with difficulties created by these inconsistencies. Even though greater attention is being paid to the humanitarian and social demands of the foreign population, the present economic recession is a constant reminder of the fact that the economic and political aspects of the labour market situation still carry more weight in the Federal Republic than all other considerations.

The place and role of migrants in economic structures

The size and nature of the foreign population

Growth of the foreign population

The decision to stop recruitment in November 1973 and the ban on the employment of new arrivals failed to produce the expected results. These should have been the consolidation of policies on the treatment of foreigners and the alleviation of the problems of the labour market. It must be added that there was an unexpressed desire to check the growth of the resident foreign population (and even reduce it) in order to forestall an increase in the demands on the social infrastructure and an aggravation of such problems as may arise when Germans and foreigners live side by side. But none of these objectives was fully realized.

In 1967, five years after the erection of the Berlin Wall, the foreign population had doubled by comparison with its size in 1961. By 1970, the figure had been multiplied by 3.5, and by 1973, the year when recruitment was stopped, it had been multiplied by 5.5. In 1978, the foreign population accounted for 6.5 per cent of the total population as against 1.2 per cent in 1961 (see Table 1).

Instead of reducing the population, the decision to stop recruitment had exactly the opposite effect. The foreign population in the country reached its highest level in 1974 with slightly more than 4 million persons. This upswing was due to the arrival of an enormous number of families in 1973. The effects of the stopping of recruitment were not felt until after 1974: the population decreased between 1974 and 1976, but never reverted to the level of 1973.

Despite the stability of the figures observed in the years after 1973/74, the composition of the foreign population was significantly affected by

TABLE 1. Growth of the foreign population and of the total population and percentage of foreigners in relation to total population—1961–79 (in thousands)

	1961	1967	1970	1973	1974
Foreign population	686	1 807	2 977	3 966	4 127
Index (1961 and 1973 = 100)	100	263	434	578/100	602/104
TOTAL POPULATION	56 175	59 926	60 907	62 089	62 048
Percentage of foreigners in relation to total population	1.2	3.0	4.9	6.4	6.7

	1975	1976	1977	1978	1979
Foreign population	4 090	3 948	3 948	3 981	4 144
Index (1961 and 1973 = 100)	596/103	576/100	576/100	580/100	604/105
TOTAL POPULATION	61 746	61 490	61 389	61 332	61 337
Percentage of foreigners in relation to total population	6.6	6.4	6.4	6.5	6.8

Sources: Ausländer 1979, published by the Statistisches Bundesamt, Stuttgart/Mainz, 1980; our calculations.

TABLE 2. Distribution of foreigners by nationality—1961–79 (percentages)[1]

Country	1961	1970	1974	1977	1979
Europe	77.9	91.5	91.6	90.0	89.1
Italy	28.7	19.3	15.3	14.5	14.4
Other EEC countries	15.5	7.2	6.2	6.7	6.7
Greece	6.1	11.5	9.9	8.3	7.2
Yugoslavia	2.4	17.3	17.2	16.0	15.0
Portugal	0.1	1.8	3.0	2.8	2.7
Spain	6.4	8.2	6.6	5.1	4.4
Turkey	1.0	15.8	25.0	28.3	30.6
Major recruitment countries (incl. Italy)	44.7	73.9	77.0	75.0	74.3
Europe, other countries	17.7	10.4	8.4	8.3	8.1
Africa	1.1	1.3	1.7	1.9	2.1
Others	21.0	7.2	6.7	8.1	8.8
TOTAL	100	100	100	100	100

1. Annual figures as at 30 September of each year.
Sources: Ausgewählte Strukturdaten für Ausländer 1974, 1976 and *Ausländer 1979*—both published by the Statistisches Bundesamt; our calculations.

TABLE 3. Migratory flows of nationals of certain countries
between 1974 and 1978

Nationality	Entries	Departures	Balance
Greek	94 823	256 898	−162 075
Portuguese	36 427	60 195	−23 768
Spanish	38 553	162 421	−123 868
Turkish	610 604	591 265	+19 339
Yugoslav	239 030	385 722	−146 692
Italian	366 126	458 891	−92 765
TOTAL	1 385 563	1 915 392	−529 829

Sources: *Ausgewählte Strukturdaten für Ausländer 1978*, published by the Statistisches Bundesamt,
Stuttgart/Mainz, December 1979; our calculations.

the decision to stop recruitment, with respect to its age structure,
employment rate and countries of origin. This development can be
explained by two factors: (a) a change in the patterns of immigration
and remigration (the return flow), as shown in Table 3; (b) an increase
in the number of births among the resident foreign population.

Between 1974 and 1977, the total number of foreigners having left
German territory exceeded the total number of foreigners having
entered the country by approximately 550,000 persons (see Table 3).

The national composition of the foreign population changed in favour
of the Turks (30 per cent of the foreign population), followed by the
Yugoslavs (15 per cent) and the Italians (some 14 per cent). The proportion of foreigners from the 'recruitment' countries remained remarkably stable (74 per cent).

As regards the age structure, it was modified by the arrival of young
people. At the same time, about 300,000 additional births were recorded,
and this development offset, to some extent, the decline in immigration.
Thus, between 1973 and 1979, the percentage of the foreign population
under the age of 15 increased by one-half (from 16 per cent in 1973
to 24 per cent in 1979).

Trends in the employment of foreigners

After immigration had been stopped, there was a marked decrease in
the size of the population of working age, which dropped from 82.6 per
cent of the total foreign population in 1973 to 73.9 per cent in 1979.

At the same time, the foreign workforce was diminishing and it
lost one-fifth of its strength between 1973 and 1978.

The employment of foreigners was therefore cut back in two ways:
indirectly, through the reduction of the potential active population (as
a result of the changing pattern of migratory flows and the hardening of

TABLE 4. Active foreign population and total labour force—1967–80

	1967	1970	1973	1975	1978	1979	1980
Total labour force							
(in 1,000s)	26 276	26 719	26 921	26 340	26 153	26 322	26 435
index (1973 = 100)	98	99	100	98	97	98	98
Active foreign population							
(in 1,000s)	1 073	1 863	2 580	2 284	2 045	2 078	2 092
index (1973 = 100)	42	72	100	89	79	81	81
Proportion of active foreign population in relation to total labour force (%)	4.1	7.0	9.8	8.7	7.8	7.9	7.9
Total activity rate (German + foreign) (%)	44.3	44.1	43.5	42.5	42.7	42.9	43.1
Activity rate of foreigners (%)	68.1	76.4	68.4	57.5	51.8	50.9	49.9
Total employed population	25 817	26 570	26 648	25 266	25 160	25 442	25 490
Percentage of wage-earners in relation to the above total	81.0	83.4	84.4	84.4	85.6	86.0	86.4
Number of foreigners employed (in 1,000s)	1 057	1 858	2 560	2 133	1 941	1 985	1 990
Percentage of foreign wage-earners in relation to the above total	95.9	97.3	97.6	96.6	95.7	95.7	95.7

Sources: Der Arbeitsmarkt in der Bundesrepublik Deutschland 1980. *Mitteilungen aus der Arbeits-markt- und Berufsforschung 4/1979* (joint authorship); our calculations.

work permit legislation) and directly, by inducing unemployed immigrant workers to return to their home countries. In these ways, the proportion of foreigners in relation to the total labour force was brought down from 9.8 per cent in 1973 to 7.9 per cent in 1980. Furthermore, the activity rate of foreigners declined sharply during the same period, since it fell from 68.4 per cent in 1973 to 49.9 per cent in 1980, whereas the activity rate of the German population remained relatively stable (around 42 or 43 per cent).

Time spent in the Federal Republic of Germany by foreign residents

The decision to stop immigration and the new regulations that accompanied it radically altered the behaviour of foreigners and affected, in particular, the time they spent in the Federal Republic. Whereas, in 1973, about 48 per cent of foreigners had been living continuously in the country for over four years; in 1979, this was true of 78 per cent. In 1980, 80 per cent of all foreigners had been residents for over five years, and about half of that group had been residents for over eight years.

Distribution of the active foreign population by sector

Immigrant workers are not distributed among the economic sectors in the same proportions as the total labour force. In 1977, 60 per cent of the foreign workers were employed in the processing industries (as against a national average of 38 per cent) and about 75 per cent were concentrated in the processing industries, mining and construction (as against a national average of under 50 per cent); the remaining 25 per cent were unevenly distributed throughout the services sector: many of these workers had jobs in the hotel and restaurant industry.

In recent years, the distribution by sector has remained remarkably stable, even though there has been a tendency for foreign workers employed in the manufacturing and construction industries to move into the services sector and into commerce and mining. There is no denying that the distribution pattern of foreign manpower amply confirms the allegation that immigrants are employed to perform tasks considered to be demeaning, particularly in periods of unemployment.

TABLE 5. Distribution and structure of the active foreign population by sector (percentages)

Sector	Structure						Foreigners total	
	1972		1974		1979			
	Total	Foreigners	Total	Foreigners	Total	Foreigners	1974	1979
Agriculture, etc.	7.2	1	6.7	1.0	5.5	0.9	1.3	1.2
Mining, gas, water, electricity	2.1	3	2.0	1.3	2.0	1.8	5.7	6.9
Processing industries	38.4	62	38.4	62.5	36.0	58.7	14.1	12.0
Construction	7.7	14	7.4	12.0	7.1	10.3	14.0	10.6
Distribution	12.1	5	12.0	5.2	12.0	6.1	3.8	3.7
Transport, communications	5.7	2	5.7	3.5	5.8	3.7	5.3	4.7
Insurance, banking	2.8	1	2.9	0.6	3.2	0.7	1.7	1.5
Other services	13.6	4	14.4	11.5	16.6	14.7	6.9	6.5
Non-profit organizations, households	1.5	3	1.5	0.5	1.8	0.7	3.1	2.7
Central and local government, social security	9.0	5	9.1	2.1	10.1	2.4	2.0	1.7
TOTAL	100	100	100	100	100	100	8.7	7.3

Sources: Statistisches Bundesamt: *Stand und Entwicklung der Erwerbstätigkeit*, Stuttgart/Mainz, 1977; *Wirtschaft und Statistik 3/1980* (total employment figures); Bundesanstalt für Arbeit, *Repräsentativuntersuchung 1972—Beschäftigung ausländischer Arbeitnehmer*, Nuremberg, 1973; social security statistics; our calculations.

Table 5, which shows, *inter alia*, how foreigners are concentrated in certain sectors, also illustrates that fact. In the processing industries sector, the heaviest concentration of foreigners is found in the smelting works, where they account for 26 per cent of all personnel. The hotel and restaurant industry comes second with 21 per cent and the textile industry third with 19.3 per cent. The jobs filled by foreigners are associated with poor working conditions (heat, noise, dust) and irksome working methods (shift work, inconvenient hours, etc.).

Distribution of the active foreign population by occupational category and level of qualifications

A study of the socio-occupational distribution of immigrants also shows quite clearly that they do the hardest and most degrading work. Between 1972 and 1977, the pattern of distribution changed as more and more foreigners were employed to perform manual jobs or repellent tasks. The largest proportion of foreigners was found in the category of 'fitters and assemblers' (*Montierer*): one-third were foreigners. Moreover, immigrants accounted for 26 per cent of all manual workers.

The findings of a survey of the situation of foreign workers in the processing industries which was based on a representative sample, were recently published in the Federal Republic of Germany.[17] The survey also compared the qualifications of foreign workers with those of German workers and confirmed that the former were far less qualified than the latter.

Table 6 summarizes the findings of this survey as regards the level of qualifications of foreigners employed in industry. Workers holding a vocational training certificate (or its equivalent) were considered to be skilled; those having had more than three month's training were classified as semi-skilled; those having had less than three month's training were classified as unskilled.

The proportion of skilled foreign workers is practically identical in the two samples. On the other hand, the FLD sample shows a higher percentage of semi-skilled foreign workers than the other sample. The difference is explained by the fact that the FLD included in the semi-skilled category all workers without certificates who had had some training (even if it had lasted less than three months).

Table 6 also shows that over one-half of foreign workers are unskilled and that only one foreigner out of seven can be considered to be skilled. The table does not take into account the various levels of proficiency of skilled workers.

It should be noted that the pattern as regards qualifications varies within each industrial sector depending on the type of work considered. This is true for German workers, but it is particularly true for foreign

TABLE 6. Classification of industrial wage-earners by level of qualifications: comparison of two samples (percentages)

	Samples			
	Industrial sample[1]			FLD sample[2] (foreigners)
	Total	Germans	Foreigners	
Unskilled	36.1	33.3	52.0	31
Semi-skilled	28.8	27.3	33.5	41
Skilled	35.1	39.4	14.5	14
TOTAL	100	100	100	86

1. Based on a survey of 1,428 industrial firms.
2. *Repräsentativuntersuchung 1972*, p. 64, Bundesanstalt für Arbeit (Federal Labour Department—FLD), Nuremberg, 1973. The remaining 14 per cent comprise: shop foremen and gang foremen (1 per cent), clerks (11 per cent) and apprentices (1 per cent).
Source: Gaugler et al., *Ausländer in deutschen Industriebetrieben. Ergebnisse einer empirischen Untersuchung*, p. 74, Königstein/Taunus, 1978.

workers. Thus, in the processing industries sector, the proportion of skilled workers is especially high in the chemicals industry and in the mechanical engineering and car industry (49.3 and 57.6 per cent respectively). However, only the mechanical engineering and car industry has a high percentage of skilled foreign workers: there the figure is 30.5 per cent, while in the chemicals industry it is only 8.6 per cent. In industry as a whole, a much smaller proportion of skilled workers is accounted for by foreigners than by Germans.

Employment of foreigners and the wage structure

The argument that foreigners are responsible, in the long run, for slowing down the upward trend of wage rates does not stand up to close examination.[18] What is needed, in fact, is a thorough study of the comparative growth of the incomes of some representative social groups. Moreover, interesting conclusions might be drawn from a comparative study of wage trends in different sectors of economic activity which originally had comparable wage structures but now employ foreign labour in different proportions.

On the whole, it can be said that the immigration of workers has made it possible to maintain a very finely adjusted wage structure.[19] However, as far as wage-earners are concerned, the structure has proved to be extremely rigid. Although some steps have been taken towards a revision of wage rates, it seems that they have been limited to the development of standard rates and have been neutralized by the general movement of wages. Thus, the wages of skilled, semi-skilled and unskilled workers

TABLE 7. Unemployment among foreigners

	1970	1971	1972	1973	1974	1975	1976	1977
	(in 1,000s)							
Total unemployed	148.8	185.1	246.4	273.5	582.5	1 074.2	1 060.3	1 030.0
Germans	143.8	173.3	229.4	253.7	513.4	922.7	954.2	937.9
Foreigners	5.0	11.8	17.0	19.8	69.1	151.5	106.1	92.1
Migratory balance of the active population	+414.7	+228.8	+139.1	+205.4	−140.1	−194.3	−98.1	
	Changes in relation to previous years (%)							
Total unemployed	−16.7	+24.4	+33.1	+11.0	+113.0	+84.4	−1.3	−2.9
Germans	−18.0	+20.5	−32.4	+10.6	+102.4	+79.7	+3.4	−1.7
Foreigners	+51.5	+136.0	+44.1	+16.5	+249.0	+119.2	−30.2	−13.2
	Unemployment rate							
TOTAL	0.7	0.8	1.1	1.2	2.6	4.7	4.6	4.6
Germans	0.7	0.8	1.1	1.2	2.5	4.6	4.7	4.6
Foreigners	0.3	0.6	0.7	0.8	2.9	6.8	5.2	4.9

Source: DIW-Wochenbericht 13/78, Berlin 13-3-78.

developed on parallel lines. During the 1950s, there was a slight tendency to adjust the pay rates for men, but during the 1960–73 period (which witnessed a sharp increase in foreign employment), a very definite process of differentiation set in to the detriment of the wages of semi-skilled workers in particular.

Unemployment among foreigners

Until 1973, the rate of unemployment among foreigners was always lower than that recorded for the total labour force. It began to rise sharply in 1974 with the worsening of the critical economic situation, and since then it has been higher than the unemployment rate of the active German population. In 1975, over 150,000 foreigners found themselves out of work and the unemployment rate stood at 7 per cent. In the same year, the net re-migration figure attained its highest level when it rose to about 200,000. It seems likely that a high proportion of these re-migrants had lost or were on the point of losing their jobs. In 1976, the foreign unemployment rate fell by 5 per cent, but not because of an improvement in the labour market situation. The drop was largely due to the exportation of unemployment and the restrictions placed on immigration. The fact of the matter is that 1976 witnessed a decrease not only in the number of foreign workers employed, but also in the proportion of the total labour force of the Federal Republic of Germany which they accounted for (see Table 7).

Since recruitment was stopped, the unemployment rate among EEC nationals has also been particularly high. This is one of the consequences of the free movement of labour in the Common Market. However, in contrast to the general immigration trend observed in the country, the number of EEC nationals entering German territory has been steadily increasing.

Integration of migrants
and their families into the host society

The participation of immigrants in political and associative life

Laws concerning the activities of foreigners

Foreigners do not have the political right to vote and are forbidden to participate in legislative elections throughout the territory of the Federal Republic of Germany.[20] The provisions of Paragraph 6 of the Aliens

Act also impose restrictions on other political activities. Such activities can be prohibited on the following grounds:

... if this is necessary in order to ensure public safety or defend public interests or in order to prevent acts prejudicial to the development of a political consensus in the Federal Republic of Germany or to any other important interests of the Federal Republic of Germany.

Moreover, a foreigner is not permitted to engage in any political activity if it:

(1) is incompatible with international law, (2) endangers the fundamental system of liberal and democratic government of the Federal Republic of Germany or (3) aims at supporting parties or other associations, groupings or endeavours which transgress this Act and are incompatible with the constitutional principles of the fundamental system of liberal and democratic government.

According to the jurisprudence of the courts applying the Aliens Act (Ausländergesetz), activities such as agitating in factories or distributing leaflets or pamphlets outside universities or in a busy street can constitute 'acts prejudicial to public interests'. As for acts 'prejudicial to the development of a political consensus in the Federal Republic of Germany', these can consist in efforts to exert pressure on Members of Parliament or influence parliamentary debates by demonstrations or stay-in strikes, or in holding protest meetings in front of the premises of a government department or a political party.

If an authority responsible for controlling the movements of aliens establishes that an act performed by a foreign worker falls into any of the categories enumerated in Paragraph 6 of the Ausländergesetz, it can place restrictions or a total ban on that worker's political activity. Under certain circumstances, it can even order his expulsion.

The same paragraph of the Aliens Act stipulates that foreigners shall enjoy all the fundamental rights of the Constitution (Grundgesetz) with the exception (in accordance with the Constitution) of those rights which are the prerogative of Germans. Consequently, the following rights are not granted to a foreigner: (a) freedom of assembly; (b) freedom of association; (c) freedom of movement; (d) freedom to choose and exercise his occupation.

Moreover, unlike Germans, a foreigner can be expelled from the territory of the Federal Republic.

On the whole, the laws concerning foreigners seem to be neither more liberal nor more restrictive than the laws in force in other countries of Western Europe. However, the worker himself is in a very insecure legal situation. One of the reasons for this insecurity is that many important decisions concerning him (work permit, expulsion, restrictions on political activities, etc.) are not subject to judicial review but fall within the competence of the administrative authorities responsible for controlling the movements of foreigners in the country.

The representation of immigrant workers' interests on official bodies

Up to the present, few opportunities have been offered to foreigners to participate in political life. When such opportunities do exist, they are due to *de facto* situations rather than to rights defined by law, except for joint decision-making procedures in firms (*Mitbestimmung im Betrieb*). More often than not, this form of participation consists simply in attending conferences about the employing firm's policy.

Representation at federal level and Länder level

Foreigners have no means of participating in political life at either of these levels. No serious efforts have ever been made to demand that foreigners be granted, possibly after a minimum residence period, the right to vote in elections to the Bundestag or to the *Länder* parliaments. There is, however, a slender possibility that nationals of EEC member countries will be accorded that right at some future date, although this may seem utopian at the present time.

Although 'co-ordination groups for foreign workers' exist, the workers concerned are not represented thereon. The same holds good for the very official Government Commission for Aliens which was set up in 1978 at federal level (see the beginning of this chapter).

Representation at municipal level

At municipal level, foreigners have more opportunities for exerting some influence when their political interests are at stake. As a rule, however, their influence is limited to giving advice and information to the municipal authorities who deal with the problems which directly affect foreign workers. Some time ago a campaign was launched to promote the establishment of an 'Aliens' Parliament' and an 'Aliens' Advisory Council' (Ausländerbeirat). The role of this type of 'parliament' is, for example, to consult the municipal council on all matters concerning foreigners. In the Ausländerbeirat, the specific problems of foreigners are discussed either by the municipal councillors or by representatives of immigrant workers' aid associations, in the presence of the foreigners' representatives.

Foreigners are only entitled to be consulted and to provide information; this does not mean that they have a right of participation, for such a right would presuppose the recognition of a right to vote in municipal elections. Up to now, only a few voices have been heard demanding that foreigners should be granted this right.

Representation at works and trade-union level

According to the Act on the formation of companies (*Betriebsver-fassungsgesetz*), foreign workers have active and passive voting rights in elections to the Works Council (*Betriebsrat*).[21] In the Federal Republic, any firm employing five or more persons must have a works council. Among other functions, the council has a say in the formulation of many of the internal rules governing the following matters: general regulations to be observed by employees, work schedules, temporary shortening or lengthening of the employing firm's working hours, holiday arrangements, health regulations, questions relating to the firm's wage structure, special measures concerning individual employees, etc.

Experience has shown that successful foreign candidates to works councils have been nominated, in almost all cases, by the Deutscher Gewerkschaftsbund (DGB) unions. The DGB is open to all foreign workers and its influence over them has steadily increased. Today, some 20 to 25 per cent of foreign workers are unionized, but this percentage gives no indication of the extent to which the interests of foreign workers are defended within the DGB and, with its aid, inside the employing firms. So far, the interests of immigrant workers have tended to be represented by German union officials and members of the works councils, who regard immigrant workers as 'experienced comrades' and consider themselves to be the 'best representatives of the interests' of their foreign workmates. No real '*Gastarbeiter* union' exists in the country.

Representation at political party level

All the major German political parties are open to foreigners. The legal status of a foreigner within a party[22] is determined by the Political Parties Act (Parteiengesetz). Paragraph 10 of this Act states that foreigners enjoy the same rights as Germans. However, that general principle does not apply to the parties' right to put forward candidates for elections to the Bundestag, the *Länder* parliaments and municipal councils. In the eyes of the law-makers, only those persons who have the right to vote in political elections should be permitted to exercise the right to nominate candidates. Thus, foreign members of a political party cannot serve as delegates or take part in the choice and presentation of candidates for election.

Inasmuch as Paragraph 2 of the Political Parties Act stipulates that a political association shall not be considered to be a political party if the majority of its members or of the members of its Executive Committee are foreigners, it follows, *a contrario*, that foreigners can be members of a party's Executive Committee at federal level or *Länder* level. That clause makes it possible for foreigners to sit on executive committees but prevents them from being in the majority.

The Act imposes no other restrictions on the political activity of the foreign members of a party, but in practice foreigners do not play a very significant role.

Foreign workers' aid organizations[23]

Among foreign workers' aid organizations there prevails a kind of division of labour according to the nationalities of immigrants. For example, workers' welfare associations (*Arbeiterwohlfahrt*) deal with the needs of Turks and Yugoslavs, Moroccans and Tunisians. The Protestant Church takes care of Greeks since the Greek Orthodox Church is a member of the World Council of Churches, a non-governmental organization (NGO) that brings together most Protestant churches. Caritas, an organization dependent on the Roman Catholic Church, looks after Italians, Spaniards, Portuguese and Croatian Catholics.

These organizations have taken over a task which no one else (neither the German employers nor the administrative authorities) was willing to shoulder—the task of attending to the needs of individuals. Unlike the German employers, they do not consider foreign workers simply as a reserve of mobile labour. Without wishing to denigrate their activities—and least of all their efforts to expose the conditions under which immigrant workers live and work—it can be said, however, that these organizations attempt what might be called 'ad hoc social engineering', that is to say, assisting individual foreigners who come up against difficulties and problems.

Such assistance takes many forms. Interpreters or mediators provided by the aid organizations intercede with employers or tackle housing problems; they contact the competent administrative authorities on behalf of immigrant workers who have problems concerning applications, certificates or other documents; they give legal advice regarding the rights of foreigners and questions of social security; they supply special information on various aspects of labour law (young people, health, family status, etc.).

Family immigration and the housing question

When the head of a family emigrates to the Federal Republic the family unit is disrupted. The separation of families has undesirable consequences such as the loneliness of the spouse, the aggravation of problems concerning the worker's social integration in the country, and a general loosening of family ties. The feelings of frustration and alienation experienced by migrant workers can be mitigated if they are joined by their families. The attitude of the German authorities towards the immigration of families has cumulative effects on the acceleration or slowing down of the integration process. The presence or absence of a migrant's spouse and/or children has repercussions on different aspects of his life such as the search for accommodation, the type of housing, the organization of free time, and social contacts.

Although immigration has been stopped, the upward trend in the immigration of families, which began in 1971, is still rising. This is no doubt due to the fact that migrants are afraid of a possible hardening of the regulations and are therefore hurrying to bring their families to the Federal Republic. Furthermore, the immigration of families has undoubtedly been encouraged by the new rules concerning children's allowances which were formulated in 1975.

These new migratory flows have placed an additional strain on the property market in the country. Because of the housing shortage, an employer having recruited a foreign worker is under an obligation to find him decent accommodation. Minimum housing standards for immigrants were laid down for the first time in the bilateral agreement concluded with Italy in 1964; in 1971, the Federal Ministry of Labour published the rules to be observed in order to meet the minimum housing requirements (see above).

In the accommodation provided by employers, several workers —usually a group of workmates—live in one room. There are separate quarters for men and women, and this means that married people cannot live together. The foreigners complain that the regulations of these hostels are designed to control and restrict their activities. These housing arrangements clearly prevent immigrant workers from getting to know how the German population lives, while making it impossible for them to follow their own way of life. Their integration is thereby retarded.

Under these conditions, it is not surprising that foreign workers are anxious to leave this type of accommodation, especially as they now tend to stay longer in the country. Workers who change jobs (and employers) must, in any case, move elsewhere. After a year's residence, foreign workers try to obtain a room of their own; after three years, they usually look for an apartment. This search is frequently motivated by the hope that they will eventually be joined by their families. The majority of foreign workers encounter the greatest difficulties in their efforts to find an apartment, for two reasons: first, the German population is prejudiced against foreigners and secondly, there is a shortage of cheap housing in the Federal Republic.

In most big German cities today there are districts with large foreign communities. Generally speaking, these districts are located partly or entirely in industrial zones where living conditions are undesirable or even quite unacceptable and housing facilities are in urgent need of renovation or reconstruction. Such districts exist, for example, in the Wedding and Kreuzberg districts of West Berlin, where foreigners account for over 30 per cent of the population. The authorities therefore decided to ban a further influx of foreigners into these districts and argued in support of their decision that it was not advisable to allow a ghetto to develop.

However, the current process of ghetto development has one of its roots in the situation prevailing in the private apartment sector of the property market. On the one hand, there are old and dilapidated apartment houses which Germans have vacated (or would like to vacate) and, on the other, there are one-room apartments to be let at rents which Germans cannot afford but which foreigners are obliged to accept because they suffer much more acutely than the Germans from the housing shortage.

Something can be said for the development of foreign districts in German towns, but there are obvious disadvantages. Very often, the foreign districts of large cities are slum areas. Even though the social situation is different from that prevailing in Anglo-American ghettos, the integration of immigrants is hampered by the differences between the housing conditions of foreigners and those of Germans and by the immigrants' isolation from the German population. Similarly, it is difficult for a foreigner leading a secluded life in a community composed exclusively of his fellow countrymen to get to know the language and customs of the host society. Lastly, town planning is also handicapped by the development of slum areas inhabited by foreigners. Landlords take advantage of the migrant workers' housing difficulties to charge very high rents for apartments in such areas and therefore have no incentive to repair or modernize them.

Conclusion

In the Federal Republic of Germany, policies concerning foreign workers are dictated mainly by four pressure groups:[24]

The trade unions. Although not fundamentally opposed to immigration, they are anxious to ensure that the unions continue to defend the rights of all workers, both German and foreign. They are in favour of the current policy of reducing the active foreign population.

Foreign workers' aid organizations. While these organizations approach immigration problems in very different ways, they are unanimous in giving frequent expression to their indignation over the immigrants' wretched living conditions.

Politicians. They have to take into account public protests against the presence of new minorities in the country.

Employers. In the final analysis, they can rely on migratory flows to develop to their satisfaction. They do not need to make frequent public statements in defence of their interests in this field, since these interests consist simply in obtaining enough labour to run their businesses.

The government is producing more and more regulations in an attempt to bring these divergent forces under control. For example, firms are under an obligation to provide a minimum of social services: they must secure housing for foreign workers and finance basic types of cultural activity (language courses, information work, etc.). These regulations have been enforced more and more strictly every year.

Foreigners are employed in the hardest and worst paid occupations. Owing to their low level of qualifications, their lack of professional experience, their cultural handicaps and their poor command of the German language, they have always had difficulty in securing skilled jobs, but now, with unemployment rising in the Federal Republic, they have no hope of obtaining anything but unskilled work.

Until now, there have been no serious minority problems in the country, even though recent conflicts—involving Turkish workers in particular—have shown that the Federal Republic is not immune to difficulties of this kind. At first, immigrants—at least a good many of them—do not aspire to become assimilated but try rather to save up as much money as possible pending their return home. They do not think of themselves as immigrants but as persons temporarily employed abroad. However, it often happens that their temporary stay is prolonged several times until living abroad becomes a permanent way of life, particularly for their children.

The government, for its part, is trying to reconcile two opposing strategies: the first is based on the idea that a foreign worker is a temporary auxiliary to be used to relieve the pressures on the labour market, and the second reflects a policy of forcing *Gastarbeiter* to become integrated, because this offers the advantage of dispensing the government from the necessity of attending to their specific problems.

In the Federal Republic of Germany, therefore, there is a 'trade unionist' type of policy regarding foreigners, in the sense that protection is afforded to those who are working on German territory whereas it is denied to those who are not.

German immigration policy today rests on many unknown factors. Three-quarters of all foreign residents in the country have been living there for over five years and half of that group for over eight years. From a purely legal standpoint, their acquired rights cannot be disregarded. No matter whether they are barely integrated or fully assimilated, they have become accustomed to the German way of life and have settled down in this country with their families.

The question, therefore, is whether these people will not eventually tire of their 'safety-valve' role (*Konjunkturpuffer*). Until now, they have tried to make sure that they would be allowed to stay in the country by performing the role assigned to them, but they will inevitably seek to rise above their present status (following the example of their German workmates). They will want to obtain higher qualifications, if not for themselves, at least for their children. They value better training not because it will help to satisfy the German employers' need for skilled manpower but because it will improve their own status. They are also certain to insist on obtaining more extensive political rights. The demands of the foreign participants in the demonstrations organized in March 1979, in West Berlin, at the time of the elections to the House of Representatives, provide evidence of the growing political consciousness of immigrant workers, who wish to be treated as human beings, not as *Konjunkturpuffer*.

Notes

1. See, in particular, Gehmacher, Kubat and Mehrländer (1978, pp. 9–17).
2. See: Ausländergesetz 28/4/65 as amended on 25/7/78; Allgemeine Verwaltungsvorschrift zur Ausfuhrung des Ausländergesetzes 7/7/67 as amended on 7/7/78; Verordnung zur Durch-fuhrung des Ausländergesetzes 10/9/65 as amended on 29/6/76, published in R. Heine and R. Marx, *Ausländergesetz mit neum Asylverfahrensrecht—Rechtsprechung zum Asylrecht mit Erläuterungen*, Baden-Baden, 1978; see also 'Act Concerning Entry and Stay of EEC Nationals 25/7/69 as amended on 17/4/74', in C. Kippes and K. Matzeder (eds.), *Neuregelung gesetzlicher Bestimmungen über Ausländerbeschäftigung*, Kessing, 1976; cf. Mehrländer (1978, pp. 116–18) and Rademacher (1975, pp. 17 et seq.). See also the following anonymous works: 'Allgemeine Verwaltungsvorschrift zur Ausfuhrung des Ausländergesetzes (AuslVwV)', Paper III/1, in *Themen. Impulse, Projekte* (Bayerisches Staatsministerium für Arbeit und Sozialordnung), No. 4, 1978; 'Änderung der Arbeitserlaubnisverordnung (AEVO)', Paper III/2, in No. 4, 1978 and 'Vollzug des Ausländerrechts—Aufenthaltserlaubnis und Aufenthaltsberechtigung', Paper III/1, in No. 1, 1979. Lastly, see E. Rasch, 'Polizei- und Ausländerrecht', *Polizei aktuell* (Stuttgart), Vol. 6, 1978.
3. This so-called 'second-line' procedure (the 'first-line' procedure being that of recruitment) authorizes entry for the purpose of taking up employment. It applies to nationals from recruitment countries (Greece, Yugoslavia, Morocco, Portugal, Spain, Turkey, Tunisia) who wish to exercise an activity specified on a special list. These people, for example, intend to follow a course of continuing or vocational training, are employed as managers or specialists by foreign firms in the federal republic, are foreign workers returning to the country after discharging their military service obligations or are frontier workers. Since immigration was cut back, doctors and nursing personnel have lost their privileged position.
4. See, among others: L. Kippes and K. Matzeder (eds.), *Neuregelung gesetzlicher Bestimmungen über Ausländerbeschäftigung*, pp. 89 et seq., Kessing, 1976; and M. Rademacher and H. Seidel, *Ausländer in Deutschland—Deutsche im Ausland*, pp. 19 et seq., Duren, 1975.
5. EEC nationals are not obliged to hold a work permit (but they must have a residence permit).
6. See note 1.
7. AFG, para. 19.
8. It should be noted that yet another type of permit exists—the *Legitimationskarte*. It is issued by the representative of the Federal Labour Department in the country of origin, within the framework of the recruitment and mediation procedure. This card has replaced the entry visa. On the whole, the same rules are applicable as those pertaining to the general work permit. Now that recruitment has been stopped, the *Legitimationskarte* has ceased, in fact, to serve a useful purpose.
9. See, in particular, Mehrländer (1978, pp. 119 et seq.) and Rademacher and Seidel (1979, pp. 49 et seq.).
10. See Mehrländer (1978, pp. 121 et seq.).

11. For more details and a critical appraisal, see Langkau and Mehrländer (1976, pp. 36–40).
12. See Rademacher and Seidel, 1975, pp. 47 et seq.
13. See *Süddeutsche Zeitung*, 22 March 1979, p. 2 and *Nürnberger Nachrichten*, 22 March 1979, p. 2.
14. Heinz Kühn, *Stand und Weiterentwicklung der Integration des ausländischen Arbeitnehmer und ihrer Familien in der Bundesrepublik Deutschland—Memorandum des Beauftragen der Bundesregierung*, Bonn, September 1979.
15. *Weiterentwicklung des Ausländerpolitik—Beschlüsse der Bundesregierung*, 19 March 1980.
16. *Nürnberger Nachrichten*, 28 February 1979, p. 3.
17. See Gaugler and Weber (1978, pp. 72 et seq.).
18. For a discussion of the effects on the wage structure of the employment of foreigners, see, among others, Salowsky (1972) and Körner (1976).
19. See Schiller (1976).
20. See Peters (1972, pp. 318–28).
21. See Lamers (1977, pp. 90–3).
22. Ibid., pp. 93–5.
23. This section owes a great deal to Mehrländer (1978, pp. 127–32).
24. Some of the ideas expressed here will be found in Gehmacher, Kubat and Mehrländer (1978, pp. 9–17).

Bibliography

ANON. Eine halbe Million ausländischer Schüler an deutschen Schulen. Ergebnisse einer Statistik für das Schuljahr 1977/78, ibv: 13 December 1978.
——. *Einige Aspekte zur Beschäftigung ausländischer Arbeitnehmer in der BRD*. Private edition, n.d.
——. *Weiterentwicklung der Ausländerpolitik—Beschlüsse der Bundesregierung, vom 19 März 1980*.
BAHADIR, S. A. Vor- und Nachteile der Wanderung von Arbeitskräften für die türkische Volkswirtschaft. *MittAB* (Nuremberg), No. 4, 1978, pp. 473 et seq.
BUNDESMINISTER FÜR ARBEIT UND SOZIALORDNUNG. *Vorschläge der Bund-Länder-Kommission zur Fortentwicklung einer umfassenden Konzeption der Ausländerbeschäftigungspolitik*. Bonn, 28 February 1977.
DEUTSCHES INSTITUT FÜR WIRTSCHAFTSFORSCHUNG. Nur vorübergehende Entlastung des Arbeitsmarktes durch Rückwanderung ausländischer Arbeitnehmer. *DIW-Wochenbericht* (weekly report), 30 March 1978.
GAUGLER, E.; WEBER, W. et al. *Ausländer in deutschen Industriebetrieben. Ergebnisse einer empirischen Untersuchung*. Königstein/Taunus, 1978.
GEHMACHER, E.; KUBAT, D.; MEHRLÄNDER, U. (eds.). *Ausländerpolitik im Konflikt. Arbeitskräfte oder Einwanderer? Konzepte der Aufnahme- und Entsendeländer*. Bonn, 1978.
IAB. Gegenwärtige Situation der Ausländerbeschäftigung in Europa. *IAB-Kurzbericht*. 9 March 1979.
——. Zur Ausbildungssituation ausländischer Jugendlicher. *IAB-Kurzbericht*, 29 May 1978.
——. Zur Entwicklung des Potentials an ausländischen Erwerbspersonen bis 1981. *IAB-Kurzbericht*, 30 May 1978.
KLEE, E. Beschwichtigen und Betreuen. Zielsetzung und Terminologie der caritativen Verbände. In: E. Klee (ed.), *Gastarbeiter. Analysen und Berichte*. Frankfurt am Main, 1972.
KÖRNER, H. De Integration der ausländischen Jugendlichen. *Wirschaftsdienst*, No. XI, 1978.
——. *Der Zustrom von Arbeitskräften in die BRD 1950-1972. Auswirkungen auf die Funktionsweise der Arbeitsmarktes*. Bern, 1976.

KÜHL, J.; PAUL, A. G.; BLUNK, D. *Überlegungen II zu einer vorausschauenden Arbeitsmarktpolitik.* Nuremberg, Bundesanstalt für Arbeit, 1978 (an English version will be available shortly).

KÜHN, Heinz. *Stand und Weiterenwicklung der Integration der ausländischen Arbeitnehmer und ihrer Familien in der Bundesrepublik Deutschland—Memorandum des Beauftragten der Bundesregierung.* Private edition, Bonn, September 1979.

LAMERS, K. A. *Repräsentation und Integration der Ausländer in der Bundesrepublik Deutschland unter besonderer Berucksichtigung des Wahlrechts.* Berlin, 1977.

LANGKAU, J.; MEHRLÄNDER, U. *Raumordnungspolitische Steuerung der Ausländerbeschäftigung, alternative Steuerrungskonzepte und räumliche Analyse der Ausländerbeschäftigung,* Bonn, 1976, pp. 36–40. ('Raumordnung' series of the Federal Minister of Regional Planning, Architecture and Town Planning.)

MEHRLÄNDER, U. 'Bundesrepublik Deutschland'. In: E. Gehmacher, D. Kubat and U. Mehrländer (eds.), *Ausländerpolitik im Konflikt. Arbeitskräfte oder Einwanderer? Konzepte der Aufnahme- und Enstsendeländer.* Bonn, 1978.

PETERS, A. Die Bundesrepublik als Beschäftigungsland für ausländische Arbeitnehmer: Ökonomische Attraktivität, rechtliche Situation und politische Mitwirkung. *MittAB* (Nuremberg), No. 4, 1972.

PICK, H. Die Muttersprache darf kein Handicap sein. Gastarbeiterkinder—eine Herausforderung für die Schule oder eine Chance für gemeinsame europäische Erziehung? *Das Parlament,* No. 3, 20 January 1979.

RADEMACHER, M.; SEIDEL, H. *Ausländer in Deutschland—Deutsche im Ausland.* Düren, 1975.

RUNGGALDIER, G. Blickpunkt: Ausländische Schüler. Keine Chance für Ausländer? *Die Demokratische Schule,* No. 1, 1979.

SALOWSKY, H. Gesamtwirtschaftliche Aspekte der Ausländerbeschäftigung. In: H. Salowsky and G. Schiller (eds.), *Ursachen und Auswirkungen der Ausländerbeschäftigung.* Cologne, 1972.

SCHILLER, G. Arbeitskräftewanderung als Herausforderung an Wirtschaftstheorie und Wirtschaftspolitik. In: G. Schiller et al. (eds.), *Ausländische Arbeitnehmer und Arbeitsmarkt.* Nuremberg, BeitrAB 2, 1976.

Zur Entwicklung des Arbeitsmarkts in der Bundesrepublik Deutschland 1980. *MittAB,* Nuremberg, No. 4, 1979.

The status of immigrant workers in Sweden

Jonas Widgren

Immigration policy and regulations in Sweden

Trends in migratory flows

Between 1840 and 1960, approximately 1.2 million Swedes emigrated, mostly to the United States. A reversal of migratory movements occurred in the late 1920s with the arrival in Sweden of an increasing number of immigrants. Since that time, Sweden's migratory balance has been positive, except in the years 1972 and 1973 (see Figure 1). It must be made clear, however, that the positive balance recorded in the 1930s (39,000 people) resulted from the return of Swedish emigrants who had previously left to settle in the United States.

The Second World War and its aftermath entailed an appreciable rise in immigration. More than 200,000 refugees arrived in Sweden from Finland, Denmark, Norway, Estonia, Germany, Lithuania, Poland and other countries; the total number of foreign residents in Sweden rose from 24,000 in 1939 to 185,000 in 1944. Some of these refugees returned to their home countries after the war and others re-migrated to the United States, Canada or other countries overseas, but a substantial proportion of them settled permanently in Sweden.

During the war years, the Swedish economy expanded enormously and the labour market was unable to meet its demands, despite the positive migratory balance, the influx of refugees, the market increase in the employment of women, the decline in the proportion of the active

Jonas Widgren is Head of Department, Swedish Ministry of Labour.

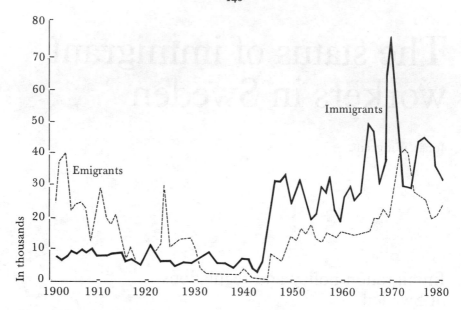

FIG. 1. Migration from and to Sweden since 1900 (including Swedish nationals).

population employed in agriculture (the rate of decrease being approximately 2 per cent per year) and the ensuing high rate of urbanization. From 1946 onwards, the shortage of labour obliged employers in the industrial sector to recruit workers from other European countries. They were recruited in the Nordic countries (initially in Finland and Denmark) as well as in other countries of continental Europe (initially in Italy, Hungary and Austria). As a result of the influx of refugees during the first five years of the decade, followed by the immigration of workers during the latter half of the decade, the migratory balance for the 1940s was three times higher than the balance recorded in the 1930s and represented a total of 134,000 people.

The migration pattern established during the 1940s was also typical of Sweden in the 1950s. The immigration of refugees continued within the framework of a transfer programme carried out under governmental supervision, which enabled 11,000 refugees to enter Sweden (including 8,000 Hungarians and 1,000 Yugoslavs). As immigration restrictions between the other Nordic countries (Denmark, Finland, Iceland, Norway and Sweden) were gradually removed, culminating in 1954 in the agreement on the common Nordic labour market, the immigration of workers from these countries progressively increased. Moreover, during the 1950s, the Swedish labour market authorities continued to recruit labour outside the Nordic countries. At the beginning of that decade, workers were initially recruited in Italy, the Federal Republic of Germany and the Netherlands; during the latter half of the 1950s, workers were recruited mainly in Italy, but also in

Austria, Belgium and Greece. In the course of the whole decade, approximately 14,000 workers were recruited in European countries. The migratory balance was lower than it had been during the 1940s and represented a total of 106,000 people.

During the 1960s, there was a sharp rise in immigration from southern Europe and, later, from Finland. At the end of the decade, the migratory balance was twice as high as it had been during the 1950s with a total of 235,000 people. The first wave of immigrants, between 1964 and 1966, consisted mainly of workers from Yugoslavia, Turkey and Greece who came to Sweden on their own initiative. In 1967, this uncontrolled flow, combined with an economic recession, compelled the Swedish authorities to impose restrictions on immigration from non-Nordic countries. One of the effects of these restrictions, which was not foreseen by the Swedish authorities, was that many jobs became available to Finnish workers at the time of the 'boom' during the late 1960s, and this encouraged immigration from Finland, which reached unprecedented levels. The record number of emigrants resulted in a drop of approximately 1 per cent in the population of Finland for the first time in a hundred years. Between 1968 and 1970, Finnish nationals accounted for 100,000 of the 167,000 aliens who entered Sweden. The percentage of Finns in relation to the total number of immigrants had never been so high since the war.

As regards immigrants from southern Europe, their percentage in relation to the total number of immigrants recorded at the end of the 1960s was unaffected by the restrictions imposed in 1967. However, most of the people who immigrated at that time were close relatives (the spouses and children under age) of immigrants already in employment before the restrictions imposed in 1967, or else had been forced for political or economic reasons to leave Greece, which was governed at that time by a military junta, and had been permitted to take refuge in Sweden on humanitarian grounds. Between 1965 and 1970, government-supervised procedures for the recruitment and transfer of labour from southern Europe concerned only 4,500 workers, 4,000 of whom came from Yugoslavia.

In addition to the immigration of families and of workers from Finland and Mediterranean countries such as Yugoslavia, Greece and Turkey, large numbers of refugees immigrated during the 1960s. Nearly 19,000 people (mostly from East European countries) were transferred from European refugee camps to Sweden between 1960 and 1969, and some 2,000 Czechoslovaks and 4,000 Poles fled to Sweden in the late 1960s and early 1970s following the events of 1968 in Czechoslovakia and as a result of rising anti-Semitism in Poland. About 1,000 American conscientious objectors and deserters who had refused to serve in the Viet Nam War were also granted asylum in Sweden for humanitarian reasons.

TABLE I. Nordic and non-Nordic migratory flows in Sweden, 1967–79

Year	Immigration					Emigration			Balance		
	Nordic	Percentage of total	Non-Nordic	Percentage of total	Total	Nordic	Non-Nordic	Total	Nordic	Non-Nordic	Total
1967	14 100	52.0	13 000	48.0	27 100	9 500	5 100	14 500	4 600	7 900	12 500
1968	21 800	66.3	11 000	33.7	32 900	10 200	7 000	17 200	11 600	4 000	15 600
1969	44 300	72.7	16 500	27.3	60 800	9 300	5 100	14 400	35 000	11 300	46 300
1970	48 000	65.3	25 600	34.7	73 600	15 600	5 700	21 300	32 300	19 900	52 200
1971	20 700	53.5	18 000	46.5	38 700	23 800	7 600	31 400	—3 000	10 400	7 400
1972	13 600	53.1	12 000	46.9	25 600	22 200	10 100	32 300	—8 600	1 900	—6 700
1973	12 700	51.0	12 200	49.0	24 900	20 000	10 200	30 200	—7 400	2 000	—5 400
1974	18 000	56.4	13 900	43.6	31 900	13 900	6 300	20 200	4 200	7 600	11 800
1975	25 400	66.8	12 600	33.2	38 000	13 300	7 100	20 400	12 100	5 500	17 600
1976	22 200	55.8	17 600	44.2	39 800	12 200	6 500	18 700	10 000	11 100	21 100
1977	19 600	50.6	19 100	49.4	38 700	10 600	4 300	14 900	9 000	14 800	23 800
1978	15 300	48.3	16 400	51.7	31 700	10 100	5 500	15 600	5 300	10 800	16 100
1979	16 400	50.6	16 000	49.4	32 400	10 700	5 600	16 300	5 700	10 400	16 100

During the 1970s, the immigration pattern was affected by two important trends which had not been in evidence during the two previous decades. The first of these trends emerged during the years 1972 and 1973 when, for the first time since 1929, Sweden showed a negative annual migratory balance of 6,000 for each of those years (see Table 1). This figure was the result of a sudden recession in the Swedish economy, which compelled a large number of Finnish immigrants, who had arrived in the late 1960s, to leave the country. For this reason, 36 per cent of all Finnish immigrants who had arrived in 1970 left Sweden in 1972. The sudden reversal of migratory trends showed for the first time on a large scale that migration between Finland and Sweden was very sensitive to changes in Sweden's economic cycles.

The second important trend observed in the 1970s was the rise in immigration which occurred between 1975 and 1977, despite a serious deterioration of the employment situation in Sweden. It was the first time since the war that immigration increased during a period of recession. The development of this upward trend despite the extremely restrictive regulations facing foreigners anxious to find work in Sweden is explained by the far-reaching changes which had taken place in the immigration pattern: there was an appreciable increase in the number of refugees and migrants authorized to take up residence in Sweden, despite restrictions concerning their employment, particularly in the case of nationals of non-European countries. In fact, the proportion of Nordic immigrants in relation to the total number of immigrants fell in 1978 to its lowest level for the past ten years.

Table 1 shows that, in recent years, about half of the migratory flows were composed of non-Nordic immigrants. The new immigration pattern for 1977 was analysed by the Swedish Commission on Immigration Research. Its analysis revealed that only 9 per cent of non-Nordic immigrants could be described as migrant labour (see Table 2).

Table 3 shows the current composition by nationality of migratory flows to and from Sweden; it reveals the growing proportion of non-European immigrants. In 1977, Finnish migrants represented 38.2 per cent of the total number of people entering Sweden and 35.3 per cent of the total number of people leaving Sweden. Turkish nationals, most of whom belong to a Christian ethnic minority from eastern Turkey, accounted for 7.1 per cent of the total number of immigrants. Immigration from other Mediterranean countries (Greece, Italy, Portugal, Spain and Yugoslavia) has remained at the same level for the last five years and represents about 3,000 people, most of whom are relatives of immigrants already settled in Sweden. Immigration from Chile and other Latin American countries has been particularly high. Since the coup d'état in Chile in 1973, Sweden has given priority to Latin American refugees, within the framework of the transfer programme which the government has put in hand.

TABLE 2. Pattern of immigration in 1977

Category		Percentage of total immigration	Percentage of non-Nordic immigration
Citizens of Nordic countries	19 640	51	
Citizens of non-Nordic countries:	19 070	49	
Family members	9 230	24	48
Refugees chosen and brought to Sweden on the initiative of Swedes	930	2	5
Other refugees	3 360	9	18
Adopted children	1 920	5	10
Migrant labour	1 650	4	9
Students on a temporary visa	790	2	4
'Humanitarian reasons'	240	1	1
Re-migrating Swedes who have acquired a foreign nationality	190	1	1
Miscellaneous (details not available)	760	2	4
TOTAL	38 710	100	100

TABLE 3. Migratory flows in Sweden in 1977

Country of origin	Immigration	Emigration	Balance
Nordic countries	19 638	10 617	9 021
Finland	14 825	5 253	9 572
Mediterranean countries	5 614	1 817	3 797
Greece	926	672	254
Italy	217	177	40
Portugal	119	59	60
Spain	316	119	197
Turkey	2 753	157	2 596
Yugoslavia	1 283	633	650
Other countries	11 104	1 319	9 785
Chile	1 732	59	1 673
Poland	1 517	27	1 487
Iran	515	30	485
TOTAL: all countries	38 710	14 860	23 850

Objectives of Swedish immigration policy

In view of the figures shown in the above tables, and mindful of the fact that post-war immigrants and their descendants account for approximately one million persons out of a total population of 8.2 million, it would seem logical to suppose that the Swedish authorities have encouraged immigration since the war as part of a long-term development strategy. Strange as it may seem, however, no decision based on economic or demographic development objectives has ever been taken by the Swedish Parliament or Government concerning desirable or acceptable quotas of immigrants from certain countries to be allowed to enter Sweden. In fact, no attempt has been made, since the end of the Second World War, to examine the question of fixing annual immigration quotas in a broad economic context. This is mainly due to the fact that Sweden, unlike other immigration countries, has never adopted a comprehensive population policy.

During the 1950s, immigration was considered to be a transient phenomenon. It was only after 1960 that external migratory movements were taken into consideration as a demographic factor of the future in the population forecasts established regularly by the Swedish Central Bureau of Statistics. The latter half of the 1960s saw a growing political awareness of the need to consider immigration in a wider context, mainly with a view to reducing it so as to enable underemployed national groups to have access to the labour market. In recent years, this tendency to restrict the immigration of foreign workers has become more pronounced, while at the same time the immigration of refugees and foreign nationals permitted to enter Sweden for humanitarian reasons has been increasing.

Contrary to generally accepted views, Swedish immigration policy is not the outcome of a detailed survey of conflicting interests and of all the questions which may eventually arise in that connection. However, there does exist a set of correlated objectives which depend on the policies adopted by the Swedish political authorities and which influence the volume of migratory flows. The guidelines of current immigration policy, as defined in the Immigration Policy Act of 1975, in the Act of 1976 on amendments to legislation concerning aliens and in a series of other documents and official statements, may be summarized as follows:

Freedom of movement within the common Nordic labour market, but immigration of Finnish nationals to be regulated through the channels of the official employment services of Finland and Sweden.

No immigration of workers from non-Nordic countries.

Unrestricted immigration of the close relatives of immigrants already settled in Sweden.

Unrestricted immigration of political refugees and a liberal policy as
regards the admission of de facto refugees.
Strict control of the immigration of temporary residents such as foreign
students.

Immigration legislation and procedures

Legislation concerning foreigners in Sweden was first introduced in 1914,
at the outbreak of the First World War. As it was of a temporary nature,
it was replaced in 1927 by a more systematically constructed set of
regulations defining the entry and residence rights of aliens seeking
admission to Sweden. This legislation of 1927 was recast in 1937, 1945
and 1954.

The Aliens Ordinance which is currently in force in Sweden
is based on the Aliens Act of 1954 as amended in 1964, 1966, 1968
and 1976. In 1975, the government appointed a commission on legislation concerning aliens to be responsible for revising the existing
provisions.

At the present time, a foreigner may not reside in Sweden for more
than three months unless he holds a residence permit; nor may he work
in Sweden without a work permit. All nationals of Nordic countries
(Denmark, Iceland, Finland and Norway) are exempt from the obligation to hold a residence permit and a work permit. The 1954 agreement on the establishment of a common Nordic labour market authorizes
all Nordic nationals to take up employment in any of the Nordic
countries without formalities. However, a non-Nordic national holding
a work permit valid in one of the Nordic countries does not have a
right to work in the other Nordic countries without first obtaining
special authorization to do so, which is granted on an individual basis
in accordance with the legislation concerning aliens currently in force
in the Nordic country concerned. The Nordic countries have also
signed an agreement on reciprocal frontier controls. This means, for
example, that the Danish authorities, acting on behalf of their Swedish
counterparts, inspect the passports of non-Nordic travellers entering
Sweden through Denmark.

The increase in migration movements between Finland and Sweden
in the late 1960s compelled Finland to urge Sweden to play a more
active part in the regulation of immigration, so as to stop the drain
of Finland's skilled labour force.

In 1973, negotiations between Finland and Sweden resulted in an
agreement aimed at channelling the migratory flow between the two
countries through the official employment services, in order to ensure
that Finnish workers intending to emigrate to Sweden knew what
jobs were available in Finland before leaving their country. Under the

terms of the agreement, Swedish employers may not employ Finnish nationals who have not previously contacted the official employment services of one of the two countries. This agreement has led in recent years to an increase in the number of workers who pass through the official employment services, but the number of Finnish job-seekers who find employment through those services has fallen to an unduly low level (29 per cent in 1977).

The basic rule concerning the immigration of non-Nordic foreigners into Sweden is that those who intend to take up employment must have obtained their work permit before entering Sweden. Work permits and residence permits can be applied for at all Swedish consulates and embassies abroad (by filling in a form). The application must be accompanied by a specific offer of employment provided by a Swedish employer (in most cases, the offer of employment is procured by relatives or friends in Sweden). The application for a work permit and residence permit is forwarded to the National Immigration and Naturalization Office in Stockholm (Statensinvandrarverk) which examines it and consults the National Labour Market Board (Arbetsmarknadsstyrelsen) about the work permit. The Labour Market Board will then consult the appropriate regional services, which contact, on the one hand, the employer concerned, so as to check the particulars regarding the nature of the employment offered, the remuneration proposed, etc., and, on the other hand, the local trade union. If the Labour Market Board gives clearance for the issue of a work permit, the National Immigration and Naturalization Office makes out both the work permit and the residence permit (provided that all the necessary conditions are fulfilled) and the applicant will be authorized to enter Sweden.

The same procedure was followed when foreign workers were recruited collectively. However, this recruitment method was never applied on a large scale, since most of the workers who immigrated to Sweden did so individually on their own initiative. Moreover, no workers at all have been recruited by the collective method since 1973 and it is highly improbable that this system will be reintroduced in the future, in view of the change in the orientation of Swedish immigration policy, the present pattern of migratory flows and the new policies of the emigration countries.

The first work permit is usually issued for a period of one year and is valid for only one specified type of activity. The first residence permit is also issued for a period of one year.

After one year, the worker is given a work permit valid for all types of activity in Sweden. However, most foreigners obtain a permanent residence permit after one year's residence in Sweden. This permit confers on the holder an unrestricted right to live and work in Sweden.

As already indicated, since 1974 there has been practically no immigration into Sweden of non-Nordic workers, whether recruited collectively or admitted on an individual basis. By the end of the 1960s, the recruitment offices in Ankara, Athens and Rome had all closed; the last collective recruitment operation was conducted in Yugoslavia in 1973 and involved no more than a hundred or so workers. The Belgrade office was closed in 1977.

Thus, in the main, non-Nordic immigration into Sweden does not conform to the general rules laid down in 1967 concerning the organized immigration of workers. The immigration of families is a case in point. Family members can obtain a residence permit and a work permit after they have arrived in Sweden. Theoretically, no entry restrictions are imposed when immigrants wish to be reunited with their families. The following are considered to be family members: the spouse, children living with the parents when the latter took up residence in Sweden (provided that the children are not married) and any other close relatives (provided that they had previously lived with the immigrants currently established in Sweden).

Exceptions have also been made for another important category, namely that of refugees and other aliens who are granted entry for humanitarian reasons. Sweden ratified the Geneva Convention of 1951 and the Protocol of 1976. The definition of a political refugee contained in the Geneva Convention was accordingly incorporated into Swedish legislation on aliens, so that any person corresponding to the criteria established in the definition would enjoy an inviolable right to live in Sweden and would be able to obtain the work and residence permits. Since the mid-1960s, Sweden has begun to grant entry, on a large scale, for humanitarian reasons, to people who are refugees in fact although they do not meet the Geneva criteria. Provision was made for this practice in the Aliens Act of 1976 which introduced the notion of de facto refugees; Sweden is one of the very few countries to have given legal recognition to this concept.

Refugees are admitted into Sweden in groups transferred collectively by the Swedish authorities from refugee camps situated in different parts of the world (with the help of UNHCR and ICEM), or on the basis of documentation concerning urgent individual cases submitted to the Swedish authorities by UNHCR or when they approach the Swedish authorities, on their own initiative, with a request for refugee status. In recent years, the collective transfer system has concerned about 1,300 refugees per year from various Latin American countries, and to this figure must be added a large number of family members. However, the majority of refugees come to Sweden on their own initiative. Since 1950, 55,000 refugees have settled in Sweden and of this total 25,000 came in groups transferred collectively and 30,000 arrived on their own initiative.

A residence permit can only be withdrawn for quite exceptional reasons (when the permit has been fraudulently obtained, when the holder commits a criminal act, etc.). A work permit is not withdrawn in the event of the holder becoming unemployed.

A foreigner who holds a residence permit has, broadly speaking, the same rights and obligations as a Swedish national. This is true, for example, as regards social services and social security, taxation, education, housing and security of employment. The main points on which the status of foreigners differs from that of Swedish nationals are the right to vote in parliamentary elections (this will be discussed more fully below), compulsory military service and, in the case of nationals from countries with which Sweden has not signed an agreement, the entitlement to certain retirement benefits.

The naturalization rate in Sweden is one of the highest in Europe. Naturalization has the effect of removing the remaining restrictions on a foreigner's rights (this will also be discussed more fully below).

Effects of immigration on demographic, administrative and economic structures

Demographic effects of immigration on the structure of the Swedish population

It is only in the course of the last few years that the authorities have taken the demographic effect of immigration into consideration. The current debate is centred on two themes. The first is the role of immigration in the future growth of the population. Given that immigration accounted for 45 per cent of the increase recorded between 1940 and 1977—during which period the Swedish population rose from 6.4 to 8.2 million—and that the birth rate has never been as low as it is today (96,000 births in 1977, representing a birth rate of 11.6 per thousand), the question to be considered is whether immigration might not militate against the decrease in population which is forecast for the coming decades. Most experts doubt, however, whether a standstill in population growth is, in fact, a serious handicap for a nation, as has been asserted hitherto. Moreover, they point out that a policy of stimulating immigration would not be a good solution, demographically speaking, inasmuch as the major problem—that of the unbalanced age structure of the population—would remain unsolved. While it is true (see Figure 2) that the age structure of the foreign population is much more evenly balanced than that of the Swedish population, its positive effect is minimized from the long-term point of view by the fact that many foreigners who were born in their country of origin are over 60 years of age. Given the gross annual immigration figure of

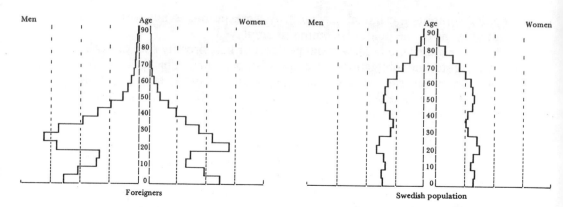

FIG. 2. The total Swedish population and the foreign population in Sweden in 1977, by sex and age.

about 30,000 aliens and the fact that their fertility rate is higher than that of the Swedes, the imbalance in the age structure of the Swedish population is likely to persist.

This emerges clearly from Figure 3, which shows what the age structure of the Swedish population is likely to look like in 2025, with and without the annual intake of 30,000 immigrants (a=without immigration; b=same fertility rate for foreigners and for Swedes; c=immigrants' fertility rate higher than 10 per cent; d=immigrants' fertility rate higher than 25 per cent).

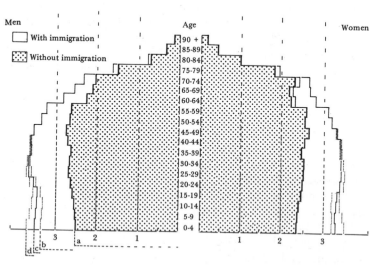

FIG. 3. Structure of the Swedish population in 2025 with and without immigration, by sex and age.

TABLE 4. Structure of the population of Sweden at the time of the 1975 census

	Born in Sweden	Born abroad	Total
Swedes	7 566 000	232 000	7 798 000
Foreigners	92 000	319 000	411 000
TOTAL	7 658 000	551 000	8 209 000

For these reasons, the experts are inclined to favour a more realistic policy of boosting the birth rate among the Swedish population. They also maintain, with good reason, that an increase in immigration would be detrimental to the emigration countries and that, furthermore, such an increase would be undesirable from the point of view of social equality.

The second theme of the current debate is the effect of immigration on the ethnic composition of the population. The census conducted in 1975 revealed the profound changes which had occurred in the structure of the population owing to post-war immigration movements. The results showed that about one million people—out of the 8.2 million of the Swedish population—were migrants or descendants of migrants.

Despite a marked upward trend in immigration, the total number of foreigners living in Sweden remained relatively stable during the 1970s (1970: 411,000 foreigners; 1971: 416,000; 1972: 407,000; 1973: 397,000; 1974: 401,000; 1975: 411,000; 1976: 418,000; 1977: 424,000). The high naturalization rate explains why the foreign population has remained stable despite a positive migratory balance. On the other hand, as shown in Table 5, the large number of children born to immigrants in Sweden offsets the high naturalization rate.

The foreign population in Sweden is made up of more than forty groups of different nationalities, each group numbering at least 500 persons. The last two years have seen a rise in the number of foreign nationals belonging to about ten countries hitherto not very well represented, so that these groups are now composed of more than 500 persons. This trend will probably continue, whereas the number of nationals from countries such as Finland, Yugoslavia and Greece will remain

TABLE 5. Trends in the foreign population in Sweden, 1976–77

	1976	1977
Immigration	+39 700	+38 700
Emigration	−18 700	−14 900
Foreigners born in Sweden	+9 200	+9 000
Foreigners who have died in Sweden	−1 200	−1 200
Naturalizations	−22 100	−24 900

relatively stable. The total number of foreigners will continue to rise steadily, as a result of immigration from a large number of non-European countries. It is self-evident that these changes in the pattern of migratory flows will eventually affect the ethnic and racial composition of the Swedish population which, only a few decades ago, was one of the most homogeneous populations in Europe from the ethnic point of view (together with the populations of Portugal, Iceland and Norway), except for the comparatively insignificant Lapp minority living in Norway and Sweden.

Effects of immigration on administrative structures and the development of social programmes

Administrative structures established to implement immigration-control legislation and promote the social adaptation of immigrants

In the early 1960s, the administrative structures set up by governmental and municipal authorities in order to implement the immigration legislation were extremely rudimentary. There was no state department responsible for promoting the adaptation of immigrants to Swedish society. The considerable volume of migratory flows in the latter half of the 1960s showed that it was necessary to establish an administrative structure which would be better equipped to regulate immigration movements and meet the social, educational or other requirements of the newcomers.

It was not until the 1970s that a complete network of administrative services was established in order to meet the needs created by the increase in immigration and promote special reception programmes designed to introduce migrants to Sweden's information, social and educational systems. The main features of this administrative network are presented in diagram form in Figure 4.

Information, social and educational aid programmes for immigrants

Until the mid-1960s, immigrants had very few opportunities to learn Swedish. However, the high level of immigration in the years 1964 and 1965 induced the government to release funds to be used by voluntary associations in order to organize language courses (some of these associations are affiliated to political parties and the largest have close ties with the workers' movement and the Social Democrat Party). This is the only area of social action on behalf of immigrants in which non-profit Swedish associations have participated to any great extent. Every year, approximately 100,000 immigrants attend these courses, which are given free of charge and are financed by the government. A total

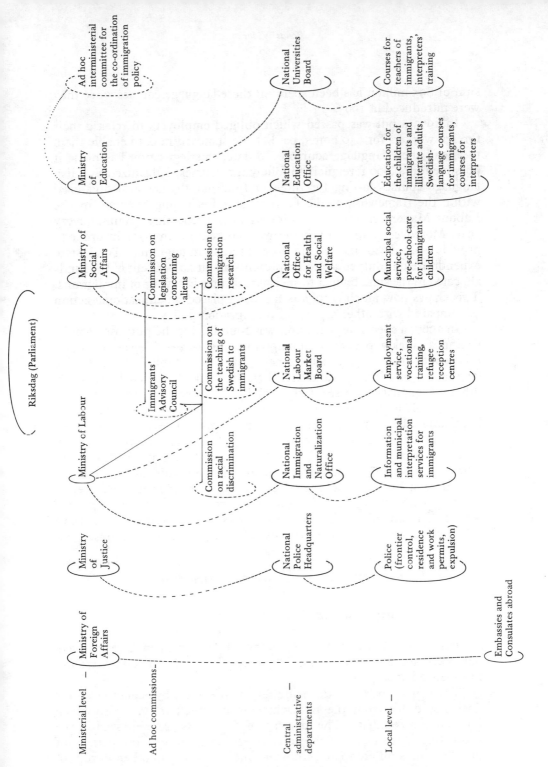

FIG. 4. Administrative structure for the formulation and implementation of a Swedish immigration policy.

sum of $95 million has been spent on these language courses since they were introduced in 1965.

In 1973 a bill was passed which obliged employers to release their foreign workers for 240 hours, paid at the standard rate, to enable them to attend these language courses. To date, this legislation has made it possible for 30,000 foreigners to follow the courses. Subsidized Swedish language courses lasting for three or four months are also organized within the framework of the Government Retraining Scheme for the Labour Market; at least 15,000 immigrants attend these courses every year. Moreover, a special scheme was worked out in 1977 in order to provide subsidized instruction for illiterate immigrants. Total state expenditure on adult education represents about 20 per cent of the funds allocated in the state budget to special measures in favour of immigrants. This shows how much emphasis has been placed on educational action as compared with other aspects of immigration policy.

In 1967, a special organization was founded for the purpose of publishing a weekly paper for immigrants, *Invandrartidningen*. In 1977, this paper had 40,000 subscribers and was published in twelve languages. In addition, large numbers of booklets issued in fourteen different languages are regularly sent by different government departments to all foreigners living in Sweden, thanks to the computerized Population Register. At local level, interpretation services have been operating since the mid-1960s. At the present time, there are eighty immigrants' aid offices distributed throughout the country and financed by the municipalities. Their main function is to provide information and interpreters. In 1968, training courses were established for interpreters working with immigrants. During the 1970s, 7,000 such interpreters were able to attend special university courses, interpretation courses in folk high schools and courses run by adult education associations.

Effects of immigration on socio-economic structures

Distribution of immigrants in the labour market

Statistics on the employment situation of foreigners in Sweden have only been available since 1977. The active foreign population currently numbers 225,000 persons.

The general pattern of distribution of foreigners by economic sector does not differ from the one which is observed in most European immigration countries. The majority of foreigners are employed in the processing industries and the services sector. However, the pattern of distribution is differentiated from the one prevailing in other European immigration countries by three distinctive features which deserve close examination. Firstly, a high proportion of immigrants are employed in

TABLE 6. Active foreign population by nationality, in 1978

Algeria	200	Portugal	1 000
Austria	2 400	Spain	1 900
Finland	103 000	Tunisia	400
Greece	9 200	Turkey	4 200
Italy	2 800	Yugoslavia	25 800
Morocco	600	Miscellaneous	73 800
		TOTAL	225 300

the public sector (hospitals, social services, etc.); this trend is likely to become much more pronounced during the coming decade. Secondly, no immigrant workers at all are to be found in agriculture in Sweden. Swedish agriculture has never been dependent on seasonal foreign labour (except in southern Sweden, for historical reasons). Lastly, there are very few immigrants in the building sector, which is distinguished by a high rate of unionization and also by high wages.

With the restriction of immigration and the growing tendency of immigrant workers to stay longer in Sweden, the general trend has been towards an alignment of the socio-occupational structure of the foreign population with that of the Swedish population. There are many more foreign workers in 'white collar' jobs today than there were ten years ago. Recent research has nevertheless shown that second-generation foreigners opt for manual work much more often than their Swedish counterparts. It is clear that this tendency may have the effect of perpetuating many of the social inequalities associated with immigration.

The employment situation of immigrant workers

The unemployment rate in Sweden stands at present at about 2 per cent of the active population. This figure is higher than it was up to the mid-1970s.

Generally speaking, unemployment among foreigners is more than twice as high as it is among Swedish nationals. At the beginning of 1978, the rate of unemployment among foreigners rose to almost 5 per cent. Finnish nationals and workers from the Mediterranean countries have been the hardest hit in the last few years.

Among young immigrants too, the unemployment rate is nearly twice as high as among young Swedish workers. Among immigrants between the ages of 20 and 24, there is an unemployment rate of 8.1 per cent, whereas the rate for Swedes in the same age-group is 4.3 per cent. In 1977, unemployment among young immigrants between 16 and 19 years of age rose to 14.4 per cent, whereas it was only 6.8 per cent for young Swedes in the same age-group.

TABLE 7. Foreigners in the active population of Sweden, by type of activity and nationality (first quarter of 1977)

Type of activity	Men		Women		Total including:		Finns	Other Nordic nationals	Other foreigners
	No.	%	No.	%	No.	%	%	%	%
Miscellaneous (e.g. hospitals)	18 700	13.7	17 200	17.5	35 900	15.2	11.5	20.7	17.3
Administration	1 600	1.2	0	0.0	1 600	0.7	0.3	0.4	1.3
Office work	2 100	1.5	10 300	10.5	12 400	5.3	5.4	5.7	4.9
Trade	4 500	3.2	2 800	2.8	7 300	3.1	1.5	5.0	4.0
Agriculture	2 800	2.1	400	0.4	3 200	1.4	1.9	1.9	0.6
Transport	7 200	5.3	1 500	1.5	8 700	3.7	3.0	4.7	4.1
Industry	88 600	64.6	34 600	35.2	123 200	52.3	58.8	43.4	48.5
Building	7 600	5.7	100	0.1	8 000	3.4	4.1	5.8	1.6
Services	11 200	8.2	30 600	31.2	41 900	17.3	16.8	17.6	18.9
Unidentified	400	0.3	800	0.9	1 300	0.5	0.7	0.6	0.3
TOTAL	137 300	100.0	98 200	100.0	235 500	100.0	100.0	100.0	100.0

TABLE 8. The employment situation of foreigners between the ages of 16
and 74 in Sweden (first quarter of 1978)

	Men	Women	Total
Active foreign population	129 300	95 900	225 300
In employment	123 800	90 500	214 300
Actually at work	109 100	74 700	183 800
Temporarily absent	14 700	15 800	30 500
Unemployed	5 500	5 500	11 000

This discrepancy between the unemployment rates of immigrants
and Swedes is seen to be even more critical and unjustifiable if it is
borne in mind that foreigners have twice as much experience of being
out of work as Swedes have (whether unemployment was experienced
before or after immigration).

Since immigrants are more exposed to the risk of unemployment,
they account for a large proportion of the workers affected by special
countermeasures taken within the framework of employment policies. For example, 30 per cent of the persons who are following the
vocational training courses organized by State Employment Centres are
foreigners.

The living conditions of immigrants compared with those of the Swedish population

In 1974, the Swedish Parliament decided to put in hand an extensive
inquiry into the changes which had taken place in the standard of living
in Sweden. The National Central Bureau of Statistics was therefore
instructed to conduct a continuous survey of the living conditions of
the population, to be based on a national sample of 12,000 persons,
including 925 immigrants (557 foreign nationals and 368 naturalized
immigrants). The findings of this survey provide material for an appraisal
of the differences between the living conditions of immigrants and those
of the Swedish population.

The most striking differences concern working and housing conditions as well as the general financial situation. The last-mentioned
point, however, does not refer to wages as such, but to the availability
of ready money and the cost of supporting persons who are not living
with the worker (34 per cent of immigrants from southern Europe have
financial responsibilities of this kind, as against 4 per cent of Swedish
workers). On the other hand, the differences are relatively insignificant
with regard to the other aspects of welfare, such as social contacts,
schooling, health and take-home pay.

TABLE 9. Working conditions of wage-earners by national origin and sex (percentages)

National origin	Persistently high noise level	Very dirty	Physical discomfort due to gas, dust, smoke, fumes	Work involving acids or corrosive substances	Work involving explosives or inflammables	Risk of industrial accidents
Men						
Swedish nationals	16.7	24.5	13.4	15.9	23.0	22.3
Born in Sweden	16.6	24.6	13.3	15.6	22.9	22.4
Swedish nationals of Swedish parentage	16.6	24.4	13.3	15.6	22.6	22.4
Second-generation immigrants	18.7	32.2	16.3	15.6	31.5	23.3
Naturalized immigrants	18.5	20.6	16.0	24.2	25.1	20.8
Foreigners	34.1	30.9	24.1	11.3	24.7	30.1
Nordic nationals	34.4	36.3	23.2	14.5	26.8	29.9
Finnish nationals	40.4	35.2	28.5	11.3	22.4	33.8
Non-Nordic nationals	34.0	26.0	24.8	9.4	22.7	30.1
From southern Europe	42.4	33.5	27.5	13.0	33.5	36.6
TOTAL FIGURE FOR MEN	17.6	24.8	14.0	15.7	23.0	22.7
Women						
Swedish nationals	4.8	3.0	3.6	6.7	6.2	8.5
Born in Sweden	4.5	2.9	3.4	6.6	6.2	8.1
Swedish nationals of Swedish parentage	4.5	3.0	3.3	6.4	6.0	8.3
Second-generation immigrants	4.0	2.2	6.4	11.5	14.8	4.2
Naturalized immigrants	13.0	4.3	7.7	9.4	6.9	15.2
Foreigners	18.1	5.8	10.8	9.8	7.4	17.5
Nordic nationals	19.0	5.5	12.5	7.7	7.5	19.3
Finnish nationals	19.1	4.2	10.4	8.0	8.2	18.1
Non-Nordic nationals	16.6	6.0	8.5	12.4	7.4	14.8
From southern Europe	24.9	5.2	13.8	11.9	10.0	23.0
TOTAL FIGURE FOR WOMEN	5.6	3.2	4.0	6.9	6.3	9.1
Men + Women						
Swedish nationals	11.6	15.4	9.2	12.0	15.8	16.1
Born in Sweden	11.5	15.6	9.1	11.8	15.8	16.1
Foreigners	26.7	19.5	18.1	10.7	16.8	24.2
From southern Europe	34.4	20.5	21.4	12.5	22.9	30.4
TOTAL	12.4	15.7	9.7	11.9	15.9	16.6

The findings of the survey concerning the employment situation of foreigners show that immigrants are often much more highly trained than Swedes for the jobs they perform. Moreover, they do twice as much night work and three times more shift work than Swedes.

However, the most disturbing conclusions concern the differences in working conditions which exist between foreigners and Swedes. In fact, these findings are a good illustration of the nature of the factors which determine the use of migratory flows from countries with less developed economies. The main conclusion of these inquiries is that the working conditions of foreigners are much harder than those of Swedes: the jobs open to them carry a higher risk of industrial accidents, as well as being dirtier, more monotonous and more exhausting, and frequently expose workers to a fast pace of work and a high noise level. They offer workers fewer opportunities for improving their skills and thus less hope of obtaining promotion within the employing firm.

Table 9 gives an example of the methods used in this survey to evaluate the working conditions of foreigners compared with those of Swedes. It brings out very clearly the differences which exist between the working conditions of Swedish-born nationals and those of foreigners from southern Europe.

On the other hand, the overall material living and housing conditions of foreigners are not very different from those of Swedes, apart from the overcrowding prevalent in dwellings occupied by immigrants. A number of items pertaining to material living conditions were selected from

TABLE 10. Material conditions and accommodation by national origin (percentages)

National origin	Car	Telephone	Colour TV	Overcrowded accommodation	Modern accommodation	Single family house	High-rise apartment building
Swedish nationals	75.7	95.9	48.7	6.9	94.2	47.5	15.3
Born in Sweden	75.9	95.9	48.3	7.0	94.1	48.0	15.0
Swedish nationals of Swedish parentage	75.9	95.9	48.3	6.9	94.1	48.0	15.0
Second-generation immigrants	76.4	94.2	49.3	9.8	94.6	45.5	16.5
Naturalized immigrants	70.2	97.3	60.9	3.5	96.3	35.2	24.6
Foreigners	63.2	80.5	44.7	27.6	93.8	17.8	33.3
Nordic nationals	67.4	82.3	47.4	23.1	96.0	19.0	26.8
Finnish nationals	68.4	79.7	51.1	25.3	96.2	14.4	28.7
Non-Nordic nationals	58.6	78.5	41.8	32.4	91.5	16.6	40.3
From southern Europe	72.6	69.8	47.0	46.7	89.5	8.8	38.4
TOTAL	75.1	95.2	48.5	7.8	94.2	46.1	16.2

many different tables and were grouped together in one table in the interests of clarity (see Table 10 above). Accommodation is officially considered to be overcrowded when there are 'more than two occupants per room, excluding the kitchen and living-room'.

Integration of migrants and their families into the host society

The new policy introduced in 1975

It was generally felt in Sweden, until the mid-1960s, that the linguistic and cultural characteristics of ethnic minorities should disappear as quickly as possible. The difficulties experienced by immigrants seemed to be associated with problems of adaptation. However unacceptable this attitude may be from the standpoint of human rights, it simply reflected the fact that, for centuries, the Swedish people was one of the most homogeneous in the world.

In 1964, a great discussion on the cultural rights of immigrants was opened in Sweden both by the mass media and at parliamentary level. The question at issue was whether an all-out effort should be made to assimilate the immigrant population or whether, on the contrary, immigrants should be given the opportunity to integrate into Swedish society while retaining their own language and cultural heritage. The government was unable to give Parliament a satisfactory answer to this question and therefore decided, in 1968, to appoint a commission to study the immigration problem, which included members of all the major political parties and undertook to draw up proposals for long-term projects aiming at the integration of immigrants into Swedish society.

The commission's final report was submitted in 1974 and was widely accepted. It was taken as the basis for the new guidelines for a policy on immigration and ethnic minorities, which were laid before Parliament—in the form of a bill—in the spring of 1975. In this bill, the government laid stress on the importance of maintaining strict control over immigration so as to guard against any adverse effects that it might have on the development of the labour market. In addition, however, the government defined, for the first time, the objectives of a new official Swedish policy on the rights of immigrants and ethnic minorities.

These objectives are based on the three principles of equality, freedom of choice and solidarity. The principle of equality implies that Swedish society must make a substained effort to secure for immigrants the same social conditions and opportunities, together with the same rights and obligations, as the rest of the population. It also implies that all ethnic groups in Sweden should have an equal chance of cultivating the use of their mother tongue and enjoying cultural activities. The immigration policy must therefore offer members of linguistic minorities real opportunities for developing their own linguistic and cultural identity in a spirit of mutual respect to be fostered throughout Swedish society.

In order to observe the principle of freedom of choice, it is necessary to ensure that immigrants have a real choice (uninfluenced by the state, which must remain neutral) between the possibility of preserving and developing their own cultural identity and that of assuming a cultural identity of Swedish origin. Steps must also be taken to enable immigrants to keep in contact with their country of origin and to facilitate the decision when the time comes for immigrants and their children to choose between settling in Sweden and becoming reintegrated into their country of origin.

The principle of solidarity also implies that co-operation should be established in all fields of activity between the various groups of immigrants and the majority of the Swedish population. It therefore calls for mutual tolerance and an awareness of the immigrants' need to be in a better position to influence decisions affecting their status.

These principles were incorporated into various legal documents concerning the rights of immigrants and ethnic minorities. They were also included in the new Swedish Constitution (Regeringsformen) which stipulates (in Chapter 2, Section 1) that measures shall be taken in order to 'promote the preservation and development of the specific cultural and community life of each ethnic, linguistic and religious minority'. Moreover, the legal freedoms and basic rights of foreigners have now been given formal recognition in recently amended clauses of the Constitution.

This new policy of promoting the rights and satisfying the demands of immigrants and minorities places Sweden in a half-way position between the countries which pursue a consistent *Gastarbeiter* policy and those whose permanent immigration policy is aimed at encouraging the settlement of foreigners.

As already indicated, however, Swedish immigration policy is not based on demographic considerations, and immigration is generally considered to be a 'necessary evil' rather than a 'national asset'. The new policy introduced in 1975 is therefore justified by the desire to restore their human rights to immigrants and by the overriding resolve to prevent the development of a social situation rife with ethnic conflict and tension, as is the case in many countries.

A further aim of this policy is to facilitate the immigrants' return to their home countries by preparing the ground for their full reintegration into their cultural, social and linguistic environment.

Implementation of the new policy

In pursuance of the objectives of the new ethnic policy proclaimed by Parliament, the government drew up a set of measures aimed at encouraging ethnic pluralism and increasing the immigrants' opportunities for exercising their democratic rights.

The first category of measures is designed to promote the formation of associations of immigrants and ethnic minorities. Estonians and Finns had already formed their own organizations in Sweden during the 1940s and 1950s. This example was followed in the late 1960s by Yugoslavs, Italians and Greeks. There are probably about a thousand ethnically-based associations in Sweden at the present time, of which approximately 120 are organized on a nationwide basis while the others have been formed at the local or regional level. The Finnish, Yugoslav, Greek and Italian national organizations, which together represent about 80,000 people, have begun to co-operate and take joint action on crucial issues affecting immigrants. Immigrants' organizations which were already in existence at the end of the 1960s receive financial aid from the state as well as from the municipalities. The new programme introduced in 1975, which is being implemented by the National Immigration and Naturalization Office, aims to provide every ethnic association organized on a nationwide basis with the financial aid it needs in order to procure its own administrative staff and equipment. The government bill emphasized that organizations formed by migrants and minorities in Sweden 'play a most important part in community life and satisfy their members' special need for an ethnic identity'. Today, the funds granted by the state to ethnic organizations total approximately $1 million per year. In addition, the municipalities provide the local organizations with financial aid totalling some $3 million per year.

The 1975 programme also includes a series of measures specifically intended to maintain and preserve the cultural and linguistic heritage of new ethnic groups. It provides for state subsidies to local public libraries to help them to purchase books written in the languages of the minorities. Since 1977, subsidies have also been granted to ethnic organizations and their publishers, to help ethnic minorities to create their own literary tradition in Sweden. Similarly, in 1977, the government introduced a state-sponsored plan for giving financial support to newspapers and journals published by immigrants' organizations in languages other than Swedish. This aid is even more substantial than that allocated to the ordinary Swedish press (a Finnish paper receives $300,000 per year under this scheme). The theatrical activities of Finns and of other minority groups are also state-subsidized. All these cultural programmes are run by the National Council for Cultural Activities (Statens Kulturråd).

New measures have also been introduced in the field of education.

The most important reform in this respect is the 1976 bilingualism programme, the aim of which is to promote languages spoken by the minorities established in Sweden and to improve the educational opportunities available to second-generation immigrants.

Lastly, a fourth series of measures concerns the opportunities available to immigrants for influencing political decisions. In this connection, it is relevant to refer again to the financial aid given to migrants' organizations and to the establishment of an Immigrants' Advisory Council on which all the major organizations are represented (see Figure 4). However, the most important reform carried out in this field was the one which made it possible to grant foreigners the right to vote for local and regional bodies in the 1976 elections and to amend the legislation concerning citizenship in such a way as to make it easier for foreigners to acquire full political rights.

The political power of immigrants

The most obvious sign of the political impact of immigration on the development of Sweden in recent years is, perhaps, the electoral reform adopted in 1976 which gave aliens the right to vote and to stand for election in municipal elections (in effect, this means in local and regional elections), provided that they had been resident in Sweden for the three years prior to the elections. This reform, which is unique of its kind, was first introduced at the time of the general elections held in 1976. General elections take place in Sweden every three years and concern the composition of municipal councils as well as the choice of Members of Parliament. The reform conferred the right to vote on a total of 218,000 aliens, representing 3.5 per cent of the entire electorate in 1976. Finns constituted the largest national group with a total of 102,019 new voters, accounting for 46.7 per cent of all foreigners who had recently obtained the right to vote. Yugoslav voters numbered 24,374 (11.2 per cent). In addition, of course, every immigrant who had acquired Swedish nationality had the same right as any other Swedish citizen to participate in the parliamentary elections.

At the preparatory stage, it was feared that the reform would come to nothing and that very few foreigners would participate in the elections. Parliament therefore established a special fund to finance an information campaign. During the spring of 1976, pamphlets were published in fifteen languages and sent to all immigrant households. Radio and television networks broadcast special programmes, and study groups on the questions at issue were organized by voluntary educational associations (most of which depended on the political parties). The national associations of various ethnic groups also took an active part in the campaign.

TABLE 11. Participation of foreigners in the communal elections of 1976, by country of origin

Country of origin	With the right to vote			Actually voting			Rate of participation (%)		
	Men	Women	Total	Men	Women	Total	Men	Women	Total
Denmark	9 368	6 476	15 844	5 198	3 762	8 960	55.5	58.1	56.6
Finland	49 504	52 515	102 019	27 252	30 111	57 363	55.1	57.3	56.2
Norway	7 324	8 259	15 583	4 172	5 089	9 261	57.0	61.6	59.4
France	788	299	1 087	466	177	643	59.1	59.2	59.2
Greece	5 622	4 095	9 717	4 282	3 113	7 395	76.2	76.0	76.1
Italy	2 468	1 083	3 551	1 537	628	2 165	62.3	58.0	61.0
Yugoslavia	12 688	11 686	24 374	8 273	7 863	16 136	65.2	67.3	66.2
Netherlands	873	447	1 320	600	338	938	68.7	75.6	71.1
Poland	1 578	2 404	3 982	879	1 663	2 542	55.7	69.2	63.8
Switzerland	805	488	1 293	567	374	941	70.4	76.6	72.8
Spain	1 198	654	1 852	610	360	970	50.9	55.0	52.4
United Kingdom	2 075	1 234	3 309	1 398	808	2 206	67.4	65.5	66.7
Czechoslovakia	1 188	899	2 087	807	669	1 476	67.9	74.4	70.7
Federal Republic of Germany	5 527	4 079	9 606	3 676	2 776	6 452	66.5	68.1	67.2
Hungary	1 530	838	2 368	672	507	1 179	43.9	60.5	49.8
Austria	1 606	655	2 258	1 174	452	1 626	73.2	69.0	72.0
United States of America	1 741	1 230	2 971	860	480	1 340	49.4	39.0	45.1
Turkey	1 721	1 397	3 118	1 202	747	1 949	69.8	53.5	62.5
Other countries	7 728	4 499	12 227	4 560	2 750	7 310	59.0	61.1	59.8
TOTAL (all countries)	115 329	103 237	218 566	68 185	62 667	130 852	59.1	60.7	59.9

The success of this campaign can be measured by the number of foreigners participating in the elections. The rate was in fact much higher than had been forecast: a total of 130,000 persons, representing 60 per cent of the foreign population entitled to vote, cast their vote at these elections. Of these foreign voters 68,000 were men, representing a turn-out of 59 per cent, and 63,000 were women, representing a turn-out of 61 per cent, while the total rate of participation in the municipal elections for the electorate as a whole was 90 per cent. The turn-out of foreign voters differed appreciably from one region to another, ranging from 51 per cent in Jämtland county to 66 per cent in Kronoberg county. Contrary to expectations, the participation rate of immigrants proved to be lower in counties where they represent a high proportion of the population.

The participation rate of foreigners from the Nordic countries was below average, as was that of American citizens, Spaniards and Hungarians. The rate was remarkably high for the majority of immigrant groups from the Mediterranean countries (which are predominant among manual workers): 76 per cent for Greeks, 66 per cent for Yugoslavs, 62 per cent for Turks and 61 per cent for Italians. It was only in the Turkish community that the participation rate was lower for women than for men (53 per cent as against 70 per cent). Swiss immigrants, most of whom hold 'white collar' jobs, had the highest participation rate of all foreign voters with 72.8 per cent. These results are shown in Table 11.

The Political Science Department of Stockholm University is at present conducting a survey, partly financed by the Ministry of Labour, of the participation in the 1976 elections of the 218,000 immigrants who had obtained the right to vote. A preliminary report on the findings of this survey (together with a summary in English) was issued in February 1977. The report contains a very interesting study of the immigrants' preferences as regards political parties, which is based on a series of interviews with some 900 immigrants living in Stockholm, who had come to Sweden from Finland, Yugoslavia, Poland and Turkey, as well as interviews with a sample of the Swedish electorate. On the basis of these interviews, which were organized long before and shortly after the elections, estimates were made of the immigrants' preferences as regards political parties according to the voters' social status (see Figures 5 and 6).

The pattern which emerges from these figures corresponds, on the whole, to the forecasts made by most of the experts before the elections. Since the bulk of the immigrant population is employed in industry and the services sector, it could be assumed that many of them would vote for the socialist parties. Immigrant manual workers tend to vote socialist more often than Swedish workers: this tendency is more pronounced among Yugoslavs and Turks than among Finns and Poles. The findings

Socialist parties
Non-socialist parties
Sweden
41%
59%
Poland
34%
66%
Finland
42%
58%
Turkey
65%
35%
Yugoslavia
87%
13%

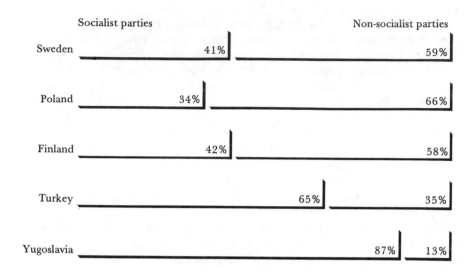

FIG. 5. The preferences of Swedish and foreign voters as regards the socialist and non-socialist parties, by country of origin (white-collar workers).

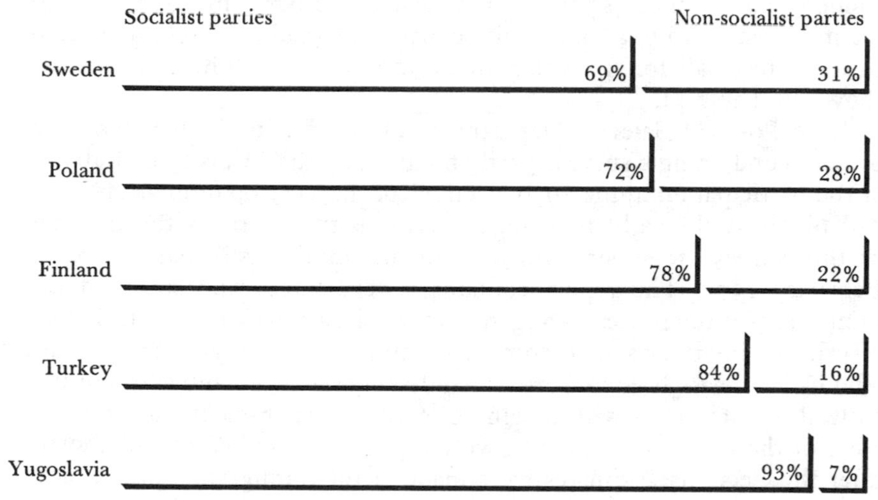

Socialist parties
Non-socialist parties
Sweden
69%
31%
Poland
72%
28%
Finland
78%
22%
Turkey
84%
16%
Yugoslavia
93%
7%

FIG. 6. The preferences of Swedish nationals and foreign voters as regards the socialist and non-socialist parties, by country of origin.

of the survey also show that the longer a foreign national has lived in Sweden, the more he tends to adopt the same political positions in elections as Swedes of the same social class and origins and with the same educational background. It should be made clear, however, that the data presented here only refer to the commune of Stockholm.

In all, slightly more than 1,000 immigrants stood as candidates in the municipal elections after their names had been included in the lists of the various political parties; about half of them were candidates for the Social Democrat Party. As a result of the elections, almost 400 immigrants became members of local parliaments and municipal councils. In some communes, the granting of the vote to immigrants had the effect of changing the balance of parties in local government in favour of the socialist parties (in Göteborg, for example).

The success of this electoral reform prompted certain influential political circles to call for an investigation into the possibility of giving aliens the right to participate in national parliamentary elections. This proposal was put forward, for example, by the trade unions (both the Confederation of Swedish Trade Unions (LO) and the TCO) and by the two socialist parties represented in Parliament. However, Parliament decided instead to liberalize the legislation concerning nationality as being a convenient way of enabling immigrants to participate in the political life of Sweden.

The decision to confer the right to vote on immigrants has also had the effect of increasing their participation in trade-union activities. Since the early 1960s, Swedish employers have usually advised newly arrived immigrants to join the relevant trade union. This explains why the level of trade-union membership among immigrants is particularly high. Until the beginning of the seventies, however, they were not extensively represented on the executive committees of local trade unions. After the LO had introduced a more active policy as regards immigrant workers, the occupational unions urged local trade-union officials to see to it that immigrants were elected more often as trade-union representatives.

Discrimination and prejudice

It is disturbing to see that prejudice, racialism, racial discrimination and racial conflicts seem to be on the increase in Swedish society. The economic recession which has affected Sweden over the last few years is obviously one of the contributing factors, but the major causes are deeply rooted in the defensive reactions of a society to the rapid changes taking place in a highly industrialized nation. However, a movement of opinion in favour of taking vigorous measures against these racialist tendencies is coming to the fore in Sweden today.

There can be no doubt that immigration creates the danger of a development of discriminatory and hostile attitudes based on racial prejudices. For this reason, special measures concerning activities directed against ethnic groups, which also covered any form of illegal discrimination, were added to the penal code in 1970. Furthermore, the new Constitution stipulates that no Act or regulations shall countenance discrimination against any citizen—in terms of race, colour or ethnic origins—because he belongs to an ethnic minority. In this respect, every foreigner present on Swedish territory enjoys the same safeguards as a Swedish citizen.

In its 1974 report, the Immigration Commission presented an exhaustive scientific survey of forms of prejudice against immigrants which are prevalent in the Swedish population. In response to the commission's proposals, Parliament decided, in 1975, to introduce new programmes for helping the Swedish public to understand immigrants better. The National Immigration and Naturalization Office was charged with putting the new programmes into effect. However, there is a general feeling in political circles that these measures do not go far enough. Parliament has been deeply disturbed by incidents caused by racial discrimination and racial conflicts. In August 1978, the government therefore appointed a special commissioner whose task consists entirely in determining what measures should be taken to guard against the development of prejudice and discrimination against immigrants and ethnic, linguistic, national and religious minorities settled in Sweden.

Conclusions

This study has reviewed the effects of the migratory flows which have developed in Sweden since the last world war. These effects have been felt in five different areas:

From the juridical standpoint, the rising trend in immigration, coupled with the change in political attitudes, has compelled the country to adopt a more restrictive immigration policy, particularly with regard to the right of entry into Swedish territory.

From the administrative standpoint, this policy has entailed the establishment of an extensive network of administrative services—at both the local and the national levels—to be responsible for regulating immigration, but also for meeting the specific social and educational needs of immigrants.

From the demographic standpoint, immigration has accounted for almost half of the increase in population recorded since the war and it has radically changed the composition of the Swedish population.

From the socio-economic standpoint, immigration has had the effect of
accelerating the trend within the labour market towards a dualistic
structure characterized by the existence of sectors in which disadvantaged social groups, and particularly immigrants, are in the
majority. It has thus contributed to creating a situation which
fosters socio-economic differences between immigrants and the
indigenous population, particularly as regards social mobility, the
unemployment rate and working conditions. Since second-generation
immigrants have less chance of finding employment than Swedish
nationals, they are in imminent danger of suffering from the
persistence of these social inequalities.

From the political standpoint, the current national discussion on immigration has given an important place to the question of policies
regarding immigrants and ethnic minorities. Furthermore, a new
policy has been introduced to promote ethnic pluralism and
co-operation with the emigration countries, and formal recognition
has been given to the political rights and the political power of
immigrants.

Although policies on immigration and ethnic minorities have developed
on very positive lines over the last ten years in Sweden, there is still an
urgent need to revise the present policies and programmes so as to
enable them to meet the more serious and far-reaching challenges which
will undoubtedly have to be faced in the future in both these very
dynamic and interdependent areas.

The author of this study holds the view that the systematic efforts
which will have to be made over the next five or ten years should be
focused on the following seven priorities:

1. A full parliamentary inquiry into the change in world migration
   patterns and their long-term implications for Swedish immigration
   legislation and procedures; a detailed analysis of the objectives to be
   set for Swedish immigration policy, particularly as regards the acceptable volume of immigration, bearing in mind long-term immigration
   capacities and the need to neutralize the causes of involuntary
   emigration.

2. A more systematically constructed administrative system for the
   regulation of immigration, including the establishment of a regional
   branch of the National Immigration and Naturalization Office, and
   an improvement in the co-ordination at ministerial level of measures
   concerning the different aspects of migration policy.

3. A plan of action for combating the social inequalities which exist
   between immigrants and the Swedish population, to be based on
   measures designed to promote social mobility and sexual equality
   and to improve wage scales and working conditions for all under-
   privileged groups of society.

4. Long-term strategies for developing bilingual teaching programmes

for second-generation immigrants with a view to improving their social, educational and employment opportunities.

5. Efforts to be made, at a national level, to check the spread of discrimination, prejudice and racial conflicts.

6. Long-term programmes for the development of bilateral and multilateral co-operation with emigration countries in order to facilitate the reintegration of migrants who return home and to contribute, in economic terms, to the creation of jobs in these countries.

7. A systematic research policy to be introduced with the aim of studying all phenomena related to international migratory movements and ethnic problems and updating the existing policies.

Bibliography

Official statistics

Population and Housing Census 1975, Part 3:3: Population in the Whole Country and in the Counties, etc., Aliens and Foreign-born Persons in the Whole Country. SCB, 1977. (Partly in English.)

Population Projection for Sweden 1976–2000, 1976:3: Forecasting Information; Appendix on Re-migration to and from Sweden 1968–1975. SCB, 1976. 121 pp.

Population 31 December 1977, Part 3: Distribution by Sex, Age, Marital Status and Citizenship by Commune, etc. SCB, 1978. (Partly in English.)

Population Changes 1977, Part 3: The Whole Country and the Counties, etc. SCB, 1978. (Partly in English.)

The Labour Force Survey, Raw Tables, First Quarter 1978. SCB, 1978.

Living Conditions, Report No. 9: Living Conditions of Immigrants in Sweden, 1975. SCB, 1977. (Partly in English.)

Immigrant Pupils in the Comprehensive School and the Integrated Upper Secondary School, Spring 1977. SCB, 1977. (Partly in English.)

Immigrant Pupils and Immigrant Teaching in Sweden. Some Findings of Surveys in 1975, 1976 and 1977. Promemorior från SCB 1977:12. SCB, 1977.

Participation of Aliens at the Communal Elections 1976, Be 1977:5. SCB, 1977.

Governmental reports and bills

Invandrarutredningen 3, Invandrarna och Minoriteterna (SOU 1974:69), Stockholm, 1974, 452 pp.; Invandrarutredningen 4, Bilagedel (SOU 1974:70), Stockholm, 1974 (Final Report of the Immigration Commission, and Annexes; partly in English).

Proposition 1975:26 om Riktlinjer för Invandrar- och Minoritetspolitiken (Bill of 1975 on Measures in Favour of Immigrants and Ethnic Minorities).

Förslag om Åtgärder för Invandrarbarn i Förskola, Grundskola och Gymnasieskola (DS U 1975:13) (Report of the Commission on the Educational Situation of the Children of Immigrants). Stockholm, 1975.

Proposition 1975/76:118 om Hemspråksundervisning för Invandrarbarn (Bill of 1976 on the Teaching of Mother Tongues to the Children of Immigrants).

Kommunal Rösträtt för Invandrare (SOU 1975:15) (Report of the Commission on Immigrants' Right to Vote in Municipal Elections). Stockholm, 1975.

Proposition 1975/76:23 om Kommunal Rösträtt för Invandrare (Bill of 1975 on Immigrants' Right to Vote in Municipal Elections).

The Biography of a People, Past and Future Population Changes in Sweden, Figures 3 and 4. A Contribution to the United Nations World Population Conference. Stockholm, 1974. (In English.)

Other sources

HAMMAR, T. *The First Immigrant Election,* Figures 5 and 6. Stockholm, Commission on Immigration Research (EIFO), 1977.

LEINIO, T.-L. *Finska Invandrare i Sverige 1974* (Finnish Immigrants in Sweden 1974). Stockholm, Institute for Social Research, 1978. (Preliminary draft.)

The migratory phenomenon and returning migrants in Turkey

A case-study

Eric-Jean Thomas

Introduction

Theoretically, the migratory chain starts and ends in the migrant worker's country of origin. It would be useless to try to understand the migratory process without taking account of the place and role filled by the countries of origin in that process. The socio-economic position of the would-be emigrant and the powerful factors inducing him to leave are of extreme importance inasmuch as they are the very source of the migratory process. However, these circumstances exist before the actual migration is undertaken and are partly extraneous to the migratory chain. In contrast, those pressures which induce the immigrant to return to his own country or to remain in the host country lie at the very heart of the complex of immigration problems.

The immigration countries, faced with a large number of foreign workers whose labour they have accepted as a means of meeting the needs of their economies, have found in the key concept of the migrant's return home the moral, economic and social justification for their desire to reduce their foreign populations. Some countries that have never been very generous in granting economic, social and political rights to immigrants have even had the ingenuity to create a 'right' to return home. They claim that when they encourage immigrants to leave the countries in which they have settled, in some cases a very long time ago, they are recognizing their right to return to their homeland. They also claim that the countries of origin can thus benefit from the knowledge and experience gained abroad by their nationals. Lastly, it is argued that, by this means, savings accumulated abroad are brought back to the home country, thus facilitating the establishment and expansion of small local industries which strengthen the national economy.

This study will not attempt to deal exhaustively with all the questions raised by the possible return of migrants. It has a far more modest aim and will simply endeavour to define this problem area and dispel certain myths propagated by numerous studies, mainly of Western origin. Our investigation, which was largely conducted in the field, has no other end in view than to open up a field of reflection and show what role might be played by international organizations such as Unesco. By giving assistance to the Turkish research workers who are studying these questions, they can make a considerable contribution to the advancement of knowledge in a relatively unexplored field which is all too often the preserve of Western research. Since their work on such questions is done within the context of their own special subjects, those research workers tend to overlook the needs of the countries concerned.

Because of the geographical and political position of Turkey in Europe as a true meeting-point between East and West, this country has a highly specific character that does not lend itself to superficial or hasty analysis. Not quite in Europe and not quite in Asia, Turkey, although an Islamic country, is distinguished from many other Muslim countries by the achievements of the Kemalist revolution, which have helped to shape a multifaceted and rapidly changing society.

It was indeed the rich and varied qualities of that society, people and country which led us to think that Turkey deserved to be the subject of a case-study.

I should like personally to thank all my eminent hosts in Turkey who kindly guided me in my research. In particular, Dr Sehmus Güzel of the Faculty of Political Science of Ankara University opened many doors for me and his knowledge was of invaluable assistance throughout my work.

I should like, finally, to apologize to them for any errors or omissions that may be found in this study; the responsibility is entirely mine.

Emigration from Turkey

Migratory phenomena are global phenomena; in other words, it is not possible to break them down completely into their various components. Thus, before tackling the complex of problems connected with returning migrants, it is necessary to analyse the factors determining emigration from Turkey in order to understand the circumstances in which it has taken place.

A recent phenomenon

Unlike many other emigration countries, Turkey did not experience significant migratory flows before the beginning of the 1960s. The few Turks who decided, between 1958 and 1960, to go abroad, and particularly to the Federal Republic of Germany, in order to take up paid employment there, helped to trigger a phenomenon that was to swell to large proportions very rapidly. In 1961, a bilateral agreement on the recruitment of workers was signed with the Federal Republic of Germany. As early as 1962, immigration was used by the Turkish authorities as a means of relieving pressure on the labour market and was at the same time expected to provide migrants with a training and a standard of qualifications which would benefit the country on their return. Accordingly, the first five-year development plan (1963–67) officially assigned a role in economic development to emigration.[1] Subsequently, many bilateral agreements were signed with other European countries—and even with Australia (see Table 1)—while thousands of workers emigrated illicitly, that is to say without going through either the National Labour Office or the missions of the various immigration countries in Turkey which were responsible for organizing, in collaboration with the National Labour Office, the recruitment of Turkish workers.

It is obvious that these agreements were, in theory, of very great importance in many fields: recruitment, transport, possible return, integration of migrants into the host society and transfer of funds to Turkey. It seems clear, however, that these agreements were looked upon and used by the immigration countries mainly as a means of recruiting workers. In the absence of adequate information, Turkish workers abroad could not exercise the few rights granted to them, particularly at the beginning of the great wave of emigration which was to last for some ten years, from 1963 to 1973. As for the question of remittances, which will be examined more closely below, we need only note here that such transfers of funds were hardly regulated by these bilateral conventions although they were very soon regarded as one of the chief advantages that Turkey was expected to derive from emigration.

TABLE 1. Bilateral agreements concluded by Turkey

1. Federal Republic of Germany:	30 October 1961	5. France:	8 April 1965
2. Austria:	15 May 1964	6. Sweden:	10 March 1967
3. Belgium:	16 July 1964	7. Australia:	5 October 1967
4. Netherlands:	19 August 1964	8. Libyan Arab Jamahiriya:	5 January 1975

N.B. Difficult negotiations are being conducted with a view to signing an agreement with Saudi Arabia.

Lastly, as regards the migrants' right to draw the various social benefits provided by host countries, several conventions were concluded between Turkey and the countries concerned. The implementation of those conventions does not seem to have presented any difficulties, but it should be made clear that immigrant workers have always encountered discrimination in many forms when they have actually applied for these benefits. The origin and legal justification of such discrimination are to be found in the immigration regulations. For example, the right to receive unemployment benefits is very often subject to certain conditions regarding the period of residence and the period of employment. Similarly, the entitlement to family allowances is very often reduced for workers whose families live in Turkey, while the same workers are often denied the right to send for their families to join them in the country where they are working.

It emerges from Tables 1 and 2 and particularly from Table 2, that the pattern of Turkish emigration is changing: while the number of Turkish workers who have emigrated to European countries has been decreasing or has remained steady since 1973–74, it is increasing very appreciably in Arab countries such as the Libyan Arab Jamahiriya

TABLE 2. Trends in the active Turkish population in the main host countries

	Federal Republic of Germany	France	Netherlands	Austria	Libyan Arab Jamahiriya[1]
1961	—	250	100	50	—
1962	18 558	250	180	200	—
1963	42 116	300	380	1 100	—
1964	94 054	350	3 200	2 500	—
1965	134 708	350	5 300	4 500	—
1966	142 532	350	8 000	5 000	—
1967	131 309	375	8 200	6 000	—
1968	152 905	400	9 900	6 500	—
1969	244 345	600	14 000	7 500	—
1970	353 898	9 500	20 700	11 000	200
1971	453 145	17 000	27 600	18 450	600
1972	528 000	27 000	29 900	19 600	1 200
1973	605 000	40 000	32 700	20 400	2 400
1974	570 000	45 000	37 400	30 700	3 800
1975	522 669	43 200	39 000	26 400	5 000
1976	520 000	42 000	38 700	26 000	7 500
1977	517 000	42 000	41 434	26 933	12 500

1. In reality, the Libyan Arab Jamahiriya ranks eighth among the countries receiving Turkish emigrants. It is included in this table because it is one of the new host countries—like Saudi Arabia—which are gradually taking the place of the traditional host countries.
Sources: Offices of labour counsellors and attachés in embassies and consulates abroad, National Labour Office and Ministry of Foreign Affairs.

TABLE 3. Turkish nationals abroad and distribution of families, by country, in 1977

Country	Active population	Wives	Children by age-group		Total
			0–6	7–18	
Federal Republic of Germany	517 467	227 833	178 700	241 700	1 165 700
Netherlands	43 992	21 275	13 809	15 115	94 191
France	39 000	17 874	11 100	12 550	80 524
Austria	26 055	7 000	6 000	7 500	46 555
Belgium	16 937	12 211	12 478	17 780	59 406
Switzerland	16 662	3 400	4 868	5 688	29 618
Denmark	7 352	1 000	2 100	2 900	13 352
Sweden	4 760	2 341	3 563	3 832	14 496
Saudi Arabia	35 000	2 000	1 000	2 000	40 000
Libyan Arab Jamahiriya	20 000	1 500	800	1 200	23 500
Australia	14 000	1 000	1 000	1 500	17 500
Others	15 000	1 000	1 500	2 500	20 000
TOTAL	751 225	298 434	236 918	314 265	1 604 842

Source: Sabri Kumbaroclu, *Yurtdisindaki Turk Gençlerinin Mesleki Egitimi*, Ankara, Ministry of Labour, 1979.

and Saudi Arabia. It seems, in fact, that the world economic crisis and its effects on the flow of remittances from emigrants have forced Turkey to redirect its emigration policy towards new countries, and in particular towards the oil-producing countries, which are both rich and closer to them, both geographically and culturally.

The economic stakes

It should be emphasized that the attitude of the Turkish authorities towards migratory movements has very often been determined largely by considerations based exclusively on the substantial financial advantages accruing from emigrants' transfers of funds. Thus, the strictly financial aspect of emigration has taken precedence over its more slowly perceived socio-political effects. This state of affairs accounts for the absence of a truly Turkish emigration policy and explains why no official body has been vested with supreme authority in matters relating to migration. The multiplicity of decision-making centres has certainly hindered any attempt at rationalization and made it difficult to define a common attitude to the various problems created for Turkey by migratory movements.

It is true that little by little, and especially from 1965 onwards, the amount of money transferred became very substantial, for in 1972 it was larger than the external deficit. The total amount transferred increased from $8,112,000 in 1964 to $740,155,000 in 1972, attaining its highest level—$1,426,211,000!—in 1974. It must also be pointed out that these sums do not represent all the savings made in the host countries. To give an even more precise idea of the significance of these remittances for the Turkish economy, we need only say that by 1974 they had risen to a figure roughly equal to that of the export revenue (f.o.b.) and equivalent to 63.5 per cent of the foreign trade deficit.

From 1975 onwards the value of remittances declined steadily, while the external deficit worsened. In 1977 remittances represented no more than $982 million as compared with a foreign trade deficit of $4,043 million. In 1978, after drastic measures had been taken, this deficit was reduced to $2,311 million while the remittances increased by only 1 million dollars, bringing them up to $983 million.

The fall in remittances seems to be in great part due to the deterioration of the economic situation and the fact that Turkish workers abroad had lost confidence in the value of the Turkish lira.

The second factor in order of importance in determining the attitude of the public authorities towards the emigration question is the state of the labour market.

With a population of 42,130,000 inhabitants and a growth rate higher than 2.5 per cent, Turkey has to contend with a particularly high unemployment rate: at least 13.5 per cent in 1979, representing 2.2 million unemployed. This situation is aggravated by the large imbalances that exist in the distribution of the population and by runaway urbanization, which, in social terms, is very costly. It is therefore understandable that emigration should have been regarded as a panacea, especially since it was a profitable source of foreign exchange. However, the axiom that emigration reduces unemployment is being seriously questioned today, for people are beginning to realize that mistakes have been made because nothing was known about the structures of migratory flows. This question will be examined later, but it is necessary to point out how this approach to the migratory phenomenon has contributed to making the solution of the major domestic problems of the Turkish economy depend even more on the economic policies of immigration countries.

The fact that the Turkish economy is so dependent on its emigrant population partly explains the extreme vulnerability of the Turkish balance of payments and the dependence of the economy itself on the European countries. We must, of course, be wary of generalizations based on the problem of emigration: true, Turkey is handicapped by an unfavourable world economic order, but its role as a supplier of manpower to many Western countries is perfectly in line with the balance of economic power in the world. It is a meaningful image of Turkey's position within that economic order.

Identifying the emigrants

A striking divergence exists between the statistics relating to the level of qualifications of migrants which are published by host countries and those supplied by the countries of origin. This is particularly true in the case of Turkey. In France, the 1975 census returns show that out of 1,385 Turks, 770 (or 55.5 per cent) were classified as *ouvriers spécialisés* (i.e. unskilled workers) or labourers. To this figure can be added agricultural workers (45) and services personnel (65). This makes a total of 70 per cent unskilled workers.[2] Yet the figures communicated to us by the Turkish National Labour Office show that, overall, during the period from 1973 to 1975, only 58.7 per cent of the workers who found jobs abroad were unskilled. Since that time this divergence has become more pronounced. Thus, while the level of qualifications of Turkish emigrants has improved very appreciably—from 1976 to the end of the first six months of 1979, 67.5 per cent of Turkish migrants were skilled[3]—we find, paradoxical though it seems, that in the two main countries receiving Turkish emigrants, which are the Federal Republic of Germany and France, the level of qualifications has remained unchanged.

This fact calls for two comments.

First, it must be pointed out that the high number of skilled workers recorded at the time of emigration is not the result of chance, especially in a country like Turkey where the illiteracy rate is 65 per cent. It is the immigration countries, acting through their local recruitment missions, that define the criteria whereby the prospective emigrants are to be selected. It must be acknowledged that these criteria are exacting but bear no relation to the job that the migrant is likely to be given in the host country. Everything goes to show that the immigration countries set a very high standard in order to cream off the best of the labour force and so be sure of obtaining good-quality immigrant workers, even though the actual employers may not take their level of qualifications into account when allocating jobs.

Second, we must draw attention to the fact that this type of emigration represents a real 'brain drain' as far as the active population is concerned, since it is the best workers who leave, that is to say those who are the most qualified and who are also the most enterprising. This being so, it becomes clear that emigration is not the panacea it was thought to be. The people who emigrate are the younger and most qualified members of society; usually they already have a job and in many cases they command the highest pay.

The fact that this considerable drain on manpower was a threat to the country's economic development began to be recognized at the end of the 1960s by the Turkish authorities, who tried to ensure that migrants were selected in a manner more in keeping with the national interest. To this end, a system of lists was established in order to assign priority to certain categories of prospective emigrants, according to criteria based on the applicant's occupation, level of qualifications, region of origin and whether or not he was unemployed. But this system had to be abandoned because it was unwieldy and had the effect of drastically lengthening the waiting time for applicants: a million and a half people were still waiting two years after putting in their applications.

The problems created by the return of migrants

The return of migrants, whether voluntary or not, is a subject on which a great deal of often conflicting information is in circulation. Its actual or merely hypothetical occurrence presents such problems to the country of origin that it seems hardly possible to ignore it. As regards Turkey, it is a striking fact that no concerted policy exists in respect of the return of migrants. There are various reasons for this. They must be examined if we are to discern and understand the specific features of the Turkish model.

Return: a myth or a reality?

If there was one question that received a unanimous reply at the time of our survey in Turkey, it was the one which concerned the volume of the homeward flow and its effects on the country's socio-economic life. All the specialists questioned—administrative authorities, university teachers, research workers, and others—took the view that this was a non-problem, because, contrary to a very widespread opinion, hardly any Turkish workers return to Turkey. Admittedly, this view should be taken with a pinch of salt, but the fact remains that the figures concerning the return of migrants, in so far as they are known, fall far short of those implied by Europeans when they discuss this phenomenon.

But the main problem is to find out what figures are available and what they signify.

A highly interesting study published in 1971[4] revealed that, in the final analysis, the 1966/67 recession in the Federal Republic of Germany had had only limited repercussions on the Turkish workers, despite the harsh policy adopted by the employing firms and the government. So far as we know, a study of this kind has not been undertaken in respect of the world economic crisis that began in 1973. It is probable, however, that some of the author's analyses are still relevant, although the two crises are not quite of the same kind. This is particularly true of the analysis of the immigrant workers' reaction to the recession and the economic 'repression' directed against them.

The restrictive measures taken in 1966–67 were reintroduced in the mid-1970s. Nermin Abadan summarized them as follows: 'The employer refused to renew the work contract; a shortening of working hours resulted in unacceptably low wages causing workers to leave; workers lost their enthusiasm for a job when the working day was organized so as to give no opportunity for earning overtime pay or output bonuses.'[5]

Alongside these measures that can be described as subjective, both in their origin and in their effects, more objective measures were taken by the authorities. In particular, regulations were drawn up in order to limit the number of workers officially recruited, through the missions of the immigration countries, in the workers' countries of origin, and to reduce the number of residence or work permits being issued for the first time or renewed. These measures were an integral part of a restrictive immigration policy which was to be introduced in all the European countries and which had already been reflected in the attitude adopted by the Federal Republic of Germany during the 1966–67 recession. In the article she wrote in 1971, N. Abadan noted that the Turkish workers were among those who were least affected by the measures in question. The explanations that she put forward still seem to be partly true today. However, in the absence of comparable statistical data covering the two periods, it is essential to proceed very cautiously when noting the occurrence of apparently identical phenomena. Furthermore, the statistics may conflict with each other according to whether the figures under review were obtained from Turkey or from the immigration countries. In this connection, when the different unemployment rates are compared we see how difficult it is to use sources of statistical material.

According to the figures provided by the study on the Federal Republic of Germany, the unemployment rate for foreigners was 4.9 per cent in 1977—roughly the same as the rate for nationals. Yet the figures obtained in Turkey from the National Labour Office give an unemployment rate for Turks in the Federal Republic of Germany of about 3 per cent. A hiatus becomes apparent when we know that the national studies show that 'the unemployed are not evenly distributed by nationality: North Africans and Turks are the most affected'.[6] Thus, according to the figures not obtained from Turkey, the unemployment rate for Turkish nationals should be higher than 4.9 per cent in the Federal Republic of Germany, whereas the figures provided by the Turkish authorities point to an unemployment rate of only 3 per cent. This example is symptomatic of statistical discrepancies and of the difficulty of interpreting data taken from different sources. These divergences are due mainly to the fact that the populations covered are not necessarily the same and that the concepts used do not necessarily correspond to the same reality.

In any event, the unemployment rate of Turks abroad is undoubtedly higher today than it was at the beginning of the 1970s. Yet, far from

TABLE 4. Migratory flows and active population abroad

| Year | Active population abroad | Departures | | | Total returns |
		Total	Emigrants intending to take up employment	Tourists	
1972	648 850	802 635	663 520	73 925	699 820
1973	762 400	843 741	773 951	105 364	838 235
1974	758 400	1 011 444	782 371	178 939	1 041 764
1975	710 000	1 116 216	734 978	224 187	1 160 482
1976	707 900	1 158 339	628 099	343 755	1 054 961
1977	715 047	—	—	—	—

Source: Republic of Turkey, *Tourism Statistics 1976*, Ankara, Prime Ministry State Institute of Statistics, 1978.

leading to an increase in the number of returning migrants, this state of affairs has resulted in a decline in the number of seasonal trips to Turkey. Fearful of being laid off during their absence, those workers who have jobs prefer to forgo their holidays, especially as they can thereby earn more money, which is an absolute priority for them, since they are uncertain as to whether they will be able to keep their jobs. As for the unemployed, they prefer to stay abroad to look for a job and not to run the risk of being turned back at the frontier when they travel back, jobless, to their host country.

Table 4 shows quite clearly that the decrease in the active Turkish population abroad is not very pronounced. The size of that population even increased in 1977 (the last year for which figures are available), attaining 715,047. In addition, the total number of returns was lower in 1975 and 1976 than the total number of departures. It should be noted that this increase in departures from 1974 onwards is not due, officially, to decisions taken by workers, since the number of persons registered as such has very definitely declined owing to the reduction in the number of workers officially recruited by the immigration countries. On the other hand, the number of tourists has very appreciably increased, since it rose from 73,925 in 1972 to 343,755 in 1976. It is obvious that a number of these 'tourists' are in fact migrants who gain entry in this way to countries that have closed their frontiers to immigration. It is difficult, however, to assess the relative proportions of 'true' and 'false' tourists.

The breakdown of total returns, as shown for 1976 in Figure 1 (from Republic of Turkey, *Tourism Statistics 1976*, Ankara, Prime Ministry State Institute of Statistics, 1978) yields some highly interesting information concerning the composition of the return flow. Out of a

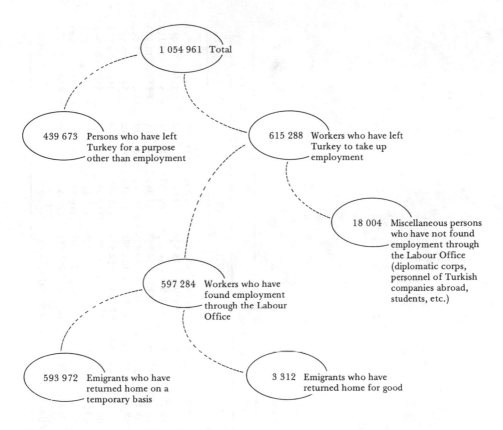

FIG. 1. Breakdown of total returns in 1976.

total of 1,054,961 returning migrants, 597,284 were workers who had found employment through the National Labour Office. According to statements made by the migrants on their return, 593,972 were intending to leave again, while only 3,312 workers considered that they had come back for good. It is difficult, of course, to gauge the accuracy of this type of data, since it is practically impossible to know how many of these 're-migrants' actually left again and how long their 'temporary' stay lasted. However, these figures are an invaluable guide to the intentions of migrants which indisputably reflect their job situation. There is every reason to suppose that those who express a desire to leave again have a job to return to abroad or have a good chance of obtaining one. This hypothesis is based on two facts. First, a comparison of the monthly statistics of inward and outward flows (Tables 5 and 6) shows that the highest figures for returns are recorded at the time of the annual holidays—Christmas and the months of June, July and August—whereas the highest figures for departures are recorded in January and in July, August and September. Moreover, the figures for returns and those for

TABLE 5. Turkish nationals leaving Turkey, by month of departure

Year	Total	Month											
		I	II	III	IV	V	VI	VII	VIII	IX	X	XI	XII
1966	155 293	6 487	7 407	37 280	9 938	9 999	7 991	14 452	22 612	16 269	10 189	7 045	5 624
1967	130 140	6 413	13 736	10 471	8 003	8 769	8 853	13 589	25 584	12 967	8 752	7 516	5 487
1968	186 449	4 725	36 804	8 882	10 937	10 261	8 949	20 906	31 033	19 908	13 321	10 570	10 153
1969	270 417	12 632	38 545	17 038	14 197	12 836	15 956	21 581	51 698	34 355	22 611	14 585	14 383
1970	515 992	60 815	25 184	30 005	34 614	31 109	38 167	41 504	80 939	75 519	40 719	29 470	27 947
1971	559 786	47 543	35 544	46 776	35 891	28 040	35 631	45 816	104 882	72 283	53 222	27 628	26 530
1972	802 635	54 300	41 913	90 737	45 503	34 046	42 394	67 769	152 534	111 338	64 030	43 316	54 755
1973	943 741	62 127	69 104	77 760	45 623	48 732	57 789	82 719	169 726	117 033	72 817	59 348	80 963
1974	1 011 444	71 046	70 365	62 494	42 489	48 929	53 950	90 051	246 736	128 419	73 222	71 508	52 235
1975	1 116 216	114 959	74 034	66 324	46 437	65 318	68 764	116 310	198 196	119 720	103 275	77 589	65 290
1976	1 158 339	130 256	72 723	65 686	61 408	70 270	84 619	130 854	162 853	120 462	120 304	65 820	73 084

Source: Republic of Turkey, *Tourism Statistics 1976*, Ankara, Prime Ministry State Institute of Statistics, 1978.

TABLE 6. Turkish nationals returning to Turkey, by month of arrival

Year	Total	I	II	III	IV	V	VI	VII	VIII	IX	X	XI	XII
1966	214 701	13 140	6 341	15 271	29 607	10 357	10 974	33 054	23 935	16 531	12 700	12 999	29 792
1967	210 036	10 621	8 659	22 625	18 942	14 660	14 706	37 606	23 701	18 490	11 242	9 640	19 144
1968	191 985	5 832	7 275	25 860	9 815	12 571	12 316	40 140	24 872	15 107	11 238	11 264	15 695
1969	266 888	7 368	9 344	31 385	13 328	14 895	19 874	54 331	33 548	20 378	13 643	14 503	34 291
1970	444 799	14 998	57 512	24 823	18 433	24 596	26 269	93 516	54 455	30 310	22 819	25 171	51 897
1971	498 874	32 739	31 607	20 157	21 124	29 490	20 267	104 987	65 212	34 524	32 287	31 370	75 110
1972	699 820	38 940	39 807	36 489	31 325	28 197	48 696	159 395	91 786	59 029	38 365	28 758	99 033
1973	838 235	55 236	38 719	36 498	36 953	41 277	67 829	189 964	81 912	63 687	49 381	38 335	138 444
1974	1 041 764	65 524	35 012	48 695	44 066	51 737	63 549	279 900	116 626	71 275	59 816	53 057	152 507
1975	1 160 482	43 079	48 586	65 511	55 533	80 158	106 891	217 188	133 205	102 886	76 184	64 349	166 912
1976	1 054 961	52 244	53 494	60 703	68 615	70 647	104 364	159 760	139 413	111 173	63 581	61 654	109 313

Source: Republic of Turkey, *Tourism Statistics 1976*, Ankara, Prime Ministry State Institute of Statistics, 1978.

departures are found to be very much the same. True, we may ask whether they really are the same migrants who leave again to go abroad. In order to answer this question, we must take into consideration a factor which, furthermore, is the second reason for our initial hypothesis, namely, the regulations of the immigration countries. As has been shown by the five country studies, foreigners are forbidden to enter the territories of those countries in order to look for work (except when they are nationals of EEC countries going to other EEC countries). In addition, since it is necessary to hold a work permit—and consequently a job—in order to be issued with a residence permit, only those workers who possess the necessary papers, or who know that they can obtain them, will go back to the host country. As the number of new work permits issued in Europe is minimal, it is clearly the same workers who leave again.

We should not, of course, overestimate the significance of such figures. The fact remains, however, that, in the absence of more precise statistics, Tables 5 and 6 give an idea of the volume and pattern of migratory flows.[7] Moreover, it is regrettable that the broken-down statistics which are available stop at the year 1976, because it is not possible, for that reason, to discern with any certainty the later trends in departures and returns. We gathered, however, from our conversations with one of the directors of the Institute of Statistics,[8] that few changes have occurred since the end of the 1970s. This fact was confirmed for us by the Chief of the Social Affairs Division of the Turkish Planning Organization.[9]

The Turkish immigrant and the economic crisis

The survey by N. Abadan already referred to showed that Turkish workers were 'affected to a minimum'[10] by the 1966–67 recession. This does not by any means signify that the German authorities did not apply a restrictive immigration policy or that the firms employing Turkish workers did not lay off large numbers. The phenomenon may be explained, in reality, by the specific political, social and economic characteristics of the Turkish immigrant population and of its origins.

A statement of this kind should be approached with extreme caution, however, because, on the one hand, it is not based on studies conducted with a view to checking such a hypothesis and, on the other hand, it tends to subjectivize and isolate a phenomenon that is normally tied up with the whole complex of problems relating to immigration and returning immigrants. What we should seek to do here, then, is not to reduce the situation prevailing in Turkey to a series of epiphenomena and deny the existence of a world economic order that is unfavourable to Turkey, but rather to bring out the specific character of the Turkish model. Since the purpose of this study is not to present firm conclusions, we shall set out in a simplified form the reasons that seem to us to explain the small number of immigrant workers who return home to Turkey.

The public image of the Turkish worker abroad

It is a fact that, in the major immigration countries, the Turkish worker enjoys a good reputation with employers. As is pointed out by N. Abadan, the Turks are credited with 'not joining trade unions, not making any demands, having acquired a strong sense of discipline in their work, and being content with very modest accommodation'.[11]

Accordingly, a Turkish worker who has lost his job has a relatively better chance of finding employment in another factory—or even in another economic sector—than an immigrant of another nationality, except for nationals of EEC countries. (In this context, it would be desirable to study the horizontal occupational mobility of Turkish workers.) Moreover, German industry is well established in Turkey and, as a result, it may often happen that North African, Spanish or Portuguese nationals are laid off before the Turks, or that the latter are the first to be taken on again in the event of a recovery of economic activity. There is no need to dwell on the ambiguity of this 'public image' of the Turkish worker, but it is necessary to bring out the fact that this 'privilege' goes hand in hand with an infra-legal status that can be accepted by Turks only because of their country's very difficult economic situation, which makes them see that they have no alternative but to keep their jobs abroad.

The sense of solidarity among the immigrant Turkish population

Generally speaking, immigrant communities of all nationalities display a sense of solidarity. However, in the case of the Turks, the fact that they are highly concentrated in certain countries—and, within those countries, in certain sectors of activity—may intensify the effect of this spirit of solidarity in periods of economic crisis. In addition, the immigrant population in each host country tends to have a homogeneous regional origin. Thus, in the case of France, 51.3 per cent of the Turkish immigrants are from central Anatolia, whereas in the Federal Republic of Germany, 45 per cent are from the most industrialized region (Marmara and Aegean).[12] As regards the Netherlands, the majority of Turkish migrants seem to have come from the region of Istanbul and Thrace.[13] Lastly, it is likely that there is a greater concentration of Turks than of other nationalities in the various sectors of activity. However, we have not been able to verify this hypothesis.

In any event, a Turk who has been dismissed will seek first of all to find another job, before even thinking of going back to his country.

In the meantime, he will be able to rely on the help of his fellow countrymen as he goes from town to town in search of a new job.

Several studies have shown how well the traditional Turkish family structure based on village endogamy—which is particularly strong in Anatolia—has lent itself to the consolidation or reconstruction of networks of alliances, sometimes on new bases, among people who have been uprooted as a result of the rural exodus, or among immigrants.[14] It is not surprising, therefore, that Turkish workers in difficulty seem to receive more support from their fellow countrymen than do immigrants of certain other nationalities for whom the same types of matrimonial exchanges and the same kinship structures do not exist.

Political and economic conditions in Turkey

While the immigration countries are having to contend with an economic crisis that makes the future of immigrants in those countries uncertain, it is a noteworthy fact that for several years Turkey has been passing through an extremely difficult period from both the political and the economic standpoints. It lies outside the scope of this study to pass judgement on the political developments that have taken place in Turkey in recent years, but it is necessary to point out that these developments have had something to do with the desire of many migrants to return—or not to return—to their country of origin. The fact, for instance, that a state of siege has been declared in several provinces certainly does not encourage immigrants originating from those provinces to return home for good. This problem was often mentioned in the talks we had with several migrants who had temporarily returned to their country for the holidays.

To this should be added the fact that the Turkish lira has proved to be very unstable in recent years. Thus, between April 1979 and January 1980, the Turkish lira was devalued by about 107 per cent! As for inflation, it has been steadily increasing: retail prices are reported to have risen by approximately 53 per cent in 1979 in the Ankara region (44.5 per cent in 1977 and 42.03 per cent in 1978).[15] As regards the prices of raw materials and semi-manufactured goods, the rate of inflation was as high as 70.52 per cent in 1978.[16] In these circumstances, it is easy to understand why those immigrants who have accumulated savings abroad hesitate to return to Turkey and invest their money in the Turkish economy. It must be emphasized that the Turkish authorities started at a very early date to look into the problem of emigrants' savings and endeavoured to set up various schemes designed to attract those savings back to Turkey. These attempts will be examined in a later section.

The social significance of the return of migrants

The way in which a migrant approaches the possibility of returning home depends not only on his original plan but also on the degree to which he has been integrated into the society of the immigration country. Thus, the first and second generations of immigrants will have totally different attitudes towards the prospect of returning to their country of origin.

In the case of Turkey, it should be noted that the second generation consists of very young people because the immigration of Turkish workers is a recent development, in contrast to Algerian immigration into France, for example. This applies to the second generation in the strict sense of the term. But we must also take into account those young people born in Turkey who have come to join their parents, having availed themselves of the facilities for the reuniting of families that were provided for a time under certain laws. As we might expect, these young people are less well integrated than those born in the host country. The way in which they view the possibility of returning home may therefore differ quite appreciably from that of their own parents. It should not be inferred from this, however, that the inclination to return home grows in inverse proportion to the degree of integration. Thus, a sample survey of young North Africans has revealed that 'the more educated young people are, the more they express an inclination to leave (for young people who have not attained a high level of training do not have the same hopes of advancement)'.[17] This sentence is important, for it makes it clear that the basic condition for returning home is in fact the hope of advancement. But, as we have already observed, the political and economic conditions prevailing at present do not appear conducive to a harmonious re-integration of 're-migrants', who prefer therefore to stay abroad and wait until the time is ripe. It is possible, however, that the time will never be ripe and that the plan for returning home will never progress beyond the stage of day-dreaming. This is certainly the reason for a marked tendency among immigrants to stay much longer.

In these circumstances, only those who are forced to return will do so. In many cases the return home will be regarded as tantamount to failure. Admittedly, external reasons may justify the decision to return. For instance, the immigrant worker may be ill or there may be family difficulties, but even these causes are viewed, to some extent, as evidence of a weakness in the migratory plan of the worker who is obliged to return from abroad. This tendency is particularly strong since many of the people who are thus forced to return home find themselves in this situation in the early years, and even in the early months, of their experience of immigration. A survey conducted in Turkey in 1975, in the district of Bogazliyan, showed that 're-migrants' were those among

TABLE 7. Length of time spent abroad by the resident immigrant population as compared with the immigrant population that has returned to Turkey

Length of stay	Returned migrants (%)	Residents abroad (%)
Less than 6 months	4.7	0.3
6 months to 1 year	3.9	4.0
1–2 years	11.8	8.6
2–3 years	18.1	9.6
3–4 years	15.0	9.1
4–5 years	14.2	13.4
5–6 years	11.8	12.1
6–7 years	3.1	12.6
More than 7 years	15.0	30.3
No reply	2.4	—
TOTAL	100.0	100.0

Source: Republic of Turkey, *Tourism Statistics 1976*, p. 190, Ankara, Prime Ministry State Institute of Statistics, 1978.

the emigrants who stayed abroad for the shortest period.[18] It also revealed that 27.6 per cent of them had returned for health reasons, while 24.4 per cent said they had done so for family reasons. This phenomenon is a constant one and is observed among other nationalities. A study carried out in Yugoslavia, in 1970, revealed that 'those who expect to stay abroad the longest are those who have already spent the longest periods there'.[19] There would thus appear to be a 'gradual change in the intentions of emigrants concerning their return home'.[20] These findings of the study on Yugoslavia seem to tally fairly well with our field observations in Turkey.

In conclusion to this section, we must lay stress on a factor which weighs heavily with a migrant when he is deciding whether or not to return to his country of origin and which makes all the difference between a return perceived as failure and a return perceived as success. An immigrant's ideal objective in returning to his country is to benefit from social advancement, and this is bound up with the possibility of having a job in which he will be his own master and which will provide him with an income comparable to what he was earning abroad.[21] The economic consequences of the behaviour prompted by this objective will be examined below. But we must emphasize here that the deterioration of economic conditions in Turkey makes a migrant's chances of achieving this objective more and more remote and more and more unfavourable. Accordingly, the hope of social advancement should be regarded as one of the important factors contributing, on the one hand, to the tendency to stay longer abroad and, on the other, to the immigrant's feeling, after he has returned home in spite of his hesitations, that he has been unsuccessful, in so far as his actual experience does not correspond to the imaginary world on which his migratory plan has been founded.

It is precisely in order to enable immigrants to return to their home country and to take up an economic activity both satisfying their aspirations and profitable to the Turkish economy that the authorities have tried to establish schemes designed to attract immigrants and, together with them, the capital in foreign exchange that they may have accumulated.

The Turkish model for the re-integration of emigrants

Action taken by the Turkish authorities

The development co-operatives

At the beginning of the 1960s the Turkish authorities became aware of the economic stakes represented for the country by the migratory flow that had just begun. Turning to account the attractiveness of emigration for the Turks, they set up a system of development co-operatives in 1964. People who paid a subscription to these co-operatives and thus became members were given priority if they wished to emigrate.[22] The basic idea was that these workers, once they had emigrated, would invest their savings in these co-operatives and would thus be sure of employment on their return to Turkey. The link between these emigrants and the development co-operative was maintained by the emigrants' obligation to pay a contribution to the co-operative at regular intervals. The amount of the contribution was sufficiently high to ensure that a migrant who had started to invest in a co-operative never lost interest in the scheme.

However, these co-operatives were very soon looked upon as an excellent means of obtaining the right to emigrate. Of the hundreds that were set up, few represented anything more than a bundle of administrative documents. In addition, it proved extremely difficult to collect contributions, so that, in the event, the results of this experiment never measured up to the expectations of the Turkish authorities. The main aim, which was to tap the savings of emigrants, was never achieved. For instance, some ten years after the co-operatives had been established, the average accumulated amount of the individual contributions stood no higher (over the period 1965–73) than 3,298 Turkish lira, as compared with an average amount of remittances standing at 17,400 lira over the same period.[23] Furthermore, the number of persons applying to emigrate increased so much that the anticipated quotas were greatly exceeded.

The workers' joint-stock companies

Originally, these companies were founded spontaneously and were created exclusively on the initiative of private individuals. They were formed, in fact, by three possible methods.[24] According to the first, workers from the same region and employed in the same firm decided to pool a certain amount of money in order to invest in Turkey and thereby set up a business with equipment purchased abroad. After a few attempts of this type had been made, Turkish scouts travelled deliberately to the emigrants' places of work for the purpose of collecting their savings and establishing a business of that type. Unfortunately, a swarm of confidence-tricksters took advantage of the credulity of some workers, who were thereby divested of large sums of money. The third method seems to have given the best results. The first step was taken by members of the Turkish élite living abroad—students or businessmen—who offered to collect the savings of migrants according to a well-constructed plan, the objectives of which were far more precise and realistic than those of the immigrants themselves. As a general rule, two types of shares were offered to those who were interested: the first category could be bought only with foreign currency while the second could be bought with Turkish lira.

At the end of the 1960s the Turkish authorities and the authorities of the Federal Republic of Germany began to take an interest in these initiatives: the former regarded them as a means of channelling savings to Turkey, and the latter saw that they could be used to encourage immigrant workers to return home, while, so it was believed, creating the conditions for their re-integration in the country of origin. An agreement was signed in Ankara on 7 December 1972 (the Ankara Agreement). This agreement provided for the establishment of two complementary sets of measures designed to encourage the return and re-integration of immigrants. The first consisted in making vocational training facilities available for immigrants. But this arrangement did not meet with much success because very few immigrants knew enough German to follow the training courses to good advantage. Furthermore, the content of those courses did not seem to be in keeping with the real needs of the immigrants, but rather with what had seemed desirable to the authorities.

The second part of the agreement was more successful, however. The main concern was to promote and assist these workers' companies with a view to making them into the best instrument for implementing a policy for encouraging the return of emigrants and developing the

Turkish economy. To this end, very thorough studies were carried out by the Institut für Entwicklungsforschung und Sozial Planung GmbH (ISOPLAN) in order to determine the nature and potentialities of these workers' companies. A joint fund was set up for the purpose of helping to finance the workers' companies.

Today, this plan has progressed and a provisional evaluation can be made.

The basic aim of the system set up by the Turkish authorities is to promote regional development and the development of certain economic sectors by channelling and optimizing the savings of emigrant workers. To this effect, a front-line role has been assigned to the State Industry and Labourer Investment Bank (DESIYAB), which was established on 27 November 1975. The special aims of this bank, which is responsible for promoting the development and industrialization of Turkey, are to 'transform domestic savings and particularly the savings of migrant workers into economic power' and to 'channel these savings towards profitable and effective investments, particularly in the industrial sector'.[25] The following information has been drawn from the DESIYAB annual report for 1978.

The great importance attached by the authorities to the workers' companies is highlighted by the fact that they are considered to be the 'third dimension of the economy'. These companies were defined as follows in the Annual Development Programme for 1979: (a) the individual shares of small savers may not exceed 2 per cent of the total capital; (b) at least 80 per cent of any private individual's shares must be taken out in his name; (c) no preferential shares are issued; (d) at least 40 per cent of the total amount of shares issued must return, in the future, to the public sector and to savers; and (e) these investment companies must comprise at least 300 shareholders.

DESIYAB's action takes several forms: (a) allocation of funds, in accordance with the evaluation made of the project and with the directives of the plan; (b) identification of profitable investment areas, in accordance with the objectives of the plan and the annual programme; (c) preparation of feasibility studies; (d) preparation of projects; (e) assistance for the efforts required in order to make suitable investments and settle any operational problem; (f) training of management personnel; (g) additional financing; and (h) utilization of foreign currency paid in by migrants in order to import machinery and equipment to be supplied to the companies.

As can be seen, this bank's activities cover all the operations that have to be carried through before a company project can materialize. Such a degree of centralization—which represents a considerable saving of time and energy—is exceptional in Turkey. By the end of 1978, sixty-six projects had been accepted by DESIYAB and were under way, as is shown in Table 8.

TABLE 8. Analysis and studies of projects by DESIYAB in 1976, 1977 and 1978

Year	Number of applications	Applications outstanding from previous year	Number of revised projects	Total number of projects	Number of projects examined	Approved	Rejected	To be examined in the following year
1976	66	—	—	66	14	2	12	52
1977	115	52	4	171	121	57	64	50
1978	70	50	28	148	93	37	56	55

Source: State Industry and Labourer Investment Bank of Turkey, *Annual Report*, p. 18.

Of the thirty-seven projects that were accepted in 1978, twenty-three were carried out in regions that were to be developed on a priority basis. These projects entailed an investment of 2,589,000 lira and led to the creation of 3,290 jobs. The fourteen other projects were to be carried out in developed regions, entail an investment of 5,534,000 lira and create 3,448 jobs. The last-mentioned projects used technologies requiring intermediary goods and were capital-intensive, whereas the projects to be carried out in the underdeveloped regions were slanted mainly towards the production of consumer goods and were labour-intensive.

In 1978, the Turko-German joint fund was used for the first time and 25,632,000 lira were thus loaned to workers' joint-stock companies.

Despite its many positive aspects, this experiment is not proof against criticism. There can be no question here of undertaking an exhaustive study of the problems encountered by the companies. It is necessary, however, to consider briefly whether the basic aims that are at the origin of this system have been achieved. We are obliged to note, in the first place, that there is no direct link between the persons who hold the jobs that have been created and those who hold shares in the companies. There are at least two explanations for this. The first is the fact that hardly any emigrants return home, owing, as we have seen, to several reasons which we do not need to go over again. The second is the fact—closely linked with the previous one—that the jobs created do not satisfy the immigrants' aspirations. As we have already pointed out, immigrants aspire to be autonomous and independent and this, in their minds, is not compatible with a job that fits into an industrial process and involves submission to a hierarchy. A gulf is thus created, which is becoming steadily wider, between the shareholders and the managers on the one hand and the employees on the other. This is due to the fact that the former are resident abroad while the latter are living in Turkey, which is contrary to the aim originally pursued.

In the second place, there is an obvious disproportion between the total funds collected through these companies and, on the one hand, the total amount of remittances and, on the other, the total amount of savings accumulated abroad. If the financial resources of the thirty-seven companies founded in 1978 are broken down (see Table 8), it becomes clear that the total sum of the shares held by private individuals is 2,717,000 lira, distributed among 34,555 shareholders. These figures should be compared with the amount of the remittances sent home by migrant workers in 1978, which stood at $983 million, and with the amount of the savings accumulated abroad, which was assessed, in 1978,[26] at some DM7,000 million for the Federal Republic of Germany alone.[27]

It would be an exaggeration to regard this experiment as a failure. It is still being pursued and should, in fact, be further developed in the coming years. However, it would be a mistake to overestimate its effect on the homeward flows of men and capital.

As regards the indirect effects of the establishment of these companies, we cannot endorse the findings of a study published in 1978[28] which assesses the 'indirect employment multiplier' at 2.0–2.5 times the number of jobs directly created by these companies. It does not seem to us possible to use this notion of an employment multiplier in a country like Turkey whose economic structures are very far from resembling those of a developed country. Nor do we know of any statistics that would enable us to check such a statement. Furthermore, the talks which we were fortunate enough to have with economic programme officers and trade-union officials impressed upon us the importance of approaching this subject very prudently. At all events, it would be highly desirable to do some thorough macro-economic research in this field.

Returning migrants and development

Countless studies establish a close link between emigration and development, laying emphasis on the argument that emigrants acquire better qualifications abroad and use them in the service of their country of origin when they return home. At the same time it is asserted that the savings accumulated abroad contribute to the economic development of the village, town or even region in which the migrant settles when he returns from abroad. In reality, however, the situation is not quite so satisfactory, and the migrant's return, when in fact he does return, is not always beneficial to his home country. Sometimes even the opposite is true.

Returning migrants and professional qualifications

As already stated, Turkey sends more skilled workers abroad than are actually employed there. We are forced to the conclusion that the job held by an immigrant does not necessarily match the qualifications that he possessed when he left Turkey. Consequently, the most highly qualified of the workers who go abroad have to submit to the law of supply and demand on the labour market. As a general rule, it is clear that the supply situation is not favourable to them. As for the unskilled workers, it might seem reasonable to hope that emigration would be their opportunity to come into contact with the industrial world and thereby gain not only a worthwhile personal experience but also, and most important, better qualifications. This would betray one's ignorance of the living and working conditions that are offered to immigrant workers. All too often, the migrant is excluded from the national life of the host country. First of all, his unfamiliarity with the language contributes to his isolation. Then the difficulties of every kind that he encounters keep him even longer inside a ghetto that he will find very hard to leave. This 'ghettoization' has become more pronounced since the slump of the 1970s, for a very large number of Turks do paid work but do not possess a work permit and are consequently at the mercy of unscrupulous employers who do not hesitate to take advantage of their precarious situation in order to exploit them to the hilt. The strike movement in France in February 1980, which was started by certain Turkish workers employed in illicit sewing shops, tells us a great deal about the infra-legal situations in which immigrants may find themselves. In addition, immigrants are always more interested in adding to their savings than in attending a vocational training course whose purpose they do not clearly understand. In many cases, a worker with spare time at his disposal therefore prefers to use it to earn overtime pay rather than devote it to vocational training courses, particularly since his poor knowledge of the foreign language does not make it easy for him to follow such courses. The training experiment tried out by the authorities in the Federal Republic of Germany, under the Ankara Agreement, and its poor success show that there is indeed a gulf between the arrangements that may be made for a migrant's benefit and the latter's own priorities, which are determined by his migratory plan.

In the last analysis, there are three reasons why immigration is not a profitable experience as regards professional qualifications. First, the fact that the migrant is relegated to the fringes of society prevents him from following the paths traditionally open to the host country's workers who wish to obtain vocational training. Second, the migrant's prime objective is to practise an independent and preferably non-manual occupation after he has returned to his country. Third, all vocational training, including on-the-job training, is geared to an overdeveloped and highly technical industrial society that the migrant will not find waiting for him when he returns to Turkey. There is no such thing as a transfer of technology that can be attributed to the emigrant worker's return to his country of origin. The industrial structure of Turkey is not comparable to that of France, the Netherlands or the Federal Republic of Germany. There is no continuity between the occupation practised by an emigrant in the host country and the occupation which may be practised in the country to which he returns, especially as a 're-migrant' is generally a man over 40 who would have great difficulty in finding another job in a factory—assuming that he wanted to do so—at a time when there are more than 2 million unemployed out of an active population of 16.4 million persons. Consequently, it hardly seems to be the rule for migrants to be re-integrated into the productive process and still less do they seem to use the knowledge acquired abroad. From this point of view, nothing can be gained from emigration.

Returning migrants and the way they use their savings

'The confrontation between two ways of life, underdevelopment and chronic unemployment, on the one hand, and advanced technology and neo-capitalism, on the other, produces a type of immigrant worker who aspires to become his own boss.' This statement by N. Abadan sums up fairly well both the situation in which the immigrant finds himself and his deep-seated aspiration. The idea of being one's own boss seems to us very characteristic of the 're-migrant' and his place on the social ladder. When he returns home, the immigrant worker will seek to mark himself off socially from his class of origin. In this way there comes into being a new 'élite' which, although lacking initially the political influence or cultural background of the local notables, none the less possesses a measure of economic power and a measure of prestige. This social advancement depends on the success of the migratory venture and, more specifically, on the act of returning from abroad with the foreign exchange and consumer goods which are symbols of success.

There then arises the problem of how the migrant is to use the savings he has accumulated during his stay abroad.

The predominant characteristic of these investments is their disturbing impact on the Turkish economy. A brief review of the main sectors which attract the capital of migrants will show very clearly that these 'wildcat investments' have undesirable effects upon all the sectors considered.

Agriculture

Turks have a stronger urge to buy land than other migrants (see Table 9). This is no doubt a consequence of the distribution and rural origin of the Turkish population. About 68 per cent of the active population work in the agricultural sector, which accounts for 26 per cent of the GNP.[29] However, relatively large purchases of land have stimulated speculation in certain regions, resulting in a steep increase in prices at the expense of peasants who have not emigrated. Many 're-migrants' have also invested in farming equipment, and in this they are encouraged by Turkish legislation that exempts workers returning home with foreign material from the payment of customs duties. In addition, various subsidies are granted in order to promote investment in the agricultural sector. But such investments have often had untoward effects. For instance, in some regions agricultural equipment is plentiful while in others it is in short supply. In other cases, for want of adequate maintenance or spare parts, the equipment remains idle for months at a time or even becomes quite unusable. Admittedly, these are borderline cases, but they are not uncommon. Furthermore, the intensive mechanization of certain agricultural regions has had the effect of considerably tightening the labour market and increasing rural unemployment and at the same time the numbers of people drifting to the towns.

Building

Since the ultimate aim of the migratory plan is to improve the social status of the emigrant and his family, it is logical that a large proportion of his capital should very often be invested in the purchase of a house, in the construction of a new one or the renovation of an old one. A fine dwelling, in particular, reflects the social status of the owner and also constitutes a sound investment. However, although the building industry has greatly benefited from the migrants' tendency to put their savings into construction projects, such investments are not very productive and prove to be very costly in social terms, particularly in urban centres. The rampant speculation in land which is prevalent in Turkey today is not confined to rural areas—far from it. The skyrocketing prices of building plots have the effect of driving people who want to buy land farther and farther away from the town centres. For this reason, most new buildings are situated in outlying quarters, often at a very great distance from zones equipped with modern facilities and public services. The urbanization of these areas—when it occurs—turns out to be very costly to the community. A. Gokalp has described very well the relationship which exists between investment in the building sector and its consequences for investment in the transport sector. This brings us to the third of the areas in which migrants prefer to invest their savings—the small businesses which spring up particularly rapidly in the services sector.

Small independent businesses

A. Gokalp's analysis of the proliferation of small transport services run by private individuals and its parasitical effect seems judicious and certainly serves as an example. The need for public transport is made even more acute by uncontrolled urbanization. In the face of the short-comings of the public authorities and, particularly, their inability to deal quickly with the critical problems of infrastructure raised by uncontrolled urbanization, it is natural that 'the missing transport should be supplied by an immediately profitable chain of minibuses imported by immigrants'.[30] But not only does this type of activity involve imports, and hence a drain on Turkey's foreign exchange; another drawback is that 'the consumption of energy, which is multiplied in proportion to the number of such vehicles in circulation, in the absence of public transport facilities, represents a further expenditure of foreign exchange for Turkey, which is not an oil-producing country'.[31] What is more, such businesses are extremely vulnerable, both to changing economic conditions and to the manœuvres of mafias and other racketeers. These behaviour patterns, which are motivated purely by the certainty of making a quick profit, are economically absurd and result in the squandering of large amounts foreign exchange.

The purchase of consumer goods

Here again, the desire to possess external signs of wealth induces the 're-migrant' to acquire a whole array of consumer goods that are hard come by and expensive in Turkey. In addition, material produced abroad has to be bought for many small non-productive businesses, the case of the minibuses being but one example. This type of behaviour consequently stimulates the demand for goods that are not locally produced and it has destabilizing and inflationary effects, since the demand is not only for scarce goods but also for imported ones. This last point highlights the strategic importance of the capital accumulated by migrants abroad. If its movements could be brought under control, it would be possible to avoid not only flagrant wastage but also the pernicious effects on the economy of the migrants' injudicious use of their capital.

TABLE 9. Purpose to be served by savings accumulated abroad (percentages)

Purpose	Turks	Yugoslavs	Greeks
Consumer goods	33.0	49.4	40.3
Housing	44.7	51.7	54.0
Land	15.0	9.5	8.4
Setting up one's own business	29.7	10.4	22.8
Purchase of shares in a company	7.7	4.4	4.7
Other uses	2.2	1.3	—

Source: ISOPLAN 1974, quoted by Werth and Yalcintas, *Migration and Re-integration*, Working Paper, Geneva, ILO, June 1978.

Returning migrants and the modification of social structures

There can be no doubt that the migratory process has significant effects on the social structures and behaviour patterns of the emigrants' country of origin. These effects are not produced solely by the return of migrants, for emigration in itself disturbs many habits and changes particularly the distribution of roles within village communities and families.

Family immigration is also a decisive factor in the modification of social behaviour: contact with the industrial world and the consumer society alters habits inherited from a radically different type of society.

Learning about industrial relations and political life in the West should also have important consequences for the political socialization of migrants.

Lastly, when migrants come back home, the new behaviour patterns learnt in Europe should, in their turn, have some influence on Turkey's socio-political structures.

Yet, the studies that have been carried out on this subject, as we noted during our stay in Turkey, insist on the complexity of the problem and, at any event, make it impossible to conclude that there exists an obvious relationship between the migratory process and changes in the socio-political attitudes of migrants. While the modification of family structures seems to be an indisputable fact, it is still extremely difficult to judge how deeply and widely they have been altered.

These phenomena cannot be described and analysed without undertaking a thorough qualitative study, which falls well outside the scope of our essentially quantitative survey. We shall quote a few examples, however, in order to illustrate the complexity of these problems.

The first question to discuss is how far emigration is conducive to political socialization. The common belief that living abroad is a school for political participation is challenged by the conclusions of a highly interesting survey conducted by Ayse Kudat,[32] who stresses that 'the international migration of Turkish workers leads to the development of a group of non-politicized persons'.[33] Similarly, the belief that emigration is conducive to class consciousness is challenged by the conclusions of a large number of studies and in particular one of those carried out by Kudat and Abadan.

The effects of immigration on the family structure and family roles are very varied and may be analysed at several levels and at several stages of the migratory experience: before the emigrant's departure, the question is to identify the family pressures that induce the worker to go abroad; during emigration, it is necessary to know what new roles are assigned to wives and how they fulfil them, and when emigrant workers are joined by their families the question is to see how the host society will influence family behaviour patterns and alter the traditional structure of the family; lastly, when the migrant returns home, we have to consider to what extent the changes in behaviour patterns that have occurred abroad are permanent and how these new ways of behaving will in their turn influence Turkish society.[34]

However, it should not be forgotten that the significance of the socio-political effects of emigration depends largely on the return of migrants. Accordingly, we should not overestimate those effects as long as the homeward flows remain fairly weak. Nor, of course, should we underestimate those effects, and least of all the indirect consequences of the migratory process. It is precisely at this level that we encounter one of the major difficulties in the way of any attempt to ascertain how social structures in Turkey have been modified by the migratory phenomenon.

Conclusion

As we made clear in our introduction, there could be no question in this study of dealing exhaustively with all the issues raised by the return of migrants to Turkey. Nor was it possible to formulate all those issues, but it was necessary at least to highlight the main facts relating to the problem of the migrants' return home.

The first conclusion that must be drawn from this all too short study is the following: there is a wide gulf between the reality of the Turkish model and the many studies that have been devoted to the return of migrants in general. The Turkish model has its own specific features and it is difficult and artificial to seek at all costs to fit this model into a general theory about the return of emigrant workers. On the other hand, this specificness should not be pleaded as a reason for denying the value of the Turkish experience, which is of course part of the international division of labour.

Furthermore, as an emigration country, Turkey shares numerous characteristics with a large number of other labour-exporting countries. We can therefore say that many of the findings of this study hold good for other emigration countries. Since the migration problem is an international one, the solution must be international as well. It would be an illusion to think that the authorities of the emigration country can control the migratory phenomenon unaided. The reason why no migrants, or very few, return to Turkey lies precisely in the fact that the country is wrestling with one of the most serious economic and political crises that it has ever known. Furthermore, we must not be misled by the purely domestic character of the political disturbances. These are caused by the catastrophic deterioration of economic conditions in Turkey, which is happening in an international context.

A very large number of emigration countries are in exactly the same position. In this field, more perhaps than in any other, the political dimension is subordinate to the economic, but there is also the human dimension which must not be ignored.

In the final analysis, it is quite clear that the immigrant worker is thought of primarily as an economic factor both by the host country and by his country of origin. The migrant has virtually no status, neither in his homeland nor abroad. The ultimate aim of his migratory plan is, in fact, to raise himself to the envied status of the people described in Turkey, significantly enough, as the *Almanyali*, that is to say the migrants who come back from Germany and who, although not very cultivated, are very rich. As long as they have no reasonable hope of attaining the desired status, the emigrant and his family will stay abroad. As their stay lengthens, intolerable living and working conditions—which were accepted only because they were regarded as temporary—assume a permanent character and trap the immigrant in an infra-legal situation in which he is exploited, so that he is even further away from being able to carry out his plan for returning home.

The last conclusion we shall draw from our study concerns the state of research in this field. There is a shortage of the scientific data needed to understand all the aspects of the migratory chain in Turkey. This shortage is dangerous, for it leads people to underestimate the difficulties that may be encountered when steps are taken to reduce the undesirable effects of emigration or to control homeward flows and facilitate the return of migrants to their country of origin. In fact, it must be acknowledged that the absence of a comprehensive emigration policy in Turkey is due not so much to a lack of interest (quite the contrary!) as to a lack of exhaustive recent information. It is clear that in order to bring the migratory phenomenon under control it is necessary, first and foremost, to know the facts of the problem. In this area, it seems to us that international organizations, and especially Unesco, have an essential role to play, in particular by encouraging and financing field research, which should be entrusted to national research workers. Indeed, it will not be possible to find solutions to the problems created by the migratory phenomenon unless more is known about this subject, which is of capital importance for emigration countries.

Notes

1. Turkish Planning Organization, *First Five-Year Development Plan*, p. 410, 1963.
2. See Table 11 in the chapter on France.
3. 39,921 skilled workers, 19,206 unskilled (National Labour Office, Ankara).
4. Nermin Abadan-Unat, 'La récession de 1966–67 en Allemagne Fédérale et ses répercussions sur les ouvriers turcs', *Türk Yilligi* (Ankara), Vol. XI, 1971, pp. 38–61.

5. Ibid., p. 41.
6. See 'Summing Up and Points of Comparison', pp. 230–1.
7. Turkey's lack of the financial resources needed in order to carry out exhaustive statistical studies on the Turkish emigrant population is a major obstacle to any attempt to analyse and understand the Turkish migratory phenomenon.
8. Rahmi Ulu.
9. Mete Törüner.
10. Abadan-Unat, op. cit., p. 44.
11. Ibid., p. 47.
12. Altan Gokalp, *Le comportement de transfert des travailleurs immigrés turcs*, p. 137, Paris, FNSP, SEAE, 1977.
13. We must draw attention, in this connection, to the unsoundness of the theory that the majority of immigrants originate from the most disadvantaged areas and that, consequently, immigration offers a demographic solution to the problem of rural unemployment and underemployment. We shall return to this point.
14. Gokalp, op. cit., p. 145.
15. State Industry and Labourer Investment Bank of Turkey, *Annual Report, 1978*, Ankara, 1979.
16. Ibid.
17. Study by C. Camilleri, quoted by J. Manchon, in *Analyse des facteurs favorisant ou contrariant le retour à la fois dans les pays d'origine et les pays d'accueil.*
18. R. Pennix and L. van Velzen, 'Migratory Labour: Bogazliyan District', in N. Abadan et al., *Migration and Development*, pp. 189 et seq., Ankara, NUFFIC, IMWOO and Faculty of Political Science/Ajans-Türk Press, 1977, 386 pp.
19. I. Baućić, quoted by B. Kayser, in *Les retours conjoncturels des travailleurs migrants*, p. 21, Paris, OECD, 1972.
20. Ibid., p. 22.
21. The conclusions of the various studies already quoted are in agreement on this point.
22. The *Kontenjan* system under which the beneficiaries were included in the immigration quotas of the host countries.
23. H. Van Renselaar and L. van Velzen, 'Public and Private Initiatives Aimed at Using External Labour Migration for Development', in Abadan et al., op. cit., pp. 99 et seq.
24. Ibid.
25. DESIYAB, *Annual Report*, op. cit., p. 7.
26. G. Rellini, 'Les politiques du retour', *Les travailleurs étrangers et le droit international*, p. 150, Paris, Éditions A. Pedone, 1979.
27. In July 1978, 100 Turkish lira were worth: U$4.22 and DM8.63.
28. Werth and Yalcintas, *Migration and Re-integration: Transferability of the Turkish Model of Return Migration and Self-help Organizations to Other Mediterranean Labour-Exporting Countries*, Working Paper, p. 24, Geneva, ILO, June 1978.
29. *Türkiye Istatistik Cep Yilligi 1978*, Ankara, Devlet Istatitisk Enstitüsü, 1979.
30. Gokalp, op. cit., p. 133.
31. Ibid.
32. Ayse Kudat, *International Migration to Europe and its Political and Social Effects on the Future of Turkish Society*, Berlin, IIM, May 1974.
33. Ibid., p. 22.
34. The reader may usefully consult N. Abadan's study, 'Implications of Migration on Emancipation and Pseudo-emancipation of Turkish Women', *International Migration Review*, Vol. 11, No. 1, Spring 1977, pp. 31–57.

Bibliography

ABADAN-UNAT, Nermin. La récession de 1966/67 en Allemagne Fédérale et ses répercussions sur les ouvriers turcs. *Türk Yilligi* (Ankara), Vol. XI, 1971, pp. 38–61.
——. Implications of Migration on Emancipation and Pseudo-emancipation of Turkish Women. *International Migration Review*, Vol. 11, No. 1, Spring 1977, pp. 31–57.
GOKALP, Altan. *Le comportement de transfert des travailleurs immigrés turcs*, Paris, FNSP, SEAE, 1977.

KUDAT, Ayse. *International Migration to Europe and its Political and Social Effects on the Future of Turkish Society*. Berlin, IIM, May 1974.

KUMBAROGLU, Sabri. *Yurtdisindaki Türk Gençlerinin Mesleki Egitimi*, Ankara, Ministry of Labour, 1979.

PENNIX, R.; VAN VELZEN, L. Migratory Labour: Bogazliyan District. In: N. Abadan et al., *Migration and Development*. Ankara, NUFFIC, IMWOO and Faculty of Political Science/Ajans-Türk Press, 1977. 386 pp.

RELLINI, G. Les politiques du retour. *Les travailleurs étrangers et le droit international*. Paris, Éditions A. Pédone, 1979.

REPUBLIC OF TURKEY. *Tourism Statistics, 1976*. Ankara, Prime Ministry State Institute of Statistics, 1978.

SAMMAN, M. *Les étrangers au recensement de 1975*. Paris, La Documentation Française, 1977.

STATE INDUSTRY AND LABOURER INVESTMENT BANK OF TURKEY. *Annual Report, 1978*. Ankara, 1979.

TURKISH PLANNING ORGANIZATION. *First Five-Year Development Plan*. 1963.

Türkiye Istatistik Cep Yilligi 1978. Ankara, Devlet Istatistik Enstitüsü, 1979.

VAN RENSELAAR, H.; VAN VELZEN, L. Public and Private Initiatives Aimed at Using External Labour Migration for Development. In: N. Abadan et al., *Migration and Development*. Ankara, NUFFIC, IMWOO and Faculty of Political Science/Ajans-Türk Press, 1977. 386 pp.

WERTH; YALCINTAS. *Migration and Re-integration: Transferability of the Turkish Model of Return Migration and Self-help Organizations to Other Mediterranean Labour-Exporting Countries*. Working Paper, Geneva, ILO, June 1978.

Summing-up
and points of comparison

Eric-Jean Thomas

Despite certain differences, the five countries dealt with in the mono-graphs contained in this work have many points in common.

They are all European countries and all belong to regional groupings —the EEC, the common Nordic labour market, Benelux—which impose constraints on them in respect of the free movement of nationals of the member countries of those communities. These constraints could not fail to influence their general immigration strategies. A European work force immigrating from countries outside the communities is distributed according to geographical, legal and political affinities.

Admittedly, the immigration pattern is not identical in the five countries. Not only the pattern of migratory flows, but also their origin, have been extremely diversified. In addition, the reactions of the host countries to the migratory phenomenon have in many cases reflected divergent politico-economic constraints and have consequently given rise to different attitudes and policies.

But, in the final analysis, the five countries are faced with the same basic issue, since they have brought all immigration to a halt and are now confronted with a large foreign population presenting specific problems which oblige them to work out special policies for their solution. Since the migrant occupies a particular place and plays a specific role in the economic structures of the host country, it is his bounden duty to raise the question of his integration into, or exclusive from, its political and social structures as well. While this question seems to have been asked, many of the answers that have been given conflict and contrast with each other.

In this chapter we propose to review these similarities and differences.

Immigration regulations

Previous trends

The attitudes towards immigration adopted by the five countries considered were for a long time determined solely by the imperatives of economic policy or by constraints inherited from the colonial past. Migrations motivated by economic pressures began really to develop only from the end of the Second World War, and it was not until the 1970s were approaching that the countries concerned attempted to draw up a proper immigration policy. France alone had worked out, as early as 1945, a policy to promote demographic growth through immigration. But the empiricism of the 1960s led to a situation closely resembling that of the other European countries with, however, the difference that France is the only European country to have really considered itself to be an immigration country. As for Belgium, Sweden, the Federal Republic of Germany and the Netherlands, it was mainly because of their great need for manpower that they were induced, in the 1950s, to open their frontiers to immigration.

At first, workers immigrated on an individual and spontaneous basis. The first to come were therefore nationals of countries traditionally linked to the receiving country. Thus, in Sweden, the number of Nordic immigrants very soon attained a very high level, and the trend was encouraged by the signing, in 1954, of a treaty instituting a common Nordic labour market. In the Federal Republic of Germany, the first immigrants came mainly from the German Democratic Republic and Italy. The situation in Belgium is a rather special one and deserves close attention. Immediately after the Second World War, when Belgium had to rebuild its economy, its nationals displayed a growing reluctance to accept work in the collieries. A systematic recruitment policy was therefore introduced and, as early as 1943, 43 per cent of the workers in that sector were immigrants. Most of them came from Italy and Poland, the countries which accounted, between 1920 and 1947, for two-thirds of the increase in the foreign population in Belgium. In France, nationals of the French Union, together with Italians, Poles and Spaniards composed the bulk of the foreign population until the late 1950s, continuing a trend that had started between the two wars. Perhaps the Netherlands was the only country which had a more diversified experience of immigration from the very beginning of the fifties, but even so migratory flows from the Dutch territories in America were predominant.

However, in order to rationalize immigration, recruitment agreements were rapidly concluded with the main labour-exporting countries, most of which border on the Mediterranean. These events were landmarks in the development of migrations. Not only was the pattern of migratory flows transformed; significant changes also occurred in employment and residence conditions affecting immigrant workers.

The modification of the pattern of migratory flows was particularly marked as regards the distribution of nationalities. Thus, migrants from the Mediterranean basin gradually supplanted migrants from the traditional immigration countries (Italy, Poland, etc.). In addition, collective recruitment of workers in the emigration country and their collective transportation gradually replaced the spontaneous immigration of isolated individuals.

Two systems of regulations concerning foreigners now coexist: a general system for immigrants who have come on their own initiative, and a special system for immigrants recruited on the basis of bilateral manpower agreements. In many countries the latter system is tending to become ordinary law. This is because immigration countries, wishing to improve the management and organization of foreign labour in the various sectors of the economy prefer more and more often to employ workers recruited collectively on the basis of that type of agreement. The countries where the trend is most pronounced are those which, not considering themselves to be immigration countries, have decided to rationalize as far as they can the influx and distribution of immigrant workers. Considerable differences exist from one country to another in this regard.

The Federal Republic of Germany is undoubtedly the first country where the government's immigration policy was determined almost exclusively by economic imperatives. Up to 1973, the very great majority of workers entering German territory had been recruited through the Federal Employment Institute in Nuremberg and its missions in the emigration countries (the German Commissions). The distinctive feature of the Federal Republic's procedure is that it was initiated exclusively by the employers, who were largely responsible for fixing the immigrants' working conditions and pay levels themselves.

In the Netherlands, seven recruitment agreements were concluded from 1963 to 1971. The basic idea behind this system of agreements was that foreign workers from the contracting countries should enjoy priority at the recruitment stage. However, by comparison with the Federal Republic, it appears that an employer's power to recruit workers abroad was controlled more strictly by the central employment authority. The control was all the more effective because channels existed for consulting the trade unions and external factors, such as housing conditions, were taken into consideration when applications were examined.

The situation that developed in Belgium during the 1960s is not unlike the situation in France at the same period. Even though a number of manpower agreements were signed during this boom by Belgium, they scarcely served as a basis for the immigration policy which was distinguished by its great laxity. France, on the other hand, had little or no experience of such a system of agreements. The manpower agreements signed by France (at the beginning of the 1960s, with the exception of the agreement with Portugal, which dates from 1977) never aimed to define special regulations concerning the immigration of certain migrants, but simply to specify in what material conditions they would be recruited and transported. Thus, a 'wildcat' type of immigration developed, both in France and in Belgium, owing to the great tolerance displayed by the administrative authorities towards foreign job-seekers and their families.

In Sweden, immigration presents aspects that are quite specific to that country. In the first place, the immigration of Finns accounts for about half of the migratory flows. This strong trend is due to the geographical, political and even cultural proximity of Finland, which was formulated in legal terms in the agreement whereby the common Nordic labour market was instituted in 1954. In the second place, Sweden has traditionally accepted political refugees and, as a result, has become the chosen country of thousands of people since the end of the Second World War. These population movements have provided Sweden with a large proportion of the manpower required on account of the rapid development of its industry. The immigration of non-Nordic workers has always been insignificant, except from 1964 to 1966. It was in fact in 1967 that the Swedish authorities closed their frontiers to migratory flows from non-Nordic countries, except for refugees and persons accepted for humanitarian reasons. Sweden is one of the very few countries to have formally recognized the notion of a de facto refugee by incorporating it into the Aliens Act of 1976.

In a word, at the dawn of the 1970s, none of the countries under consideration—with the exception of Sweden—had defined an immigration policy. The attitude of the public authorities was largely dictated by economic imperatives and *laissez-faire* tendencies which resulted in the formation of a mass of foreign workers, generally exploited and living in wretched conditions. It was the worsening of the economic situation at the beginning of the 1970s that forced governments to turn their attention to this state of affairs and to produce, if not an immigration policy, at least a systematically constructed set of rules.

Controlling migratory flows

Just as the labour shortage in the Western countries had speeded up the migratory flow from the Mediterranean countries, the subsequent increase in unemployment in Europe induced the immigration countries to exercise far stricter control over migratory flows and gradually to deny access to the labour market to foreigners who did not qualify for special treatment.

The immigration countries began by applying the existing regulations far more strictly. The practice of regularizing the administrative situation of immigrant workers after they had gained a footing in the host country, which had been widely adopted up to that time—particularly in France, Belgium and the Netherlands—was gradually replaced by the system whereby a prospective immigrant was obliged to obtain the necessary authorizations before leaving the country of origin, failing which he was turned back at the frontier. Thus, as a general rule, permission to immigrate was granted by governments only to nationals of states with which a manpower agreement had been signed.

Very soon, however, a further step was taken to control migratory flows. Most governments decided to bar the way to immigration. Sweden, which had already reduced immigration in 1967, decided, in 1973, to put a stop to all collective recruitment and an agreement was concluded with Finland with a view to making all Finnish emigrants pass through the Swedish employment services. In the Federal Republic of Germany, the government decided, in November 1973, to suspend immigration from all countries with which a manpower agreement had been concluded. In the Netherlands, as from January 1970, recommendations were addressed to Parliament by the government in the form of 'Notes to Parliament concerning alien workers'. While no spectacular decision was taken, the number of foreigners authorized to enter Netherlands territory was greatly reduced and there was a marked decline in the recruitment of workers from countries having signed manpower agreements, with the result that, in 1972, the recruitment figure was only one-quarter of the figure for 1971. In France, by virtue of a decision taken by the Council of Ministers on 3 July 1974, the admission of immigrant workers was temporarily suspended, pending the adoption of a new immigration policy designed to 'stabilize a population of 4 million aliens'. In Belgium, as from 1967, the regularization procedure was abandoned and a royal decree, reaffirming the principles laid down in the texts of 1936, based the immigration control system on the rule that a work permit must be issued in the country of origin. This decree had the effect of halving the number of entries. It should be noted that Belgium is the only country that has not really put a stop to immigration. Today, in fact, it is the country where the population includes the highest proportion of foreigners.

It was at the very time when the national immigration laws were being tightened up that freedom of movement within the Common Market became a reality. Regulation 1612/68 and Directive 360/68 removed the last obstacles to the right of establishment for nationals of Member States of the European Economic Community. These can now freely seek employment within the Community without having to go through the employment services of the country in which they find themselves. In addition, an EEC resident's card, valid for five years and issued automatically to applicants presenting a work contract or a letter of appointment, was introduced in October 1968 and naturally facilitated immigration within Europe as from 1969.

It is not by chance, therefore, that the countries considered here —except, precisely, Sweden—established strict immigration regulations in the 1970s. The system of free movement within the EEC is one of the major reasons, together with the development of the economic crisis, for the decision to close the frontiers to migrant workers from the Mediterranean countries.

The closing of frontiers has had important consequences for migratory flows but also for the structure of immigrant populations. It is a noteworthy point that, by and large, the halting of immigration had no immediate effects: the foreign population continued to increase. This was because the halting of immigration initially concerned only the workers themselves. Accordingly, workers who were already established in the host country, foreseeing the even stricter regulations that were to be applied as from 1975, hurried to send for their families. For this reason, immigration flows, far from decreasing, even increased in some cases, following the decisions taken by governments to refuse access to the labour market to nationals of non-EEC countries. For instance, in the Federal Republic of Germany, the year which followed the decision to stop immigration was the one when the foreign population reached the highest level that has ever been recorded. Thus, instead of reducing the foreign population as a whole, the adoption of restrictive policies contributed, at first, to accelerating and amplifying immigration movements. Another important consequence was the change in the length of time spent by migrants abroad. As the conditions governing access to the territory of the host country were more strict, those migrants who had been admitted stayed longer, knowing that once they had returned home they would meet with the greatest difficulties if they tried to immigrate once again. Furthermore, the presence of a migrant worker's family makes his exile more bearable and it is therefore easier for him to extend his stay, particularly since his children can be enrolled in schools in the host country. This trend towards an extension of the period of residence is very marked in all the countries studied and is clearly reflected in the statistics concerning the number of residence permits issued. Lastly, owing to the arrival of families, foreign communities in host countries have become much younger. So it was that new situations arose, from 1973–74 onwards, for which host countries were not well prepared and which induced them to make their regulations clearer and, in some cases, to formulate a real immigration policy.

Immigration regulations

The period extending from 1973 to 1977/78 can be said to be one of tentative efforts and adjustments. The immigration countries came to realize that they could not dispense with immigration altogether. They also sought to stabilize the foreign population established on their territory and, where possible, to reduce it. Lastly, most countries decided to face up to the problems raised by the presence of the immigrants, as well as to those encountered by the immigrants, and regulations defining a number of standards were drawn up. The aim was to weave around the migrant a web of regulations, the stated purpose of which was, on the one hand, to ensure that stricter control was exercised over both the inflows and the stocks of foreigners and, on the other, to provide certain rights and safeguards for immigrants. It has to be admitted that, while the regulations regarding the policing of foreign communities achieved their purpose, those relating to human rights fell far short of what was expected of them when they were being prepared. This last point will be discussed more fully later, for the present section is concerned only with the immigration control system.

It is of course impossible, within the limits of this summing up, to undertake an exhaustive comparative study of the control mechanisms used in the five countries under review. We shall therefore highlight the guiding principles and draw attention to the specific features of some of the mechanisms.

Immigration control systems are based on many criteria that vary from one country to another. A list could be prepared on the basis of the mechanisms used, for despite different and sometimes conflicting interests and imperatives a number of common features can be observed.

In all the regulations, a distinction is made between the immigration of workers in the strict sense of the term and the immigration of members of the family. For a very long time only immigrant workers were subject to controls. However, in the last few years, increasingly strict laws have been passed to regulate the immigration of families. These two points should therefore be dealt with in turn.

The immigration of workers

With the exception of workers from a free movement zone (the EEC or the common Nordic labour market), immigrants can neither enter nor work freely in the territory of the host countries. This rule implies the existence of procedures designed to enable aliens to exercise, when appropriate, a gainful activity while residing in the country considered. They are therefore obliged to obtain both a work permit and a residence permit.

Employment controls

Nowadays no country regards itself any longer as an immigration country. Since the beginning of the 1970s immigration has been accepted only so far as it has met the labour demands of national economies. For this reason, the possibility of hiring a prospective immigrant is subject to strict control by the employment services of the host country. In all national laws on the subject the issue of a work permit is a *sine qua non* for entering the national territory. Consequently, this is issued in the migrant worker's country of origin when the agreement of the host country authorities has been obtained. This rule holds good both for an individual worker wishing to immigrate independently and for workers recruited collectively. At present, none of the five countries studied recruits workers by the collective system any more. The access of individual workers to the national territory is limited to specialized professionals and these are admitted only if the national labour market cannot meet the demand for qualified personnel in the branch in question. Conversely, immigration may be authorized for workers without any particular skill in order to fill the jobs which national workers refuse to take. Such is the case in Belgium, where immigration has not been formally stopped and foreign workers continue to be employed in jobs deemed to be 'socially unacceptable' by national workers. In such jobs, the tasks to be performed are socially degrading and working conditions are particularly arduous. It is reasonable to suppose that this situation is not confined to Belgium. In France, for instance, research has shown that a mass exodus of immigrant workers would not create a commensurate number of jobs for national workers, since the latter refuse to take the jobs generally held by immigrants. It is likely, therefore, that a certain amount of immigration will always continue but, above all, it is becoming very important for the host countries to organize the working conditions of the resident foreign population in such a way as to derive the maximum benefit from its productive labour. It was with this in mind that the regulations concerning the different types of work permit have been revised in the last few years.

In this field, two control mechanisms can be distinguished. One, the most traditional, consists in the existence of several permits issued one after the other, which gradually increase the immigrant worker's rights. This system exists in Sweden, France and the Federal Republic of Germany.

Although Sweden has an extremely strict immigration policy, it is indisputably the country that grants the greatest number of rights and safeguards to those migrants who are allowed to enter Swedish territory. Thus, the first work permit is issued for one year and is valid for one specified type of activity, thus enabling the worker to change his employer. After one year a permit valid for all types of professional activity is issued. It must be pointed out, however, that the majority of immigrants are granted at the end of the first year an establishment permit giving them an unrestricted right to reside and work in Sweden.

In France, there are three kinds of work card. A temporary card, known as Card A, is valid for a professional activity in one or more departments. It is valid for one year and is renewable. When it expires, the ordinary card, known as Card B, can be issued to the worker, giving him the right to exercise one or more professional activities in one or more departments. It is valid for three years and is renewable. Lastly, a person whose Card B expires may obtain Card C, which is valid for all paid occupations without geographical restrictions. It is valid for ten years and is renewable. It must be pointed out, however, that immigrants by no means have a right to the third type of card and an application for one can be refused by the Ministry of Labour, which can also refuse to renew a card. In this field the administrative authorities enjoy enormous discretionary powers, since they can refuse to renew the work permit of a person who has been in France for fourteen years (one year with Card A+three years with Card B+ten years with Card C). It is indeed shocking that this should be possible.

The German system is somewhat different but the discretionary powers are no less extensive. The general work permit is valid for one specific professional activity in one particular firm and in the district under the jurisdiction of the employment office which has issued it. It is usually valid for two years but it may, in exceptional cases, be extended to three years. It is issued only to immigrant workers already residing in the Federal Republic who have lost their job, on the express condition that the job they wish to take cannot be filled by a German worker. A favourable decision on an application for the extension of the permit depends on the state of the national labour market and consequently the worker's situation is extremely precarious. However, an immigrant worker who has been legally and continuously employed for five years, or who has married a German national and has settled in the Federal Republic of Germany, is entitled to a special work permit. This permit, which is valid for five years, is granted without reference to the labour-market situation, authorizes the holder to exercise any occupation and is valid, as a general rule, for the entire territory of the country. Theoretically, an application for the renewal of this permit should satisfy the same conditions as those required when it was issued.

Belgium and the Netherlands operate the second control mechanism, which requires the employer, instead of the worker, to obtain a permit. In Belgium, in fact, the regulations stand half-way between the two contrasting mechanisms and both the first system and the second system exist side by side. An employer wishing to hire immigrant workers must first obtain authorization to do so by applying for an employment permit from the services of the Ministry of Labour. This permit will be granted only after the state of the labour market has been reviewed. It is required only when the object is to employ a foreigner who does not hold a work permit. Three kinds of work permit exist in Belgium. Permit C, valid for a maximum period of twelve months, is issued for trades that do not involve a permanent attachment to the same employer, as in the case of dockers for instance. It is renewable. Permit B, valid for a maximum period of twelve months, is limited to one employer or to one specified branch of activity. It is also renewable. Lastly, Permit A, of unlimited duration, is valid for all kinds of paid work. As the renewal of Permits B and C depends on the state of the labour market, the workers holding them cannot be sure of being able to continue working when they expire. However, foreigners who have worked in Belgium for four years obtain Permit A without the state of the labour market being taken into account. This period is reduced in accordance with agreements concluded by Belgium.

While this system is very similar to that existing in the other countries, the Netherlands—in its new legislation which entered into force in 1979—has completely abolished the work permit system, replacing it by a single employment permit to be obtained by the employer. The Netherlands is currently going through a period of transition and it is therefore necessary to describe briefly the two systems. Under the former regulations, a temporary work permit valid for one year is issued taking into account the labour-market situation, so that the employment of immigrant workers is considered to be a stop-gap measure. Foreigners who have worked for five years obtain a permanent work permit which is issued without reference to the state of the labour market. It is noteworthy that a right of appeal exists for an immigrant whose application for his first work permit or for the renewal of a work permit is refused. The appeal is lodged with the Ministry of Social Affairs. There also exists a right of appeal before the Council of State. The Netherlands is thus the only country where the granting of a work permit is not a purely discretionary matter. The new provisions have abolished the work permit. There now exists only the employment permit which an employer will have to obtain in order to employ a foreigner who has worked for less than three years in the Netherlands. After three years, a permit is no longer required and the state of the labour market cannot be invoked against the worker. The main advantage of this mechanism is that control is exercised at the employer's level and the employer can be held responsible for taking on illicit workers. In addition, the foreigner does not have to cope with the procedures for obtaining a work permit and can thus become more speedily adapted to unfamiliar conditions and integrated into the society in which he is living. It is clear that this policy has been shaped by concerns which are very different from those reflected in the German and French systems, for in these two countries, and especially in France, an immigrant remains dependent on the goodwill of the authorities for many years and even up to the very end of his stay.

Residence controls

A movement is currently developing in favour of bringing work permits into line with residence permits. For a very long time, the conditions on which the two types of permit were issued and the procedures for their renewal were independent of each other. This was the cause of numerous discrepancies, and particularly the fact that a worker could have the right of residence but be refused the right to work, or vice versa. Legislative provisions today tend to align the conditions for issuing a residence permit with the conditions for issuing a work permit. As a general rule, as we have already noted, the work permit is a *sine qua non* for admission to the national territory and consequently for the granting of a residence permit. However, the granting of this permit is always subject to certain conditions and continues to depend on the judgement of the competent authorities, these being, in most cases, the police services responsible for controlling the movements of aliens, which come under the Ministry of the Interior or the Ministry of Justice.

France is the only country where three types of residence permit exist: the temporary resident's card, valid for one year, the ordinary resident's card, valid for three years, and the privileged resident's card, valid for ten years. The validity of these cards and that of the three work permits which exist in France correspond perfectly. A bill drafted in the Council of Ministers in June 1979 provides for the abolition of the first card. If it is passed, foreigners will be admitted immediately for three years and the privileged resident's card will be renewed automatically.

The Netherlands also has a system of residence permits which matches the system of work permits. Theoretically, possession of a residence permit is a condition for obtaining a work permit; but in practice, if a worker applying for a residence permit is out of work, he will not be granted the permit. There therefore exists a renewable one-year permit which, at the end of five years, can be replaced by a permanent establishment permit, but this permit is not granted automatically. It is noteworthy that, as in the case of work permits, an appeals procedure exists which immigrants can follow in the event of a refusal to issue a residence permit. The appeal is lodged with the Ministry of Justice in the first instance; if necessary, it can be taken higher and will then be heard by the Council of State.

In Sweden, the law regarding residence permits bears the same stamp of liberalism as the regulations concerning work permits. The two systems of permits are in harmony with each other, since the first residence permit is valid for one year and after that period an establishment permit is issued almost automatically, conferring on the holder an unrestricted right to work and reside in Sweden. The mechanism here is an extremely attractive one which has the advantage of being very simple and securing maximum safeguards for the foreigner.

So far as the Federal Republic of Germany and Belgium are concerned, however, there is no co-ordination between the two systems of permits. In the Federal Republic there exists a residence permit of limited duration which is issued for a period of one year in the first instance and is renewable for two-year periods. After five years of continuous residence, foreigners may apply for a residence permit of unlimited duration which, contrary to what its name suggests, is valid for five years. Many conditions have to be fulfilled before this permit can be issued: in particular, the foreign worker must hold a special work permit, which is not granted automatically. After eight years of residence and in so far as the foreigner is considered to be well integrated into German society, he may be granted a permanent resident's permit, valid for an indefinite period which, in principle, cannot be taken away from him. The system here is clearly a highly selective one, very far removed from the Swedish system.

The Belgian system is not very different from the German system, since there exists in Belgium an initial one-year permit which is renewable and foreigners may, after five years of residence, apply for an establishment permit which is issued after a favourable decision has been taken independently by the Minister of Justice. But this permit is valid for only five years and cannot be placed in the same category as the German permanent resident's permit.

It should be made clear that, in most countries, various conditions have to be fulfilled before a residence permit can be issued and that, by and large, these conditions are found to be the same from one country to another. Quite recently, possession of accommodation meeting national standards has become a widespread requirement and in many cases constitutes one of the main criteria for the renewal of permits. Another widespread requirement is that the migrant be familiar with the language of the host country or that he be well integrated into the host society. Unfortunately, it is difficult to define these conditions very precisely and there is a danger that they may increase the discretionary powers of the administrative authorities.

The immigration of families

All countries acknowledge the right of families to be reunited. This right which, moreover, is recognized in many international documents drawn up by international organizations (ILO, OECD, Council of Europe), has not been called into question by those countries that have closed their frontiers. The case of France is interesting because that country, after deciding to suspend family immigration, had to go back on that decision owing to the large number of hostile reactions which it elicited, at both the national and the international levels.

The conditions governing family immigration are different, of course, from those applying to immigrant workers in the strict sense of the term, that is to say, those persons whose sole purpose in immigrating is to take up paid employment.

As a general rule, families immigrate once the head of the family has gained a footing in the host country. This assumption is the basis of the laws that have been established in regard to family immigration. It is very rare for the simultaneous immigration of the worker and his family to be planned and permitted. Nor is it usual for a woman who is the mother of a family to immigrate alone first, but sometimes a young woman who has immigrated gets married in her country of origin and afterwards applies for authorization to send for her husband.

Family immigration raises three questions which are not answered in the same way by the laws of the various host countries. First, what does the concept of 'family' cover and who may accordingly be authorized to join the foreign worker? Second, at what point does the family obtain the right to immigrate? And third, while the members of the family who are authorized to immigrate obtain the right of residence as a matter of course, how far are they allowed to take up paid employment?

First, in all cases, the wife and the children under age are covered by the concept of 'family'. The age at which the children attain their majority is generally the one recognized by the host country and not the one fixed by the country of which the young immigrant is a national. Thus, in the Federal Republic of Germany and France, a child is considered to be a minor only up to the age of 18, whereas in Belgium and the Netherlands, a child does not attain his majority until he is 21 years old. In Sweden there is no age limit, provided that the child is living with his parents. As a general rule, collateral relatives and forebears are excluded, but they can sometimes be authorized to immigrate when they are very dependent on the worker who has already immigrated. Such is the case in the legislation of Sweden and the Netherlands.

Second, the family is authorized to join the immigrant worker when certain conditions have been fulfilled. In the first place, all countries require the immigrant to have resided in their territory for a certain length of time before he can apply for his family to join him. This is a kind of probationary period at the end of which it is hoped that the migrant will show that he has become adapted to his new environment or, better still, that he is well integrated into the host society. The only country where this system does not exist is Sweden which, as already stated, has adopted extremely liberal regulations for persons who have obtained authorization to take up residence in its territory. The Belgian system is also very flexible, since an immigrant is only required to have worked for three months in order to be entitled to send for his family. In France, as in the Netherlands, this period is one year, while the German system is the harshest since it makes the immigrant worker wait three years. The second condition which is laid down by all countries is that the immigrant be able to offer his family accommodation meeting certain standards. This condition may be very difficult to fulfil in view of the housing shortage, for the immigrant worker may take a very long time to find suitable accommodation, and this makes the prescribed waiting time proportionally longer before he can be joined by his family. In addition, the foreigner is usually required to be actually in occupation of the necessary accommodation at the time when he initiates the application procedure, which may be many months before his family arrives.

Third, the right to work brings us to a highly controversial problem. It seems to be inconsistent to authorize the family to immigrate and then refuse to allow its members to take up a professional activity, and thus to lead a normal life. This situation mainly affects wives, since the children are generally too young to work and, in any case, are allowed to do so only if they have followed a school course or a vocational training course in the host country.

The French Government had decided to stop issuing work permits to the members of foreign workers' families, but this decree was recently annulled by the Council of State. Thus, theoretically, members of an immigrant's family can work in France. However, as the state of the labour market can be given as a reason for denying them the authorization to work, the Minister of Labour still has the power to refuse to issue work permits to the members of a foreign worker's family. In the Federal Republic of Germany, the spouse can exercise a professional activity after a period of four years and the children after two years. It is also stipulated that a work permit shall be granted only for those sectors in which there is a labour shortage. As can be seen, these regulations are based largely upon the imperatives of economic policy. In Belgium, the Netherlands and Sweden, the regulations are more flexible, since members of the family are allowed to work regardless of the state of the labour market. It is necessary, however, for them to obtain a work permit. Nowhere do the members of an immigrant worker's family automatically have a right to work; they must always obtain the authorization of the administrative authorities in order to exercise a gainful activity. In the last resort, and although in some cases the state of the labour market cannot provide grounds for refusal, it is still possible for the administrative authorities to refuse to grant such authorization. In so doing, they condemn the immigrants to return to their home country.

France is the only one of the five countries studied which has instituted a system of aiding immigrant workers and their families to return home by offering them a lump sum to be used to facilitate their resettlement in their country of origin. The establishment of this system in France has been criticized because it obliges the migrant and his family to relinquish all the rights from which they benefited in France and forbids them to come back to France in the future. The question of implementing a policy of aiding immigrants to return home has been broached in most of the immigration countries, but no steps of any consequence have been taken in this direction. In particular, Belgium and the Netherlands have categorically refused to consider introducing a system of aid to return home on the French model, although this idea has been proposed several times. It is likely that these countries will tend rather to cut back family immigration and they may even make it a policy not to renew the residence and work permits of newly arrived immigrants.

By way of conclusion to this part, certain points should be stressed:

The five countries studied have put a stop to the immigration of unskilled workers, rare exceptions being made for nationals of countries having signed a manpower agreement.

In 1975 efforts began to be made to frame new immigration strategies. These efforts have now culminated in the adoption of a new generation of legislative provisions. Sweden, which has the most liberal regulations concerning the immigrants' exercise of their specific rights and freedoms, was the first country to pass its new law in 1976. The Netherlands has passed its new legislation which is gradually coming into force, while Belgium, the Federal Republic of Germany and France produced texts, which came out in 1980.

These new provisions are largely dictated by the imperatives of the current economic and political situation. In principle, this new generation of laws should take into consideration the specific needs of immigrants and aim at outlining a 'legal status for immigrants', which would provide them with certain rights and freedoms. These aspects of the problem will be considered in the third part of our summing up. The part that follows will seek to establish points of comparison as regards the situation of immigrants in the economic structure of the host countries.

The place and role of migrants in the economic structures of the host countries

The foreign population in the host countries

The migrant's place and role in the economic structures of the host countries depend in the first place, on the relative size of the foreign population. To evaluate this, it is necessary to take account of various factors, including the geographical distribution and the density of the population of the host country. These two factors are interlinked: it is generally the densely populated areas that attract immigrant workers because the major industries, which are most in need of foreign labour are usually established there. There can be no doubt that the relative size of the foreign population and the problems encountered by foreigners (as regards their housing, integration or assimilation, and so on) depend directly on the overall density of the population of the host country: the Netherlands has a foreign population that represents only 2.6 per cent of its total population and it also has the highest population density in Europe (409.6). However, the importance of this demographic factor must not be overstated. It should be borne in mind that if governments resolve to establish a policy of integration or, simply, to desist from applying excessively strict or frankly repressive regulations, this indubitably affects, to an appreciable degree, the distribution and activities of the foreign population, as is suggested by certain conclusions which can be drawn from the country studies contained in this work and which will be discussed at greater length further on in this part.

Despite the fact that frontiers have been closed to immigration, foreign populations have been steadily increasing. However, there has been a change in the pattern of immigration flows. In the first place, the increase is accounted for by the influx of families. The relative proportion of foreign labour consequently declined between 1974 and 1977: by 19 per cent in the Federal Republic of Germany, by 16 per cent in France and by as much as 29 per cent in the Netherlands. Although it has continued to increase in Belgium (by 10.5 per cent), it is none the less true that the employment rate of the foreign population has fallen to a level lower than that of the Belgian population. In Sweden, the relative proportion of foreign labour has also continued to increase, but this is due to the special situation of that country where half the immigrants are workers from the other Nordic countries. In the second place, there is a growing tendency for immigrants to be skilled workers. In the Netherlands, only skilled workers obtain work permits. In Sweden, more than one-quarter of the immigrants from non-Nordic countries are skilled workers, most of whom are political refugees. In France, refugees account for approximately half the immigration figures. However, there are no signs of such a trend emerging in the Federal Republic of Germany or in Belgium. As regards the latter country, this situation seems to be due to the fact that the economic crisis has not affected the demand for immigrant workers, the number of work permits issued having scarcely changed since the beginning of the 1970s. In the Federal Republic of Germany, the reason indisputably lies in the fact that immigrants obtain work permits only if they are to be employed in the sectors forsaken by German workers and, unlike France, for instance, the Federal Republic does not admit a large number of political refugees.

The modification of the pattern of migratory flows, and particularly the large-scale immigration of families, has contributed to the increase in the foreign population or the population of foreign origin, owing to the larger number of children born to foreigners. This trend is particularly pronounced because the birth rate of the immigrant population is much higher than that of the nationals of the host country. Thus in Belgium foreigners accounted (in 1977), for 15 per cent of the total number of births while representing 'only' 8.7 per cent of the total population.

One of the important consequences of this development is the lowering of the average age of foreign communities and the increase in the number of persons who are not of an age to work. It then becomes increasingly apparent that there is contradiction between the official positions of the European countries which still do not consider themselves to be immigration countries (this emerges both from their declarations and from the new texts of laws that are about to be published) and the development of a resident foreign population that is displaying more and more of the characteristics of immigrant communities aiming at permanent settlement. This trend is confirmed by the decrease in the proportion of workers in relation to the total foreign population and the rapid increase in the number of naturalizations. Tension is often caused by the fact that this type of community has needs that are different from those of a community of immigrant workers in the strict sense of the term, and these needs can very seldom be satisfied by the host countries.

The modification of the structure of the active population is an important phenomenon, for it gives rise to new behaviour patterns within that population which call into question quite a number of generally accepted ideas concerning the role and place of immigrant Vorkers in the economies of the host countries.

Distribution of the active population

The geographical distribution of the active population has always been determined by the demand for labour. Foreigners are therefore concentrated in highly industrialized and urbanized regions. The Federal Republic of Germany is the only country to have made it illegal for foreigners to settle in certain zones on the grounds that the foreign population was already too large there. This *Plafondierung* system was applied as soon as the percentage of foreigners in any given zone exceeded 12 per cent.

But this system was operative only from April 1975 to April 1977. The economic recession does not appear to have had any particular effect on geographical distribution, except in the case of Belgium. In that country, during the 1950s, a very large proportion of immigrants were employed in the mining regions. As deposits were worked out, foreign labour left those regions when no alternative employment was available. This phenomenon, which is due to the decline of one type of activity, is also in evidence in other countries—particularly in the north of France—but it occurred on a particularly large scale in Belgium owing to the enormous number of workers who were recruited precisely in order to work in the mines. Lastly, there is a gradual tendency for active foreign populations to move towards town centres owing to the increase in the proportion of foreigners employed in the tertiary sector.

As regards the distribution of foreign workers in the different economic sectors, an interesting development is under way, even though it does not affect all countries.

Because the relevant data are either lacking or, in some countries, inadequate (Sweden, Netherlands), it is not possible to make a close comparison between the various countries studied, especially since the statistical methods and references used to analyse the economic situation vary from one country to another. It is possible, nevertheless, to identify certain constant factors.

It is traditional for foreigners to be employed in the metallurgical, processing and building industries, civil and rural engineering and services. There was a very marked concentration of foreign labour in the industrial sectors up to 1970 in all the countries studied. But since that date, foreign labour—particularly in Belgium, the Netherlands and Sweden—has come to be distributed throughout all the economic sectors, perhaps the largest proportion being employed in the tertiary sector. Admittedly, the country studies on which our comparison is based do not provide sufficient data to enable us to make a detailed analysis of the reasons for this development. Nevertheless, a survey of the professional qualifications of foreign workers yields some very interesting food for thought.

Professional qualifications

The lowest level of qualifications is found in France and the Federal Republic of Germany. These are the very countries in which there is the greatest concentration of foreign workers in the traditional branches of activity and where there are no signs of a trend towards an even distribution of foreign workers among the various economic sectors. It would seem, in addition, that the situation as regards professional qualifications is stationary. This means that, although in Sweden, Belgium and the Netherlands the average level of qualifications is tending to rise, this seems to be constant in France and the Federal Republic of Germany or at least seems to be rising less rapidly than in the other three countries. These are only hypotheses which need to be checked in the light of a more thorough statistical survey, but other findings give us reason to suppose that they might well be confirmed. Thus, while in Belgium and the Netherlands the distribution of foreigners in the different economic sectors tends to be falling into line with that of national workers, there would appear to be in France and the Federal Republic a greater concentration of foreign labour in certain sectors only. It is true that reliable conclusions cannot be drawn without carefully analysing the state of the labour market of the countries concerned—which the five country studies do not enable us to do—but there probably exists a correlation between the trend in the distribution of foreign workers and the trend in their average level of qualifications. It is not by chance, of course, that the great majority of resident foreign workers fall into the unskilled or semi-skilled categories. The recruitment efforts of the host countries have always been dictated by a concern with economic profitability. Workers have therefore been recruited primarily in order to fill jobs which national workers are unwilling to take. It is reasonable to assume that the countries where foreign labour is tending to become more concentrated in certain sectors are those which have allowed working conditions to deteriorate in those sectors, at least in relative terms, as compared with the progress made in the other sectors. Thus, the 'dynamics of second-rate occupations' has made it possible to continue employing foreign workers at a wage lower than what would have been demanded by the national labour force. For instance, it is undoubtedly thanks to this method that the German textile industry has been able to remain competitive and survive. A cumulative process ensues whereby certain industries are continually obliged to draw on foreign labour. It is becoming more and more difficult to employ national workers, for this implies a modification of the capital/labour ratio and an upgrading of the tasks to be performed, which is especially hard to achieve because it would jeopardize the competitivity of whole sectors of the national economy.

This general trend shows that a very strong link may exist between the sectoral distribution of foreign workers and their level of qualifications on the one hand, and the regulations governing immigration on the other. It is a fact that the strictest regulations regarding work permits are to be found in the Federal Republic of Germany and France. In neither country does there exist a permanent work permit and before a foreign worker can obtain a permit giving him freedom of choice and movement, he must wait four years in France and five years in the Federal Republic. Yet in Belgium and Sweden he can apply for such a permit at the end of the first year. In the Netherlands, foreign workers have to wait five years, but the permit they obtain is valid for an unlimited period, in contrast to the rule in force in France and the Federal Republic. The case of the Netherlands is not relevant, however, because that country ceased to recruit unskilled workers many years ago. It can therefore be assumed that 'liberal' laws are, to some extent, conducive to the professional mobility of immigrant workers within the labour market. Stringent laws, on the contrary, accentuate the basic inequalities between national workers and foreign workers by increasing, for instance, the degree to which the latter are concentrated in certain economic sectors and in certain socio-occupational categories.

This assumption can be illustrated by the example of the work permit. The worker's limited freedom to move about the country, as well as his assignment to a particular occupation, or even to a particular employer, are imposed by his work permit. The more a foreign worker's freedom of movement and right of establishment are restricted, the fewer his opportunities for finding a better job and securing promotion. The same applies to the employment opportunities offered to the members of foreign workers' families. When it is easy to take up a paid activity, the household's income and the chances of social advancement are improved, which is conducive to the socio-economic integration of the migrant and his family.

These points are particularly important because migrants are tending to stay much longer in the host country and the problems encountered by the second generation are partly connected with the experiences of the first generation.

It is clear, however, that the legal immigration control regulations do not operate quite independently within the socio-economic system of the host country. Host countries have the regulations they deserve or, to be more accurate, those that they need most. It is not by chance that the effect of the regulations is to meet the demands of the host country's economy. Just as it would be desirable to know what role is played by immigrants in the process of economic development—and on this question economic theory does not have much to say today—so would it be desirable to know what role is played in the migratory process by legislation when it comes to the assistance of the economy.

Unemployment among foreigners

Unemployment trends among foreigners have been bound up with the economic recession. Until around 1973 the unemployment rate in Europe was distinctly lower among foreigners than among the nationals of the host countries. But from that time onwards, the trend was reversed. Today the active foreign population is suffering even more from the effects of the economic crisis than the national labour force. This pattern appears in the five countries studied, including Sweden where the total unemployment rate is, however, far lower than in the other countries (about 2 per cent!). It is difficult to make a valid comparison between the five countries owing to the disparity of the statistics used in the national reports. The broad lines of a general trend can nevertheless be discerned.

First, unemployment among foreigners has gradually increased to a point where it is approximately twice as high as among nationals.

Second, the unemployed are not evenly distributed by nationality: North Africans and Turks are the most affected.

Third, the structure of the population of foreign job-seekers differs from that of the population of national job-seekers, there being of course a larger number of men among the foreigners than among the nationals. This is due to the structure of the foreign population and to the fact that the 25–49 age-group is overrepresented. It should be added, however, that an extremely large number of women immigrants are unemployed. In those countries where there is a better balanced distribution of the foreign population by sex, women account for a not inconsiderable proportion of job-seekers. Thus, in Belgium, women account for about half the total number of job-seekers and their unemployment rate is 22.5 per cent! As for young immigrants, they seem particularly hard hit by unemployment, for they appear to be growing proportionately more numerous in relation to the number of job-seekers than in relation to the total foreign population. However, these projections would have to be verified. In any event, unemployment among the young is very high: in Sweden, unemployment in the 20–24 age-group is 8.1 per cent for foreigners and 4.3 per cent for nationals; in the 16–19 age-group the gap is wider, the rate for foreigners being 14.4 per cent as against 6.8 per cent for nationals, whereas in that country the average unemployment rate is only 2 per cent.

Lastly, the number of registered job-seekers can only give an imperfect idea of the actual situation, because of the phenomenon of migrants returning home. This phenomenon, which is not properly grasped by the statistical tools of the departure countries varies in scale according to the country's policy in regard to the renewal of residence permits for unemployed immigrants. In the Federal Republic of Germany, which applies in this field a policy of re-exporting its unemployed labour, the unemployment rate for foreigners decreased from 6.8 per cent in 1975 to 4.9 per cent in 1977 and thus approached the rate for nationals which was 4.6 per cent at that time. The importance of the phenomenon of migrants returning home should not be exaggerated, however, as is shown by the case-study conducted in Turkey.

In concluding this part, we must emphasize that the migrant's place in the society of the host country seems largely determined by the role—or in other words, the function—assigned to him within the system of production at the time when he gained access to the labour market. As the immigration regulations serve to keep the worker in his appointed place and, if need be, to send him back to his own country when he has ceased to make a sufficiently profitable contribution to the economy of the host country, the foreign worker's chances of advancement will depend directly on the degree of severity of the legal machinery which regulates his life in the immigration country.

Integration of migrants into the society of the host country

In raising the question of the migrant's integration into the society of the host country we are not necessarily suggesting how this complex of problems should be approached, but merely expressing our concern with the treatment meted out to foreigners in the matter of rights and freedoms. In every society, a large number of rights and freedoms are attached to the nationality of the individual. Consequently, an alien automatically finds himself in an inferior legal situation which is *ipso facto*, discriminatory. In addition, the foreigner is all too often regarded as a threat to the nation's integrity and homogeneity; special regulations are drawn up which reduce his rights even further and impose constraints upon him. A process of marginalization is then set in motion. It traps the foreigner in an 'infra-legal' situation, all the more easily because the differences in cultures and levels of development between the society of origin and the host society make it uncertain whether he will be in a position to enjoy the few rights and freedoms remaining to him.

Raising the problem of the migrant's integration means ascertaining to what extent the immigration country tries to avoid such marginalization and what place it assigns to foreigners within its society.

We have selected an indicator which reveals the attitude adopted by the immigration countries in this field; this indicator is the degree to which foreigners participate in the life of the host society. Their participation was evaluated mainly by examining the arrangements which certain states have made in order to facilitate the immigrant workers' integration.

Participation in political and social life

Reception and welfare services

All countries possess reception facilities for immigrants, but their scale and effectiveness vary considerably from one country to another. As for welfare services in the broad sense of the term, they are provided by bodies specifically concerned with assisting immigrants to cope with problems arising during their stay in the host country. The nature of such assistance and the problem areas covered depend very much on the country's overall immigration policy. This is in fact illogical, for the needs of immigrant workers and their families in this matter of social integration reveal themselves objectively, regardless of immigration policy, whether it be a question of getting to know the language and even the way of life of the host country, finding accommodation and knowing one's rights, or keeping in touch with the culture of one's country of origin, etc.

For a long time, economic profitability seems to have been the only criterion whereby states judged whether it was worth while to provide a few services to facilitate the economic and administrative integration of immigrant workers. The various reception services which were set up in this spirit were rather rudimentary, since their main function was to check that each migrant 'conformed' to the appropriate recruitment standards: health, age, qualifications, and so on. Subsequently, services were developed for the purpose of enabling migrants to meet the minimum conditions for obtaining authorization to stay in the host country, that is to say by helping them to find decent accommodation. Lastly, once it was realized that it was important for migrants to know the language of the host country, the need to teach it was recognized and this task was entrusted to certain special bodies.

Administrative guidance, accommodation and language instruction—such were the three needs that the authorities have tried to satisfy. But, in the event, only a minority of foreigners benefit from their efforts. Admittedly, this situation is partly due to financial factors, but it also owes something to political options. Countries such as the Federal Republic of Germany, Belgium or the Netherlands, which have always denied that they were immigration countries, did not set up the necessary structures to promote the integration of immigrants although large communities were settling in their territories. For this reason, action by the public authorities in this field has always taken the form of stop-gap measures.

In Sweden, on the contrary, the state has taken action at all levels to facilitate the integration of migrant workers and their families. In that country, not only have public services with very wide fields of competence assumed the task of providing reception, housing and educational services for immigrants; the state has also been guided in its action by a resolve to avoid discrimination in all its forms and a concern to improve the status of immigrants in order as far as possible to eliminate the causes of tension and conflict within Swedish society. Sweden is therefore the only country to have really developed a true immigration policy, to which we shall have occasion to refer again later.

The position of France is an intermediate one, largely because the Act of 2 November 1942 was designed to serve demographic purposes and France became accustomed long ago to large migratory flows from the former French Community, particularly from Algeria. Thus, as early as 1958, a welfare fund was set up in France to contribute to improving the living conditions of Algerian workers in France. However, while the French Government has repeatedly expressed its resolve to elaborate a true legal status for immigrants, its achievements have fallen far short of its intentions.

One of the consequences of this general situation is the extremely important role played by associations offering assistance and support to immigrant workers and their families. In the Federal Republic of Germany, Belgium and the Netherlands, most of the measures taken to promote the welfare and improve the status of foreigners are due to the work of associations set up by private initiative. True, they may be generously subsidized by the public authorities, but it is obvious that, despite the efforts they may make to co-ordinate their activities, their work cannot be as far-ranging and effective as the action that can be taken by a state desirous of promoting equality, freedom to choose from among the various cultural models and a sense of solidarity among the resident population, which are the three guiding principles underlying the Swedish policy.

The right to participate in public affairs

Party politics

It is by no means self-evident that immigrants should be allowed to participate in the political life of the host country. From time immemorial public life has been the preserve of citizens, and it is not by chance that the word *hostis* designated, in the Twelve Tables of early Roman law, both a foreigner and an enemy. Accordingly, there is nothing surprising about the fact that, as a general rule, strict regulations govern the political activities of foreigners. However, the situation differs greatly from one country to another.

France appears to be the country which is most reluctant to allow foreigners to engage in political activity. Although the principle in question is only a matter of customary law, the authorities see to it that foreigners observe an obligation to remain neutral: failure to comply with this obligation often constitutes grounds for an expulsion order. The German system is hardly more flexible: foreigners may, in theory, engage in political activities, but so many restrictive provisions exist regarding the application of this principle and the discretionary powers of the administrative authorities are so extensive when it comes to interpreting those provisions that the freedom enjoyed by foreigners in the matter of politics is very limited. Practically the same situation exists in Belgium but the systems of Sweden and the Netherlands are very different.

Thus, in the Netherlands, the authorities are quite well-disposed towards the political activities of the various foreigners' associations. Admittedly, if such activities are considered to be prejudicial to public order and national security, they can be prohibited and foreigners participating in them may even be expelled, but this is a far cry from the extreme severity that is characteristic of the French approach to this question. In addition, a debate has been in progress since 1974 concerning the desirability of granting foreigners the right to vote in local elections. A bill has even been drafted which proposes that certain clauses of the Constitution be amended so as to make it possible to grant immigrants the rights to vote and to stand for election in local elections.

Sweden has already reached this stage and has even progressed beyond it, since foreigners have now obtained the right to vote and stand for election at the local and regional levels. They were able to exercise these rights for the first time in the municipal elections held on 19 September 1976. The outcome of these elections was a success in terms of the numbers of voters, for 60 per cent of the foreigners registered went to the polls. It is noteworthy that, following these elections, many political parties and trade unions pressed for the right to vote to be granted to foreigners at national level. But Parliament preferred to make the law governing citizenship more flexible, as foreigners could then obtain access to political life at the national level by deciding once and for all to commit themselves to Swedish society.

Associative life

Foreigners can quite easily participate in public affairs by becoming members of consultative bodies or by setting up associations which serve as a collective means of expressing the concerns and demands of their adherents. But the right of association may itself be governed by regulations.

In France, foreign associations are subject to a strict rule requiring them to obtain prior authorization from the Ministry of the Interior. It is clear that this system greatly inhibits the formation of associations for foreigners, and the latter can apply instead for individual membership of French associations. In the Federal Republic of Germany, the system is even more restrictive, since no freedom of association exists for groups of foreigners; they are only allowed to take out membership of German associations on an individual basis. In Belgium and the Netherlands, where foreigners enjoy full freedom of association, they usually set up associations bringing together people of the same nationality. But while the Belgian associations are mainly of a cultural nature, foreigners' associations have become more politically active in the Netherlands where foreigners who have resided in the country for more than eighteen months enjoy great freedom in this respect. The activities of these associations must not, of course, be prejudicial to public order. This is not surprising, for is it not true that the very status of an alien and the exercise of his rights are dependent on this concept which is always the ultimate justification for the discretionary powers used by the executive against non-nationals? Once again, it is Sweden that has taken the lead in recognizing the right of association. In that country there exist about a thousand foreigners' associations organized on a nationality basis, and 120 of them are operating at national level. The state supports all nationwide associations, for it has been recognized that they play a very important role in helping to preserve the cultural identity of foreigners. Many of them are financed by the state (one-quarter) and the municipalities (three-quarters), without being required to sacrifice their independence. In addition, an Immigrants' Advisory Council has been set up, whose function is to consider how these various associations can influence and take part in the shaping of decisions which affect foreigners. The desire to grant foreigners the right to vote was the direct outcome of this effort at co-ordination. The Swedish experience shows that foreigners' associations, far from presenting a threat to public order—as is feared by the Federal Republic of Germany and France, for instance—have an extremely important role to play in the process of integrating immigrants into the host society. In particular, they can enable them to maintain a link with the society of their country of origin and help them to preserve their cultural identity to some extent. These aspects of immigration policy are very important because the conditions that must be created in order to facilitate the life of immigrants during their stay in the host country are also prerequisites for their reintegration into the society of their country of origin. The cultural and educative action of such associations undoubtedly does much more to help migrants to return home without difficulty than the allocation of a lump sum which will rapidly be spent and is only a source of bitter disappointment to many foreign workers.

The second important aspect of this associative life is the participation of foreigners in consultative bodies. In contrast to the case of associations, this mode of participation is more often due to the initiative of nationals of the host country than to that of foreigners themselves. In addition, it is viewed primarily as a substitute for political participation in the strict sense of the term. These reasons probably explain to a large extent why this system has never met with the success that its initiators hoped for. Experiments of this kind were made at the municipal level in particular. Belgium, the Federal Republic of Germany and the Netherlands set up bodies with a consultative function, in certain communes, to participate in the shaping of decisions of special importance to immigrants. These consultative bodies were distinguished by the fact that foreigners elected their own representatives who served as a channel of communication between the foreign population and the administrative authorities. Unfortunately, in the Federal Republic and the Netherlands, the immigrants' councils were a failure and the experiment was brought to an end. In Belgium it is continuing, but many communes which had also intended to set up such consultative councils finally decided to drop the plan. To the reasons that have just been outlined to explain the failure of these attempts, we may add the fact that these councils never had any real power to take decisions and that it must have been very difficult for foreigners to understand how these administrative structures could help them to solve their own problems. No doubt the same reasons account for the failure of the French experiment whose purpose was not, except in rare cases, to bring immigrants into the decision-making processes, but rather to establish municipal commissions with administrative responsibilities. In Sweden, the problem arises in very different terms, since foreigners are entitled to vote in municipal and local elections and, in some communes, even have elected representatives.

It has to be acknowledged, finally, that the efforts which have been made to associate foreigners with local public affairs have not been a success. This is not to say, however, that foreigners do not take an interest in such experiments. The Swedish experience shows, with the very high rate of participation in elections, that foreigners are anxious to look after their own interests themselves. But the Swedish experience also reveals that it is not enough to establish new structures but that it is necessary, on the contrary, to extend the rights of migrants and to bring their status closer to that of the nationals of the host country.

In 1980, an immigrant worker is still an alien in the full sense of the word. He contributes to the economic development of the country in which he is employed but he draws hardly any benefit from it. The various attempts that have been made to facilitate his social integration reflect, in reality, the contradictions of the immigration policies worked out by the immigration countries. While refusing to consider themselves as such, those countries have none the less witnessed an appreciable increase in the size of their foreign populations since the early seventies. The closing of their frontiers, decided as from 1973–74, has perhaps reduced the flow of immigrant workers, but it has contributed, above all, to modifying the structure of the resident foreign population. Consequently, the integration problems already encountered by immigrants are now assuming unprecedented proportions. And the disparity of the measures that are being taken makes them far less effective.

Conclusion

Eric-Jean Thomas

Since the beginning of the 1950s the political migrations that were the cause of the principal population movements throughout the world have slowed down quite significantly. Conversely, migrations motivated by economic pressures have considerably developed in accordance with the pattern of supply and demand on the international labour market. Thus, while the economies of the rich countries became dependent on the labour of the poor countries, the latter came to view emigration as a solution to some of their problems. The internationalization of capital has had as its corollary the internationalization of labour.

From being an exile or a refugee, the foreigner has become an essential economic factor in the economy of the host country. The foreigner is now an immigrant worker.

Even though political migrations have started up on a large scale again—refugee flows are larger now than they were at the beginning of the 1970s—the immense majority of foreigners in Europe are immigrant workers and their families.

The change in the attitudes of the host countries towards immigration and immigrants is symptomatic of a change in needs and mentalities in this field. Initially, and right up to the mid-1960s, immigration control was very loose. The pressing demand for labour in Europe, which began with the prodigious economic expansion of the 1950s, justified the non-observance of regulations designed to slow down migratory flows and the turnover of workers. This *laissez-faire* attitude to immigration went hand-in-hand with general indifference to the situation of immigrants and their families. This was the heyday of labour traffickers and 'Rachmanites', who found it particularly easy to exploit immigrants because they were actually encouraged to do so by the passive attitude of the administrative authorities and industry's need for a cheap work force. Subsequently, the gradual closing of frontiers gave the authorities occasion—somewhat paradoxically—to take an interest in the status of immigrant workers. When the authorities ceased being lax and started to apply immigration controls more strictly in the latter half of the 1960s, they realized that they could no longer tolerate labour trafficking if their attempts at the reinforcement of controls were not to prove illusory. It was at that time that people began to show that they were concerned about protecting foreign workers and improving their social status. Finally, when immigration was halted in the early 1970s, the authorities of the immigration countries declared that it was necessary to formulate a consistent immigration policy which would benefit not only the national economy—through the easing of tension on the labour market, for this was supposedly due largely to foreign workers—but also the immigrants themselves—through the elaboration of a legal status for immigrants designed to stop the process of marginalization inflicted upon them.

Reflecting these trends, there are three important stages in the development of legislation in this field. The first generation of texts regulating immigration was due to legislative action taken after either the First or the Second World War. The law-makers of those years were largely guided by a concern to regulate the movements and residence of foreigners who immigrated on an individual basis and settled for long periods in the host country. The characteristics of these immigrants—who might equally well be motivated by economic factors (the need to find work) or by political factors (population movements following in the wake of war)—were markedly different from those of the far more numerous immigrants who were to arrive around the 1960s. Thus, when the great wave of migrants attracted by the economic boom swept through Europe, a second generation of texts appeared. These provisions, which were introduced mainly by means of statutory instruments and derived their legal force from the executive, were drawn up on an *ad hoc* basis according to the needs of the moment and the various pressures to which governments were exposed. This piecemeal approach to an extremely complex field through a succession of circulars, ordinances, decrees, bilateral agreements and other texts led to the proliferation of overdeveloped and inconsistent regulations which left enormous powers in the hands of the administrative authorities. Consequently, there now exists a paradoxical situation in which, on the one hand, the immigration countries want to improve the immigrant's situation, and, on the other, there is an uncontrolled—and often uncontrollable—flood of regulations which submerges the human element. The truth is that migratory movements have all too long been viewed primarily as strictly economic phenomena. Accordingly, law-makers have endeavoured to establish a system for regulating movements of persons and to serve national economic interests as well as possible. This restrictive immigration law has been superimposed upon the law traditionally applied to aliens, which has always been of a static nature, more concerned with fixing limits and formulating prohibitions than with promoting equality of treatment between aliens and nationals. Thus, immigrant workers and their families have found that they are subject to two sets of legal texts designed entirely to limit their freedoms and rights. In this sense, the law concerning immigration and aliens can be said to be essentially negative. For this reason, declarations in favour of improving the status of foreign workers are pointless inasmuch as the elaboration of a few new rules to be superimposed upon the earlier regulations is hardly likely to change a factual situation which is due both to the unwieldiness of the existing rules and to the growth of the powers of the administrative authorities.

The halting of immigration went a long way towards destroying whatever consistency was still possessed by the regulations controlling immigration. While a new series of provisions introduced by means of statutory instruments were defining the procedures to be applied in order to stop immigration, the earlier provisions of legislative origin were becoming less and less usable. The debate which was then opened in all the immigration countries, on the desirability of enacting new measures drew attention to the precarious situation of migrants and also to the fact that governments had to obtain the agreement and support of national parliaments.

At this stage there was born the third, and currently developing, generation of texts on immigration, which are drawn up in consultation with the legislature. The basic characteristic of this generation of texts is that it considerably reduces the possible ways of obtaining access to the national labour market and, consequently, access to the national territory itself. Exceptions to the restrictive rules are made, of course, for privileged foreigners who benefit from a preferential status on account of their nationality. It is one of the paradoxical aspects of this trend that, at the same time as states were closing their frontiers to migratory flows, they were opening them to nationals of member countries of regional groupings. A variety of systems thus came to be superimposed on each other which not only sanction differences in the treatment of nationals and foreigners, but also establish new forms of discrimination even within the foreign population.

It must be stressed that this new generation of laws should enable the host countries to adopt a consistent immigration policy and at the same time to arrive at a clearer definition of the role to be assigned to foreign workers by society. For, as has already been pointed out, a legal status for foreigners cannot be elaborated unless it is based on the immigration control mechanisms. It is in those mechanisms that discrimination first finds expression. They play a leading part in determining the status of immigrants, whatever other mechanisms may be devised later.

Moving towards a legal status
for immigrant workers

Foreigners residing within a country's national frontiers are traditionally subject to strict regulations. In law, they are usually regarded as abstract and interchangeable beings who cannot benefit from most civil and political rights until they have undergone a long process of assimilation culminating in their naturalization. But this is an outmoded point of view which is characteristic of times that are no more. As we have already said, the foreigner is now an immigrant worker. The old approach is therefore changing thanks to new trends in political ideas and, more specifically, as a consequence of the great deal of work that has been done in this field by international organizations[1] and also because of the existence of privileged categories of foreigners enjoying the advantages of systems which have had some influence on ordinary law.

It is necessary to identify the various kinds of prerogative attaching to every individual but enjoyed by foreigners only within certain specified limits. We propose to establish a distinction between civil liberties and socio-political rights. Even though it is not very precise, this distinction will help us to perceive more clearly the problems which are inseparable from efforts to improve the status of foreigners.

Civil liberties

In municipal law, civil liberties traditionally consist of the prerogatives guaranteed by civil law, the enjoyment of which does not, in principle, bring the individual into a relationship with the state. It is not possible to draw up an exhaustive list of these civil liberties; however, some of the most important should be noted.

So far as immigration and the status of foreigners in the strict sense of the term are concerned, freedom of movement within the host country, together with freedom to work, appear to be the most important liberties, even though they are restricted in many cases.

Similarly, freedom to be party to a contract, particularly with an employer, is a liberty which is governed by strict regulations in the case of foreigners.

Freedom to exercise the occupation of one's choice does not always exist, particularly for members of the professions (lawyers, doctors, and so on). This freedom is particularly important for refugees.

Freedom to live with one's family is also one of the fundamental freedoms of the human person: certain trends give reason to fear that it may be reduced even further in the case of immigrant workers.

Lastly, we must mention the freedom to choose one's way of life, which
is so important for persons brought up in a society whose culture
and civilization may be quite different from those of the host society.
Taken as a group, these freedoms are the ones most affected by immigration controls. Thus, to take a simple example, the system adopted
in order to regulate the employment of foreigners—which generally
consists in issuing a work permit valid for a limited period and a limited
area—has the effect of reducing, or even abolishing, the freedom to be
party to a contract, freedom of movement throughout the national
territory, freedom to choose one's occupation and residence, etc.

The major problem that arises in connection with civil liberties is
how to decide whether it would not be advisable to break away from the
traditional line of analysis and work out a new approach based on the
specific needs of immigrants, for although these liberties are recognized
as being prerogatives attaching to the human person, this reasoning
seems to hold good only for nationals and not for foreigners. Accordingly,
we should ask ourselves whether these liberties do not also constitute
rights which, besides being safeguarded, should be conferred upon every
individual, irrespective of nationality. Such is the general trend of
international law, and more particularly of international law concerning
human rights. It would therefore be a serious matter if the European
countries, which so often claim to be the defenders of human rights,
were to refuse to put into practice principles that now form an integral
part of *jus cogens*, simply because they believe that there are good
economic reasons for not doing so.

Socio-political rights

By socio-political rights we mean rights that govern the individual's
relations both with the state and with the various institutions of the
society in which he is living. They define the individual's socio-political
status. In order for them to be exercised, these rights have to be granted
and safeguarded. They include not only the various voting rights, but
also, for example, trade-union rights, the right to participate in the
social and political life of the commune where the foreigner resides or
in the management of the firm where he is employed.

For a long time the ordinary people demanded socio-political rights
and struggled to obtain them. When they had been won, they were
conferred exclusively upon nationals. Law-makers today still refuse to
entertain the idea of elaborating a specific status for foreigners, and in
law there exists only the status of aliens. The nuance is an important one.

It would seem that the main obstacle standing in the way of efforts
to establish a legal status for immigrant workers and secure the recognition of their rights is rooted in the fact that the immigration countries

refuse to consider themselves as such. For many years, countries like the Federal Republic of Germany, for instance, refused to accept the possibility of foreign workers settling in their territory for very long periods. The host countries assumed, in fact, that since there was a turnover of the 'stock' of migrant workers, those foreigners who took up residence on a long-term basis in their territories did not need to have any particular status, as they could become integrated into the host society by becoming naturalized. This line of reasoning was inherited from the past inasmuch as the great waves of immigrants which arrived at the beginning of the century did actually result in the settlement and naturalization of very large numbers of migrants. As for the theory of the turnover of labour, not only has it been abandoned in the countries that had officially adopted it; in addition, it has always proved to be unrealistic in the sense that it would have been necessary to rely entirely on the compulsory repatriation of migrants in order to put it into practice.

The five national monographs, and particularly the case-study on Turkey, have shown that migrants were tending to stay even longer abroad. In the face of this situation, certain countries such as France have established a system for inducing immigrants to return home. It cannot be overemphasized that an exodus of immigrants having decided to return home would in no case prove to be a panacea for the problems of immigration, and this is made quite clear by the study on Turkey. But neither should such a policy provide any country having adopted it with a pretext for shirking its responsibilities and giving no thought to its duties towards migrants or to the rights which it ought to extend to them.

It is more than ever necessary to recognize and take into consideration the specific needs of the foreigner—immigrant worker. Instead of being regarded merely as an economic factor, he should now be respected as a worker who has contributed, and is continuing to contribute, to the expansion of the host country. It emerges very clearly from the national monographs that immigrant workers play a decisive and essential role in developing the economies of the host countries. Immigration has really been the Third World's aid to developed countries. For this reason, immigrant workers should be able to claim, if not a share of the power to take decisions, at least a right to participate in the political, social or economic life of the nation in which they are living and tending to settle on an increasingly permanent basis. It is in this field that the greatest gains can be made, for many experiments have already gone to show, despite the failures, that foreigners are willing—and able—to take up positions of responsibility within the national communities. However, the leading immigration countries in Europe have not yet granted immigrant workers an adequate place in their societies. There is still a great disparity between the possibilities of the rich European countries, which are also blessed by great political stability, and the infra-legal situation of the majority of foreigners in the host countries.

The way in which law-makers have traditionally perceived, analysed and determined the status of aliens is compatible neither with the economic realities of the contemporary world nor with the level of economic and social development now attained by all Western societies.

This state of affairs is due to the fact that the concept of the foreigner underlying all the laws at present in force has remained practically unchanged since the beginning of the century and is based on outdated political and legal principles.

Immigration is motivated by the migrant's desire to improve his lot. It is not natural that it should result in a worsening of his situation as regards his personal status. In short, the immigration control mechanisms are too often unsuitable and the status of resident foreigners is marked by too much discrimination. Admittedly, these two aspects of the problem—immigration controls and the foreigner's status—are largely the concern of the political authorities, but it is not reasonable to persist in setting political considerations against legal considerations simply in order to prevent the law from being developed and adapted to contemporary realities.

Note

1. See E.-J. Thomas, 'The Work of International Organizations in the Field of Immigration', *ICMC Migrations News* (Geneva), No. 4, 1978, and SFDI, *Les Travailleurs Étrangers et le Droit International*, Paris, A. Pédone, 1979.